D1575526

POETS OF
THE BIBLE

❧ ❧ ❧

From Solomon's Song of Songs
to John's Book of Revelation

Memoirs

From Hawthorne's Gloom to a Whitewashed Island
Sunday Morning in Fascist Spain: A European Memoir, 1948–1953
With Borges on an Ordinary Evening in Buenos Aires
We Jews and Blacks: Memoir with Poems
Borges at 80

Literary Criticism

Miguel de Cervantes's Rinconete y Cortadillo
The Poetics of Ecstasy: From Sappho to Borges
The Poetics of Translation: History, Theory, Practice

Libretto for Opera

An American in China (music by David Michael Hertz)

Translations

Eighty Poems of Antonio Machado
The Other Alexander: A Greek Novel by Margarita Liberaki
(with Helle Tzalopoulou Barnstone)
Mexico Before Cortez: Art, History, Legend by Ignacio Bernal
Physiologus Theobaldli Episcopi—Bishop Theobald's Bestiary
Sappho: Lyrics in the Original Greek with an English Translation
Greek Lyric Poetry
The Poems of Saint John of the Cross
The Song of Songs: Shir Hashirim
My Voice Because of You by Pedro Salinas
The Unknown Light: The Poems of Fray Luis de León
A Bird of Paper: Poems of Vicente Aleixandre
(with David Garrison)
The Art of Worldly Wisdom by Gracián Baltar
Cántico spiritual: The Spiritual Canticle of St. John of the Cross
La fianza Satisfecha: The Outrageous Saint by Lope de Vega
La cena del rey Baltazar (The Banquet of King Balthazar)
by Pedro Calderón de la Barca
Radiance and Death of Joaquín Murieta by Pablo Neruda
The Dream Below the Sun: Poems by Antonio Machado
The Courage of the Rainbow by Bronislava Volkavá
Laughing Lost in the Mountains: Poems of Wang Wei
(with Tony Barnstone and Xu Haixin)
To Touch the Sky: Poems of Mystical, Spiritual and Metaphysical Light

Six Masters of the Spanish Sonnet: Francisco de Quevedo,
Sor Juana Inés de la Cruz, Antonio Machado, Federico Garcia Lorca,
Jorge Luis Borges, Miguel Hernández

Border of a Dream: Selected Poems of Antonio Machado

Sonnets to Orpheus: Rainer Maria Rilke

Sweetbitter Love: Poems of Sappho (bilingual edition)

The Complete Poems of Sappho

The Poems of Mao Zedong

Ancient Greek Lyrics

Love Poems by Pedro Salinas: My Voice Because of You
and Letter Poems to Katherine

Anthologies / Editions

Concrete Poetry: A World View (with Mary Ellen Solt)

Spanish Poetry, from Its Beginning through the Nineteenth Century

Modern European Poetry

Eighteen Texts: Writings by Contemporary Greek Authors
(with Edmund Keeley)

A Book of Women Poets from Antiquity to Now (with Aliki Barnstone)

Literatures of Asia, Africa, and Latin America (with Tony Barnstone)

Literatures of Latin America

Literatures of the Middle East (with Tony Barnstone)

Twenty-four Conversations with Borges

The Angel of the Divine Presence Bringing Eve to Adam by William Blake.

POETS OF THE BIBLE

From Solomon's Song of Songs
to John's Book of Revelation

Edited and translated from
the Hebrew and Greek by

WILLIS BARNSTONE

W. W. NORTON & COMPANY
Independent Publishers Since 1923
NEW YORK | LONDON

for Robert Alter who led the way
Jill Bialosky for permitting me voyage
Sarah Handler whose eye lighted each word

CONTENTS

APOCRYPHA

THE NEW TESTAMENT

POETS OF THE BIBLE

The world's great poetry resides in the Bible. In the Hebrew Bible we hear Solomon carol in Song of Songs, David chant in Psalms, Job and God debate in Job, and Isaiah, Jeremiah, and Amos declaim amid the prophets; in the Greek Scriptures we hear Jesus speak wisdom verse in Gospels, Paul exult in Corinthians, John and James preach musically in Letters, and John of Patmos roar epically in Revelation. Although these are among the most familiar biblical figures, because their words are set as prose few have traditionally associated them with poetry. Consider William Blake, Walt Whitman, and Herman Melville. Melville is the greatest hidden author of the prose poem. These great poets in English capture the image and song. And those tales and harmonic resonance are immersed in their poetry and have profoundly fashioned their work. Today it seems unimaginable that the Psalms and Song of Songs were once printed as prose. Without that inspired biblical song "locked in prose," as Emily Dickinson called the concealed holy poems, would we have Shakespeare, Herbert, Milton, Blake, Whitman, Dickinson, Melville, Hopkins, Yeats, Joyce, Eliot, and Dylan Thomas? Their work would be diminished.

The Bible is a very large part of the language globe that is a people's language and culture, for both the faithful and secular. The Bible enters our language sphere through the liberating act of translation. We consume that translation, as in the King James Version, as a work born in English. Strictly speaking, it is a "reborn" version in English. The fact that so-called "literal words of the Bible" are never literal but a translation (often a translation of a translation) is lost to most readers. Bible speech is our atlas and guide to language, literature, and philosophy. The great voices in Genesis, Solomon, Job, and Psalms, and Gospels, Paul, and Revelation keep the biblical fountain flowing with magnificent speech. It continues in contemporary poetry from T. S. Eliot and Dylan Thomas to Joan Baez, John Lennon, Theodore Roethke, and C. K. Williams.

Consider the following lines. Are they from Walt Whitman's "Song of the Broad Axe"? Yes, my smart students at Wesleyan University voiced unanimously. They knew their Walt.

> The carpenter measures with a line and makes an outline with a
> marker;
> he roughs it out with chisels and marks it with compasses.
> He shapes it in the form of man, of man in all his glory, that it may
> dwell in a shrine.
> He cut down cedars, or perhaps took a cypress or oak.
> He let it grow among the trees of the forest, or planted a pine, and
> the rain made it grow.
> It is man's fuel for burning; some of it he takes and warms himself,
> he kindles a fire and bakes bread.

This passage is not, however, from Whitman but one of his inspirations, Isaiah (44.2–5), a world poet who wrote in the mid-sixth century B.C.E. Yet Whitman heard poetry concealed in prose in the Old Testament decades before the prophets' lines were set as poetry. As a son of Quakers, he knew his scriptures. The grand poets, who wrote in echoing couplets, did not need to have the Hebrew text lineated as poetry to be swayed. They were overwhelmed especially by the prophets and by Revelation. As for Old Testament verse, to any native reader of ancient Hebrew, the above passage from Isaiah is poetry, but not to most earlier European and American biblical scholars and translators. However, those who best capture the Bible's parallelistic verse in echoing couplet or tercets are the forty-seven translators of the King James Version. Though these gentlemen froze the Song of Songs into a Prose of Proses, they were following an unthreatened tradition. Nevertheless, with genius, they infused their famous version with lines of such rhythmic cadence that we hear them as we might Handel's *Messiah*.

The reason for the almost universal blindness to Hebrew poetry (and later to the Koine poetry of Jesus, where the same prosodic principles apply) is that Hebrew lyric song, chanted psalm, and prophetic wisdom verse do not follow Greco-Roman meter and rhyme. Biblical Hebrew poetry is based on parallel units of verse, anaphora, and sound patterns in which the second line repeats the sense, but varies the sound, of the first line. Reading the first thunderous sprung rhythm lines of Genesis in which roaring gales of chaos prevail and waters tear apart, one remembers the rhetorical alchemy in the Catholic poet Gerard Manley Hopkins and his "The Wreck of the Deutschland." It is amazing how Hopkins and English literature are saturated with poetic Bible speech.

Today almost every edition of the Old Testament poetry—since the first English Revised in the 1880s—lineates the poetical books as verse. The poetry is apparent. Many go to the Bible for titles and song. In the 1920s Hemingway finds the name for his first novel *The Sun Also Rises* in "The sun also riseth" in Ecclesiastes (1.5), Lillian Hellman finds her play title *The Little Foxes* in Song of Songs (2.5), Joan Baez and Pete Seeger hear the preacher Koheleth say, "there is a time to love, and a time to hate; / a time of war, and a time of peace" in Ecclesiastes (3).

As for the New Testament, it has been treated as the stepchild with respect to its magnificent poetry throughout. It has not experienced the same recognition as the parent Old Testament, though countless passages appear in the New Testament as prose that in their original verbal equivalent in the Old Testament are poems. *The Restored New Testament* does reveal the great poets of the Greek scriptures. The Jesuit *Jerusalem Bible* (Doubleday, 1966/2003) makes a step in this direction, giving all of Jesus's wisdom poetry speech as verse.

In this new translation of poets from the Hebrew Bible, I have used the same strategy as in the *Restored New Testament*. Hence *Poets of the Bible* consists of poetry from a *Restored Old Testament* and a *Restored New Testament*.

TYNDALE, KING JAMES VERSION, AND REVISED VERSIONS

The King James Version (KJV) is called a version because King James ordered his translators *not* to do a fresh translation but a version based on the model of earlier translations. Hence the revelatory title *The King*

James Version. The KJV of the New Testament is largely based on William Tyndale's 1525 translation of the New Testament and some of the Old Testament. Tyndale makes the splendid claim that both Hebrew and Greek "agreeth a thousand times more with the English than with the Latin." His aim is to convey "the same grace and sweetness as it hath in the Hebrew." In fact he renders not only the "grace and sweetness" of Song of Songs and Matthew but also the cosmic narrative power and poetry of Genesis. For his heretical act of translating directly from the original Hebrew and Greek rather than from the Latin Vulgate, Henry VIII orders him strangled and burned at the stake in 1536 at the Castle of Vilvoorde outside of Brussels. A few years later when Henry turns Protestant, the Tyndale New Testament volume is welcomed to England and becomes its most popular book. During his longish captivity, Tyndale was in a lightless dungeon room. He begged for a candle and a Hebrew dictionary. Had he time and his basic tools, we would now benefit from a true "common speech" version of the whole Jewish and Christian Bibles, more enlightened in terms of its Jewish origin than the KJV, which would have been a new delight to the world and artists and authors seeking inspiration.

The earlier Tyndale follows Erasmus's dictum to write "for the plough-boy of the fields," and his English reflects the elegant plainness of the Koine Greek. The Tyndale is a jewel of Renaissance literature, but it is too hard to read by modern readers. Between Tyndale in 1525 and the KJV in 1611, the English language changed perhaps more than it has from 1611 to the present. The KJV remains as immediately understandable as a sonnet or play by Shakespeare.

Yet consider the KJV over more recent versions, especially the various Revised Versions. Gerald Hammond writes, "Aesthetically there is no argument. Everyone concedes . . . that the Authorized Version is itself a great work of art. It marked the culmination of nearly a hundred years of English Bible translation, beginning with the Tyndale in the 1520s and 1530s."[1] He goes on to assert, "The Renaissance translators were still close to a Protestant Reformation which stressed the primacy of the Bible's literal sense, as opposed to the various allegorical readings."[2]

---

1. Gerald Hammond, "English Translations of the Bible," in *The Literary Guide to the Bible*, ed. Robert Alter and Frank Kermode (Cambridge, MA: Harvard University Press, 1987), 650.
2. Ibid., 664.

I admire the various Revised Versions, and the annotation is by far the best. The King James speech is as elevated from common speech as Ben Jonson and William Shakespeare are in their plays, and Marvell and Milton in their poetry. As for the Revised Versions, they create a sometimes elegant but strange speech not spoken outside of the text. It remains by far the best extant prose version we have of both Testaments, though they are uniformly verbose and explanatory where the original is concise and dynamic. Rather than permit an original metaphor to come through with the same analogy, they find an equivalent. Equivalents never match the powers of an original, which will ultimately dominate and change what can be said in English, the target tongue. We benefit by the new that occurs when the old is allowed to exist in a new form.

Homer and Plato used high formal Greek, not the popular Koine that always existed alongside the classical Greek written language. Despite the perceived schism dividing the spoken and the written, the grand Hebrew and grand Greek of the Bible are also the popular languages spoken in home and street. To be true then to the source scripture as the King James scholars often are, it is best to follow the speech of one's own time and so evoke the Hebrew and Greek rhetoric. I follow the same principles in the Old and New Testaments, where I use a chaste but charged poetic lexicon to reflect the plain Hebrew and Koine Greek that everyone understood, however its magnificent or vulgar turn of phrase seems to us now. In doing the Old Testament I follow the same principles as in the New Testament, so we now have a *Restored Old Testament* as well as the *Restored New Testament*.

The Bible often reads like a detective novel. The wonderful cadences grab the reader. The poetry has captured the world. It is right to distinguish for the first time all the major poets, from God (in Genesis and Job), Solomon, and Isaiah to Jesus, Paul, and John of Patmos, and enter them into the pantheon and street knowledge of the great poets of the globe. The poets understood. William Blake (1757–1827), whose work is a child of the Testaments, asserts unambiguously that "the Old and New Testaments are the Great Code of Art."[3] The Bible also gave him a uniquely marveled version of key scenes.

In this new translation of *Poets of the Bible,* my hope is to emulate the

---

3. Stephen Prickett, *Words and the Word: Language, Poetics and Biblical Interpretation* (Cambridge: Cambridge University Press, 86), 66–7.

literary beauty of earlier versions, especially the Tyndale, but to use a chaste contemporary speech (as in the *Restored New Testament*), and also be religion neutral. The speech in the KJV and in all later ones converts the set of Old and New Testaments into completely Christian documents. Making both Testaments fully Christian scriptures by way of translation is a flaw, and compromises veracity.

There is no anachronistic fiddling here with the Hebrew Bible. Both Testaments (or more accurately "Covenants") were composed by Jews about Jews. That correction to neutrality pervades here, with no religio-political preference to either side. Both are documents exclusively about this "people of the book" in a strip of land along the eastern Mediterranean coast of what is now Asia Minor. Beyond question there are historically only Jews in each book; no "gentiles" or "heathens" (the bad gentiles), no Greeks, no Europeans. The book is Asian, not European. The only non-Jews are the occupying forces of the Roman Empire in the New Testament, who along with everyone else are inexplicably speaking Koine Greek, which evokes a mountain of never answerable queries. It is my ecumenical hope that this volume of beautiful poetry will bring beauty, harmony, and wisdom to the traditional antagonists of two joined faiths. Some day a good literary scholar will extend this hope to the third Abrahamic document, the Qur'an.

Yeshua ben Josef, the last major Jewish prophet, is later seen as the Isaiah-foretold Messiah. The Hebrew *Mashiah* means "Messiah." "Messiah" in Greek is *Hristos,* that we transliterate as "Christian." We should be pleased that we derive from one conjoined religious history. Christianity began as one of many competing Jewish sects. The major champion is the Pharisee Paul, who was badgered by John, James, and especially Peter to keep him from straying too far from strict Jewish law. For all this mess of emerging combinatory faiths and their concordant texts, it is good to be enlightened and happy with our common origin. Paul, a Jew from Tarsos, essential founder of Christianity, had, until well into the second century, one available scripture: the Jewish Bible in Hebrew.

DETAILS OF THE TRANSLATION

In *Poets of the Bible,* the original Hebrew and Aramaic names of person and place will be restored, as in my earlier volumes. Hence, Joshua and Jesus are Yeshua, James is Yaakov, and Jerusalem is Yerushalayim, Paul is Shaul, God is God or Yahweh (and other names). In King James's instructions to the forty-seven translators, James specifically orders the group to render into English the closest possible approximation of the Hebrew and Greek original. They did not respect proper nouns. Rather, they Anglicized most of them. Anglicization has given us many names in English far from the original names. Indeed, it stopped woefully short of conveying an equivalent of either the Hebrew or Greek names, or that they were originally in Hebrew or Greek. "Mary" is from Greek "Maria," not, as it should be, from the original Hebrew "Miryam" (Miriam). There is no reason why in English we cannot say Shimon for Simon, Yaakov for James, Miryam for Mary, Markos for Mark, Andreas for Andrew, or Yosef for Joseph. These are all people of the Asian Near East, not from London or Rome. Bibles will attain a true harmony of authenticity with the restoration of the ethnicity and sounds of the people in their poems. However, in order to help the reader unfamiliar with the correct original names, I have used their common English names in all titles and the original names in the texts themselves. Hence, it is Adam and Eve in the garden in the title, but in the scripture itself they are Adam and Havah.

The present version is as close to the original Hebrew and Koine Greek as I can render them literarily, and in this instance without encumbering the text with annotations. I hope that these major world biblical poets will appear in an anthology of stunning poetry, whose every line is memorable poetry in English as each line is in Hebrew and Greek.[4]

Finally, I hope this work will be read independent of faith. I appeal to Jews and Christians, and to everyone, not to limit yourselves tribally. It is crucially important for Jews to read New Testament poets and Christians to read poets of the Hebrew Bible. Solomon and Matthew are universal. If you choose solely by sect, you deprive yourself of a multitude of beauty, knowledge, and wisdom. Please, dig in with a free mind.

---

4. I have refrained from extensive annotation. For example, Genesis 1.1 is contentious. The *JPS Hebrew English Tanakh* (Philadelphia, PA: Jewish Publication Society, 1999) renders it "When God began to create heaven and earth." The frequent new interpretation gives the verb a temporal meaning, yielding "started to" or "began to" create heaven and earth.

POETS OF
THE BIBLE

✄ ✄ ✄

From Solomon's Song of Songs
to John's Book of Revelation

THE OLD TESTAMENT

GENESIS

Γένεσις בְּרֵאשִׁית

The Greek word Genesis (Γένεσις), meaning "origin/birth," is a gift of the Septuagint translation of the Hebrew Bible for Greek-speaking Jews in Alexandria in the second century B.C.E. Saint Jerome in the fourth century adopted the Greek title "Genesis" for book one in his Latin Vulgate translation of the Hebrew Bible. From Latin his Genesis spread to European languages. Genesis is the title of the first of the five books of the Bible. Christians call them the Five Books of Moses or the Pentateuch from the Greek word Πεντάτευχος, meaning "Five Scrolls." Sometimes we also speak of the Hexateuch, meaning the first six narrative books, which adds the Book of Joshua to the narration of the history of Israel.

The title of the first book in the Hebrew Bible is not Genesis (origin/birth). Indeed, the earliest scrolls of the Hebrew Bible had no titles. Later generations used the first word to title the book. Hence, *Bereshit,* בְּרֵאשִׁית, meaning "In the beginning," became the title of the first book of Torah. Though "Torah" signifies specifically the first five books of the Bible, it is also a general word in Hebrew for the whole Bible. Christians call the Hebrew Bible the "Old Testament." Clearly, the purpose is to suggest fresh and greater significance to the Greek New Testament scriptures over the suspect Torah. Torah is a discourse on living a good life. The Torah commands you to love your neighbor, to provide for the poor, to be good and honorable now and on earth. These elemental ideas are elaborated in the prophets Isaiah to Amos and the stories of Babel, Noah, Moses, Abraham, Isaac, Rachel, Rebekah, Joseph, Deborah, Ruth, Samson, David, Daniel, and Jonah.

For the Jews the Jewish scripture is simply their Bible, the Tanakh, and never an old testament compared to a new one. Tanakh is an acronym, TaNaKh, formed from the first Hebrew letter of the Bible's three subdivisions: *Torah* (Teachings), *Nevim* (Prophets), and *Ketuvim* (Writings). In common usage "Torah" refers not only to the Five Books of Moses but to the entire Tanakh.

Genesis contains the foundation tales of the Bible, with two glorious creation stories. The first begins, "In the beginning God created the heaven and the earth." It requires seven days (Genesis 1.1–2.3) to complete the universe. In the second version (Genesis 2.4–6), all things of the world are created in a flash, including Adam and Eve in Eden. The ancient tale initiates the ethical schism between the powers of God and humans. God's antagonist is Eve, who seeks the freedom to acquire knowledge. For her disobedience in picking fruit from the tree of the knowledge of good and evil, come exile, time, childbirth pain, and death. The rich book of Genesis begins Torah and establishes a level of figure, tale, and metaphysical meaning that permeates the early books and is also the history of a people striving to survive well in a crowded, hostile land on the coast of Asia Minor.

In the Beginning

In the beginning God creates heaven and earth
And earth is wasteland and emptiness
And darkness lies on the face of the deep
And a wind from God roars over the face of the waters.
God says, "Let there be light!" and there is light.
And God sees that the light is good.
And God separates the light from the darkness.
And God calls the light Day and the darkness he calls Night.
And there is evening and there is morning, first day.

And God says, "Let there be a dome[1] in the middle of the waters
To separate the waters from the waters."
Then God makes the dome and separates the waters
That are under the dome from the waters
From those that are above the dome. And it is so.
And God calls the dome Sky.
And there is evening and there is morning, second day.

And God says, "Let the waters under the sky
Be gathered in one place, and let dry land appear."
And it is so. And God calls the dry land Earth,
And the gathering of the waters he calls Seas.
And God sees that it is good. And God says,
"Let the earth grow vegetation, plants yielding seed
And fruit trees yielding fruit of every kind
On the earth whose seed is in it." And it is so.
And the earth grows vegetation and plants yielding seed
Of every kind on the earth that bears seed.
And God sees that it is good.
And there is evening and there is morning, third day.

---

1. Or "vault."

And God says, "Let there be lights in the firmament
Of the sky to divide the day from the night,
And let them be as signs and for seasons and for days
And years. And let them be for lights in the sky
To spread light over the earth." And it is so.
And God makes the two great lights,
The greater light for dominion of day,
And the lesser light for dominion of night and the stars,
And God sees that it is good.
And there is evening and there is morning, fourth day.

And God says, "Let the waters be alive with swarms
Of living creatures and let winged birds fly
Above the earth through the dome of the sky."
And God creates the great sea monsters and all creatures
Of every kind that swarm in the waters
And all winged birds of every kind.
And God sees that it is good.
God blesses them, saying, "Be fruitful, and multiply,
Fill the waters in the seas, and let the birds multiply on earth."
And there is evening and there is morning, fifth day.

And God says, "Let the earth bring forth living creatures
Of every kind, cattle and creeping things, and wild beasts
Of every kind and cattle of every kind." And it is so.
And God makes wild beasts of every kind, and all kinds
Of creeping things on the earth. And God sees that it is good.

Gen. 1.1–25

Let Us Make Man in Our Image

And God says, "Let us make man in our image, in our likeness,
He shall have dominion over the fish of the sea,
And over the birds in the air and over the cattle,
And over all the earth, and over each creeping thing
That creeps on the earth."

And God creates man in his own image.
In the image of God he creates them,
Male and female he creates them.
And God blesses them, and God says to them,
"Be fertile and multiply, and replenish the earth, and subdue it,
And have dominion over the fish of the sea
And over the birds of the air,
And over every living thing that moves on the earth."

And God says, "Look, I have given you every plant
Bearing seed that is on the face of all the earth,
And every tree with seed in its fruit so you can have food.
And to every beast of the earth,
And to every bird of the air,
And to every living thing creeping on the earth,
I have given them all green plants for food."
And it is so. And God sees everything he has made,
And, look, it is very good.
And there is evening and there is morning, sixth day.

Gen. 1.26–31

God Forms Man from the Dust of the Earth

So the sky and the earth are completed
And all their multitudes, and on the seventh day
God ends all the work that he has done
And God rests on the seventh day from all the work
That he has done and God blesses the seventh day
And he hallows it because on that day God rests
From all the work he has done in his creation.
This is the story of creating heaven and earth.

On the day the lord God makes the earth and the heavens,
Before every plant of the field is in the earth
And no grasses of the field have grown

Because God has not sent rain to fall on the earth,
There is no one to till the ground,
But a mist would rise from the earth
And water the whole face of the ground
And the lord God forms man from the dust of the earth
And breathes into his nostrils the breath of life
And man becomes a living being.

Gen. 2.1–7

Adam and Eve in the Garden of Eden

And the lord God plants a garden in Eden, in the east,
And there he puts the man whom he has formed,
And out of the earth the lord God makes grow

Every tree pleasant to see and good for food:
The tree of life in the middle of the garden
And the tree of knowledge of good and evil.

A river flows out of Eden to water the garden,
And from there it divides and becomes four branches.
The name of the first is Pishon

That winds through the whole land of Havilah
Where there is gold, and the gold of that land is good.
There is bdellium and lapis lazuli.

The name of the second river is Gihon
That winds through the whole land of Cush.[2]
The name of the third river is Tigris

That flows east of the east of Assyria.[3]
And the fourth river is Euphrates.
The lord God takes the man and places him

2. Ethiopia
3. Asshur

In the garden of Eden to till it and to keep it.
And the lord God commands the man, saying,
"Of every tree of the garden you may freely eat,

But of the Tree of the Knowledge of Good and Evil,
You shall not eat, for in the day
That you eat of it you shall die."

The lord God says, "It is not good for man
To be alone. I will make him a good helper."
Out of the ground the lord God forms every beast

Of the field and every bird of the air and brings them
To Adam to see what he shall call them
And whatever Adam calls every living creature

That is its name. And Adam gives names to all cattle,
And to the birds of the air and to wild beasts.
But no helper for Adam is found.

So the lord God casts a deep sleep on the man
And he sleeps. Then he takes one of his ribs
And closes up the hole with his flesh,

And the rib the lord God takes from the man
He makes into a woman and brings her to the man.
And Adam says, "She is bone of my bones

And flesh of my flesh. She shall be called Woman
Since out of man she is taken."
So a man leaves his father and his mother,

And clings to his woman and they become one flesh,
And the man and his woman are both naked
And they are not ashamed.

Gen. 2.8–25

And your desire will be for your man
And he will rule over you." To Adam
He says, "Because you have heard the voice

Of your woman and eaten from the tree
From which I commanded you not to eat,
Cursed is the ground because of you. In toil

You will eat from it all the days of your life.
Thorns also and thistles it will grow for you
And you will eat the grasses of the field.

By the sweat on your face will you eat bread
Until you return to the ground. From it you are taken.
You are dust and to dust you will return.

The man names his woman Havah,[4]
Because she is the mother of all the living.
And the lord God makes garments of skins for Adam

And for Havah, and he clothes them.
Then God says, "Look, the man has become
As one of us, knowing good and evil,

And now he might reach out his hand
And take fruit from the Tree of Life and eat
And live forever." Therefore the lord God

Expels him from the garden of Eden
To till the ground from which he is taken.
He drives out the man, and east of the garden

4. Eve from Havah (חַוָּה), "the living one," "the source of life."

And there place the cherubim holds
A flaming sword that is turning every way
To block the way to the Tree of Life.

Gen. 3.1–24

God Sees Wickedness on Earth and Declares a Genocide

God sees that the wickedness of man is great
On the earth and that the thoughts in every mind
Are nothing but evil. And the lord regrets
That he has made man on the earth,
It grieves him to his heart, and the lord says,
"I shall blot out from the earth all those
Whom I created, all people and beasts,
Both creeping things and birds of the air.
I am sorry that I have made them."

Gen. 6.5–7

Noah Builds the Ark to Survive the Destroying Flood

Noah finds grace in the eyes of the lord.
These are the generations of Noah.
Noah is a just man and perfect in his heart
And Noah walks with God.
And Noah begets three sons, Shem, Ham, and Japheth.
The earth is also corrupt before God,

And the earth is filled with violence.
And God looks upon the earth,
And behold, it is corrupt, and all flesh
Had corrupted its way upon the earth.
And God tells Noah,
"I have decided to put an end to all flesh,

For they have filled the earth with violence.
I will destroy them along with the earth.
Make yourself an ark of gopher wood.
Make compartments in the ark
And cover it inside and out with pitch.
Here is how you should make it.

The length of the ark will be three hundred cubits
And its breadth fifty cubits, and its height
Thirty cubits. Make an opening for daylight.
Make a roof for the ark another cubit
Above. Put the entrance to the ark
On the side. Make it with a bottom

And a second and a third story. And look,
For my part I shall bring a flood of waters
Over the earth to destroy all flesh under heaven
In which there is a breath of life.
And every thing that is in the earth shall die,
But with you I will establish my covenant,

And you shall come into the ark,
You and your sons and your woman
And your sons' women with you.
And of every living thing of all flesh,
Two of every kind you shall bring into the ark
To keep them alive with you.

They shall be male and female.
Of birds of every kind, and of cattle
Of every kind, of every stirring thing
On the earth after his kind.
Two of every sort shall come
To you to keep them alive.

And take with you all kinds of food
That is eaten. And store it away
And it shall be the food for you
And for them." Noah follows all
That God has commanded of him,
He does so. And the lord tells Noah,

"Go into the ark with all
Your household. You alone I have found just
In this generation. Of every clean beast
Take with you seven pairs,
The male and his female, and of beasts
Who are not clean take two, male and female.

Of birds of the air take seven pairs, the male,
And female to keep the seed alive on the face of all
The earth. In seven days, and I will send rain
On the earth, forty days and forty nights,
And every living being that I have made
I shall blot out from the face of the earth."

And Noah follows all that God has
Commanded of him. And Noah is six hundred
Years old when the flood of waters spreads
Over the earth. And Noah goes in, and his sons
And his woman, and his sons' women with him
Into the ark because of the waters of the flood.

Gen. 6.8–7.7

The Flood

Of clean beasts and of beasts that are not clean and of birds,
And of every thing that creeps upon the earth
There go in two and two into the ark with Noah,
The male and the female, as God has commanded.
And after seven days the waters of the flood

Are upon the earth. In the six hundredth year of Noah's life,
In the second month, the seventeenth day of the month,
On that day all the fountains of the great deep
Burst apart and the floodgates of the sky break open.

And the rain falls on the earth forty days and forty nights.
On that very day Noah, and Shem, and Ham, and Japheth,
The sons of Noah, and Noah's woman and the three women
Of his sons with them all go into the ark.
They and every species of beast and of cattle
And every species of creeping thing that stirs
On the earth and every species of bird
And every winged creature of the air.

They go into the ark with Noah, two and two
Of all flesh in which there is the breath of life.
And they that go in, male and female of all flesh,
As God commands him. The lord locks them in.
The flood continues forty days on the earth
And the waters increase and bear up the ark
And it rises high above the earth. The waters swell
And expand hugely across the earth.

And the ark floats on the face of the waters
And the waters swell mightily on the earth.
All the tallest mountains everywhere below the sky
Are covered. The waters swell above mountains,
Burying them fifteen cubits deep.
And all flesh that stirs on the earth perishes;
Birds, cattle, beasts, and all swarming creatures
On the earth and every human being die,

All in whose nostrils is the breath of life,
Everyone on the dry land is extinguished.
He blots out every living thing
There is on the face of the ground,

Both man, and cattle, and the swarming things,
And the birds of the air he blots from
The earth. And Noah alone remains alive,
And those who are with him in the ark.

The waters swell on the earth one hundred and fifty days.
God remembers Noah, and all the wild beasts
And all the cattle that are with him in the ark,
And God makes a wind roar over the earth
And the waters subside. The fountains of the deep
And the floodgates of the sky are closed
And storm-rain from the sky is restrained.
The waters gradually recede from the earth.

At the end of one hundred and fifty days the waters
Abate. In the seventh month on the seventeenth
Day of the month, the ark comes to rest
On the mountains of Ararat. The waters decrease
Until the tenth month. In that month on the first day
Of the month, the tops of the mountains are visible,
And at the end of forty days, Noah opens
The window of the ark that he has made

And he sends out a raven and it flies back and forth
Until the waters are dried up from the earth.
Also he sends out a dove to observe
If waters abate from the face of the ground,
But the dove finds no resting place for her foot
And glides back toward him in the ark.
There are waters on the face of the whole earth.
Noah extends his hand to the dove

And seizes her and gathers her into the ark.
And he waits another seven days, and again
He sends the dove out from the ark,
And the dove comes back in the evening

And there in her bill is a freshly plucked olive leaf.
Noah knows that waters dwindle from the earth.

He waits another seven days, sends out the dove
But the dove does not return again to the ark.
It occurs in the six hundred and first year,
In the first month, the first day of the month,
The waters are drying up from the earth.

And Noah removes the covering of the ark
And looks and sees that the face of the ground
Is dry. And in the second month, on the seven
And twentieth day of the month,
The waters are dried up from ground.
And God speaks to Noah, saying, "Come out

Of the ark, together with your woman and your sons
And bring the women of your sons with you.
Bring out every living thing along with you,
All living flesh, birds, animals, everything that creeps
On the ground and let them abound on earth
And be fruitful and multiply on earth."

And Noah sallies out with his sons and his woman,
And his sons' women. Every beast, creeping thing,
And bird, and whatever stirs on the earth,
Every species of being departed from the ark.
And Noah built an altar to the lord,
And from each clean animal and each clean bird

He offers burnt offerings on the altar.
And the lord smells the pleasing savor
And the lord says from his heart, "I shall never
Doom the ground because of human beings,
The inclinations of men's imaginations
Is evil from his youth. Nor shall I destroy

Every living thing again as I have done.
As long as earth endures seedtime and harvest,
Cold and heat, summer and winter,
The day and the night shall never cease."
God blesses Noah and his sons, and tells them:
"Be fruitful, and multiply, and replenish the earth.

And your fear and your dread
Shall be in every beast of the earth
And in every bird of the air,
In all that moves across the earth
And in all the fishes of the sea.
Into your hand they are delivered.

Every living creature will be your food.
I have given you green grasses to eat.
But that flesh alive with its life blood
You must not eat of that blood.
I shall require a reckoning from human life
And also from every animal.

I demand a reckoning for each man's life.
Whoever sheds the blood of a man
By man his blood will be shed,
For in the image of God makes a man.
Be fruitful and multiply abundantly.
Be fruitful and abound on the earth."

Gen. 7.8–9.7

God Makes a Covenant with Noah

God speaks to Noah and to his sons saying,
"I establish my covenant with you
And your descendants and with every
Living creature with you, the birds,

The cattle and every wild beast of the earth.
As many as have come out of the ark,

I will establish my covenant with you
That never again will I have your flesh
Cut away by the waters of a flood.
Never again shall there be another flood
To destroy the earth." God declares,
"Here is the sign of the covenant

I make between me and you and every living
Creature with you, and for all coming
Generations. I set my bow in the clouds
And it will be for a sign of the covenant
Between me and the earth.
When I bring clouds over the earth

That bow will be seen in the clouds.
I will remember the covenant,
Between me and you and every
Living creature of all flesh. The waters
Will not again become a flood to destroy
All flesh. And the bow will be in the clouds.

I will see it and remember the eternal
Covenant between God and each live creature
Of all flesh that is on the earth."
And God tells Noah, "This is the sign
Of the covenant that I establish
Between me and all flesh on the earth."

Gen. 9.8–17

Noah's Sons See Their Father Drunk and Naked As If After an Orgy and Cover Him, Averting Their Eyes from His Shame

And the sons of Noah who depart
From the ark are Shem and Ham,
And Japheth. Ham is the father of Canaan.
These three are Noah's sons. From them
The whole earth is re-peopled. Noah a man
Of the soil is first to plant a vineyard.
He drinks the wine and becomes drunk
And he lies uncovered in his tent.
Ham, the father of Canaan, see his father's
Nakedness and tells his two brothers outside.
Then Shem and Japheth take a cloak

And lay it on their shoulders. Walking backward
They cover their father's nakedness. Their faces
Turn away. They do not see their father's nakedness.
When Noah wakes from wine, he knows what
His son has done to him. "Cursed be Canaan.
He will be the lowest of slaves to his brothers."
He says, "Blessed be the lord God of Shem
And Canaan will be his slave. God will enlarge
Japheth and he shall dwell in the tents of Shem
And Canaan will be his slave." And the days of Noah
Are nine hundred and fifty years when he dies.

Gen. 9.18–29

The Tower of Babel[5]

Everyone on the earth is of one language
And the same words. As they journey from the east,
They find a valley in the land of Shinar and settle there

---

5. "Babel" is from the Hebrew בָּבֶל Bavel, meaning "the Gate of God."

The Tower of Babel by Pieter Bruegel the Elder.

And tell each other, "Come, let us make bricks
And bake them in a fire and burn them hard."
They use brick for stone and bitumen for mortar.

And they tell each other, "Come, let us build a city
And a tower with its top in the heavens.
Let us make a name for ourselves

Or we shall be scattered over all the earth."
The lord comes down to see the city and the tower
That the people have constructed.

The lord says, "Look, they are one people
And they have one language. This is the beginning
Of what they can do. Now nothing they plot

Will be impossible. Come, let us go down
And confound their language so they will not
Understand each other's speech."

So the lord scatters them from there
Over all the earth. They cease building the city.
Therefore it is called Bavel.

There the lord confounds their tongue into babble
Over all the earth, and from there the lord
Scatters them over all the earth.

Gen. 11.1–9

The Lord Comes to Abram in a Vision

The word of the lord comes to Avram in a vision
Saying, "Do not be afraid, Avram. I am your shield.
Your reward will be very great." Avram replies,
"Lord God, what will you give me? I am childless
And the heir of my house is Eliezar of Dammesek."
Avram says, "Look, you have given me no heir,
And a slave in my house will be my heir."
The word of the lord comes to him, saying,
"This man will not be your heir.
Your heir will come out of your own loins."
He leads Avram outside, and says,
"Look up at the heavens and count the stars,
Count them, if you can." God tells him,
"So will your offspring be." He believes the lord
And he counts. He sees himself a good man.
Then God says, "I am the lord who brought you
From Ur of the Chaldeans to give you this land."
He answers, "Lord God, how will I know
I am to possess it?" And God says to him,
"Bring me a three-year-old heifer,
A three-year-old she-goat, and a three-year-old ram,

A turtledove and young pigeon."
He brings them and cuts them in two,
Leaning each half against the other
But he does not cleave the birds.
When birds of prey come to the carcasses,
Avram drives them away. As the sun descends,
Avram falls into a deep and terrifying sleep:
"Know in full certainty that your offspring
Will be strangers in a land not theirs.
There they will be slaves and be oppressed
For four hundred years, but I will judge
that nation whom they serve, and afterward
They shall come out free, with great wealth.
And you will go back to your ancestors in peace
And you shall be buried at a good old age."

Gen. 15.1–15

Covenant Between God and Abram to Be Circumcised and Become Abraham

When Avram is ninety years old and nine,
The lord appears to Avram, and tells him,
"I am El Shaddai.[6] Walk before me and be perfect.

I will make my covenant between me and you,
And multiply you greatly." Avram flings himself on his face.
God talks with him, saying, "Look, my covenant is with you.

I have made you father to a multitude of nations.
Your name will no longer be Avram.
Your name will be Avraham. I have made you father

---

6. El Shaddai is from אל שדי, whose meaning is uncertain. It can be "God of the Mountains" or "God of Heaven."

Of a multitude of nations. Kings will come from you
And your descendants. I will make my covenant
To be your God, and to your seed after you.

I will give you and your offspring after you
The land where you are now a stranger,
All the land of Canaan to keep forever. I shall be

Their God." God told Avraham, "Keep my covenant
Between you and your offspring after you.
Every male among you shall be circumcised

And you shall circumcise the flesh of your foreskin.
It shall be a sign of the covenant between me and you.
When he is eight days old, he shall be circumcised;

Each man child in your generations, born in your house
Or bought with money of a foreigner not of your seed
Or born in your house whom you bought with silver

Must be circumcised. So my covenant in your flesh
Will be everlasting. Any uncircumcised male
Whose flesh of his foreskin is not circumcised,

Will be cut off from his people. He breaks my covenant."
Then God informs Avraham, "Your woman Sarai
Will no longer be Sarai. Her name will be Sarah.

I shall bless her and give you a son by her whom
I shall bless. She shall be the mother of nations,
Kings of people issue from her." Avraham flings himself

On his face and laughs. He mumbles, "Can a son be born
To a man who is a hundred years old? Can Sarah,
At ninety years, bear a child?" Avraham tells God,

"May Ishmael live in your favor!" God replies,
"No, but your woman Sarah will bear you a son
And you shall name him Yitzhak,[7]

And I will my establish my everlasting covenant
With him and with his seed after him.
And as for Ishmael, I hear you. See, I have blessed him,

Will make him fruitful and multiply him exceedingly,
He will father twelve princes and be a great nation,
But my covenant I shall establish with Yitzhak.

Sarah, you shall have a son at this time next year."
When he ends speaking with him,
God leaves Avraham. Avraham takes his son

Ishmael and all born in his house,
And all bought with his silver,
And every male in Avraham's house,

And he circumcises the flesh of their foreskin.
Now Avraham is ninety-nine years old
When he circumcises the flesh of his foreskin,

And Ishmael his son is thirteen years old
When he is circumcised in the flesh of his foreskin.
On that same day Avraham circumcises his son Ishmael

And all the men of his house, born in the house
And those who were bought with silver
From a stranger. All are circumcised with him.

Gen. 17.1–27

---

7. Isaac from the Hebrew יִצְחָק, Yitzhak.

Sarah Is Laughing

The lord appears to him on the plains of Mamre,
And he sits at the tent door in the heat of the day,
      And he lifts his eyes and sees
      Three men standing near him.
When he sees them, he runs to meet them from
The tent door, and bows low to the ground,
      He says, "My lords, if now
      I find favor in your eyes,

Do not pass by your servant. Let a little water
Be fetched and bathe your feet, and rest
      Under the tree. And I
      Will fetch a morsel of bread,
And freshen yourselves so you can journey on
Since you have come to your servant." And they say,
      "Do as you have said."
      And Avraham hurries to the tent

To Sarah, and says, "Quickly prepare three measures
Of fine flour, knead it, and make cakes."
      And Avraham runs to the herd,
      And catches a calf tender and good,
And gives it to a servant, and he quickly prepares it.
He takes curds and milk, and the calf which he prepares
      And sets it before them.
      And he stands by them under the tree

While they eat. And they tell him, "Where is your woman Sarah?"
And he says, "Look in the tent." And he says, "I will return to you
      In this same season, and Sarah
      will have a son." And Sarah listens
At the tent door. Now Avraham and Sarah
      Are old and advanced in age,
      And Sarah no longer has

Her woman's monthly flow. Sarah laughs to herself,
Saying, "After I am withered. Will I have pleasure
     When my husband is also old?" The lord
     Tells Avraham, "Why
Does Sarah laugh, saying, 'Shall I really bear a child,
Now that I'm old?' Is anything beyond the lord?
     At the appointed time I will
     Return to you

In good season, and Sarah will have a son."
Sarah denies, saying, "I did not laugh." She
     Is afraid. And he says,
     "Yes, you laughed."

Gen. 18.1–15

Sarah Bears a Son She Names Isaac that Means "Laughter"

And the lord visits Sarah as he has said,
And the lord does for Sarah as he spoke,
And Sarah conceives and bears Avraham
A son in his old age at the set time
Of which God spoke to him.
And Avraham calls the son Yitzhak,
Who was born to him and whom
Sarah bore. And Avraham circumcises
His son Yitzhak when he is eight days old,
As God had commanded him.
And Avraham is a hundred years old
When his son Yitzhak is born to him.
Now Sarah says, "God made me laugh,
And all who hear will laugh with me."
And she says, "Who would have said
To Avraham that Sarah would nurse
Children? For I have borne him a son
In his old age." The child grows and is weaned

And Avraham makes a great feast
On the day that Yitzhak is weaned.

Gen. 21.1–8

God Tempts Abraham into Filicide as a Burnt Offering on Mount Moriah

After these things God tests Avraham,
And says to him, "Avraham,"
And he answers, "Here I am."
And he says, "Take your son,
Your only son Yitzhak, whom you love,
And go to the land of Moriah
And offer him there as a burnt offering
On one of the mountains
That I will show you."
And Avraham rises early
In the morning, and saddles his donkey
And takes two of his young men
And Yitzhak his son with him,
And splits wood for the burnt offering.

He rises and goes to the place
That God has shown him.
On the third day Avraham
Raises his eyes, and sees the place
Far off. And Avraham tells
His young men, "Stay here
With the donkey. The boy and I
Will go ahead and worship,
And return again to you."
Avraham takes the wood
For the burnt offering, and lays
It on Yitzhak his son, and he takes
The fire in his hand, and a knife,
And they both walk together.

Yitzhak speaks to Avraham his father,
And says "Father!" and he says
"Here am I, my son." He says,
"The fire and the wood are here,
But where is the lamb for a burnt offering?"
And Avraham says, "God will see to the lamb
For the burnt offering."
So they both walk together.
And they come to the place which God
Told him, and Avraham builds
An altar there, and lays the wood
In order. He binds his son Yitzhak,
And lays him on the altar on top
Of the wood. Then Avraham reaches out
His hand and takes the knife
To slaughter his son. But the angel
Of the lord calls to him from heaven
And says, "Avraham, Avraham!"

And he answers, "Here I am."
And he says, "Lay not your hand
On the boy. Do nothing. Now I know
That you fear God, since you have not
Withheld your son, your only son
From me." Avraham raises his eyes
And sees a ram caught in a thicket
By his horns. Avraham goes and takes
The ram, and offers it as a burnt offering
Instead of his son. And Avraham
Calls that place Yahweh Yireh,[8]
As it is called today. In the mount
Of the lord it shall be seen.

And the angel of the lord calls
To Avraham out of heaven

8. Yahweh or YHWH Provides.

A second time, and says,

"I myself declare," said the lord,

"Because you have done this thing

And not withheld your son,

Your only son, I will greatly bless you,

I will multiply your offspring

As numerous as the stars of heaven

And the sand on the seashore,

And your offspring shall possess

The gate of their enemies.

And your offspring shall from all nations

Of the earth be blessed because you

Obeyed my voice." So Avraham

Returns to his young men,

And they rise and journey

Together to Beersheba,

And Avraham lives in Beersheba.

Gen. 22.1–19

Abraham's Servant Tells of Rebecca at the Well

And before the servant finishes speaking

Rivka comes out. She was born

To Vetuel,[9] son of Milkah,[10]

The wife of Nahor, Avraham's brother.

With her water jar upon her shoulder

The young woman is a beautiful virgin

To look upon, whom no man

Had known, and she goes

Down to the spring and fills her jar, and comes up.

And the servant runs to meet her

And says, "Please tip your jar so I can sip a bit of water

From your jar." And she said, "Drink,

9. Bethuel from Hebrew בְּתוּאֵל, Betuel.
10. Milcah from Hebrew מִלְכָּה, Milkah.

My lord," and quickly
Lowers her jar on her hand and lets
Him drink. And when she has done

Letting him drink his fill, she says, "I will draw water
For your camels also until they
Have had their fill,"
And she quickly empties her jar
Into the trough, and runs again

To the spring to draw water
For all his camels, and the man
Gazes at her in silence
Wondering whether the lord has made
His journey a success

Or not. And after the camels drink
Their fill, the man
Takes a gold nose ring
Weighing a half shekel, and two bracelets
For her arms weighing ten shekels

Of gold, and asks, "Whose daughter art you?
Would there be room
In your father's house for us
To spend the night?" And she says to him, "I am
The daughter of Vetuel, the son

Of Milkah whom she bore to Nahor."
And she adds, "We have an abundance
Of straw and fodder and a place
To spend the night." And the man bows
His head low in homage to the lord.

Gen. 24.15–26

Romance of Rebecca and Isaac in the Fields

"Look! Rivka is before you, take her,
   And let her be the wife
Of your master's son, as the lord
   Has spoken." And it happens
That when Abraham's servant

Hears their words, he bows low
   To the earth.
And the servant brings out objects
   Of silver and gold,
And garments and gives them to Rivka.

He also gives her brother and her mother
   Costly ornaments. Then
He and his men who are with him
   Eat and drink
And spend the night there. When they rise

In the morning, he tells them, "Send me off
   To my master."
But her brother and mother say, "Let
   The woman stay with us
At least ten days. After that she can go."

But he tells them, "Do not delay now that the lord
   Has made my journey a success.
Send me off that I may go
   To my master." And they
Say, "We will call the young woman, and ask

Her answer." They call Rivka, and say
   To her, "Will you go with

This man?" And she says, "I will."
   And they send off their sister
Rivka and her nurse, and Avraham's servant,

And his men. And they bless Rivka, and say
   To her, "Our sister, now
Become thousands of myriads,
   And may your offspring seize
The gate of their enemies." Then Rivka

And her young women mount the camels,
   And follow the man,
And the servant takes Rivka
   And goes off. Yitzhak
Comes by way of Beer-lahai-roi,

Since he lives in the Negeb. Yitzhak goes out
   In the evening to stroll in the field,
And raising his eyes he sees
   The camels coming
And Rivka raises her eyes. When she sees Yitzhak,

She quickly alights from the camel and says
   To the servant, "Who is the man in the field
Walking to meet us?" And the servant says,
   "He is my master."
So she takes her veil and covers herself.

The servant tells Yitzhak all things he had done.
   And Yitzhak brings her
Into the tent of his mother Sarah and he takes
   Rivka as his wife. He loves her,

And Yitzhak is consoled after his mother's death.

           Gen. 24.51–67

First Romance of Jacob and Rachel
Who Is Herding Her Flocks

Then Yaakov takes up his journey, and comes to
     The land of the people
Of the East. And he looks and beholds
     A well in the field.
There are three flocks of sheep lying by it.

From that well they water the flocks,
     And a great stone is
On the well's broad mouth. And there
     All the flocks gather,
And they roll the stone from the well's mouth

And water the sheep, and put the stone again
     In its place on the mouth
Of the well. Yaakov tells them,
     "My brothers, where are you from?"
And they say, "We are from Haran." He asks them,

"Do you know Laban the son of Nahor?"
     And they say, "We know him."
And he asks them, "Is he well?"
     And they say, "He is well.
And here is his daughter Rahel, coming with

The sheep." And he says, "Look, it is still bright day
     And not time to round up
The flock, water the sheep
     And go with them
To pasture." But they say, "We cannot wait

Until all the flocks are gathered here
     And the stone is rolled
From the well's mouth.

Then we water the sheep."
And while he yet speaks with them, Rahel

Comes with her father's sheep. She keeps them.
    And it happens
  That when Yaakov sees Rahel the daughter
    Of Laban his mother's brother,
And the sheep of his mother's brother Laban,

Yaakov goes and rolls the stone from the mouth
    Of the well and waters
  The flock of Laban his mother's
    Brother. And Yaakov
Kisses Rahel, and lifts his voice and weeps.

Gen. 29.1–11

Jacob Wrestles All Night with an Angel or with God

Yaakov is left alone, and a man wrestles
With him until daybreak.
When the man sees he has not won against Yaakov,

He strikes him on the hip socket,
And as he wrestles with him
Yaakov's hip comes out of joint.

Then he says, "Let me go. Dawn is breaking."
But Yaakov says, "I will not let you go unless you bless me."
So he tells him, "What is your name?"

And he answers, "Yaakov."
And he says, "You shall no longer be called Yaakov, but Yisrael,
For you have fought with God and men

And you have won."
And Yaakov tells him, saying, "Please tell me your name."
But he says, "Why are you after my name?"

And there he blesses him.
And Yaakov names the place Penuel, saying,
"I have seen God face to face and I am alive."

The sun rises over them
But Yaakov is limping because of his hip.
Therefore, the children of Yisrael

Do not eat the thigh muscle of the hip
Because he (the nameless) struck Yaakov
On the socket of his hip.

Gen. 32.24–32

Joseph the Dreamer in His Robe of Many Colors and the Well

Yosef lives in the land of Canaan where his father
Lives as an outsider. Here is the story of Yosef.

At seventeen years Yosef tends the flock
With his brothers. He is a helper to the sons
Of Bilhah and Zilpah, his father's wives.
Now Yisrael[11] loves Yosef more than all his sons,
Because he is the child of his old age,

And he makes him a coat of many colors.
And when his brothers see that their father loves him
More than all his brothers, they hate him even more
And cannot say one kind word to him.
Then Yosef dreams a dream and tells his brothers,

11. Jacob.

And they hate him even more.
And he says to them, "Hear this dream

I have dreamed. We were binding sheaves
In the field and suddenly my sheaf woke and stood upright.
And your sheaves circled around
And bowed low to my sheaf."
His brothers tell him,
"Do you intend to have dominion over us?"
And they hate him even more.

He dreams another dream, and tells his brothers,
Saying, "Look, I have another dream.
The sun and moon and eleven stars were bowing
To me." And he tells his father and his brothers,
And his father rebukes him, and tells him,
"What is this dream you have dreamed?
Shall I and your mother and brothers,

Bow down to you on the earth?"
His brothers are jealous. His father keeps it in mind.
His brothers go to graze their father's flock in Shechem.
Yisrael tells Yosef, "Do your brothers not graze the flock
In Shechem? Come, and I will send you to them."
And he tells him, "Here I am." And he says to him,
"Go, see whether it be well with your brother

And with the flocks and bring me word again."
So he sends him out of the vale of Hebron,
And he comes to Shechem and a certain man finds him
Wandering in the fields, the man asks him, saying,
"What are you looking for?" He said, "I seek my brothers.
Tell me where they are, where they graze their flocks."
And the man says, "They have left. I heard them say,

'Let us go to Dothan.'" And Yosef goes after his brothers.
He finds them in Dothan. And when they see him far off,

Even before he comes near, they plot to slay him.
They say to each other, "See, the dream prince is here.
Come and let us slay him and devour him,
And we shall see what will become of his dreams."
And Reuven hears it,

And he delivers him out of their hands.
"Let us not kill him," Reuven tells them,
"Shed no blood, fling him into a pit in the wilderness,
And lay no hand on him"—intending to save him
But return him to his father. And it happens
When Yosef comes to his brothers, they strip Yosef
Of his robe, his robe of many colors that he wears.

And they seize him and fling him into a pit.
The pit is empty, there is no water in it.
And they sit down to eat bread, and raise their eyes
And see a caravan of Ishmaelites
Coming from Gilead with camels bearing gum, balm,
And myrrh on their way down to Egypt.
And Yehudah[12] tells his brothers, "What gain is it

If we kill our brother and conceal his blood?
Come, let us sell him to the Ishmaelites,
And let not our hand be upon him, for he is our brother,
Our flesh." And his brothers agree.
When Midian[13] merchants pass by,
They draw and lift Yosef out of the pit,
And sell Yosef to the Ishmaelites for twenty pieces of silver,[14]

And they bring Yosef into Egypt.
And Reuven returns to the pit
And Yosef is not in the pit, and he tears his clothes
And returns to his brothers, and says,

12. Judah.
13. Midianites.
14. Most probable source for tale of Judas's sale of Jesus.

"Yosef is gone. Where can I turn to?"
Then they take Yosef's robe and slaughter a goat
And dip the robe in the blood.

And they rend the robe of many colors,
And bring it to their father, and say,
"This we have found. Examine it. See whether
It is or is not your son's robe." He recognizes it
And says, "It is my son's robe! A vicious beast
Has devoured him. Yosef has been surely
Torn to pieces." And Yaakov tears his clothes,

And puts sackcloth on his loins,
And mourns his son many days.
And all his sons and all his daughters rise
To comfort him and he refuses to be comforted.
And he says, "For I will go down to Sheol[15]
Mourning my son." His father weeps for him.
Meanwhile the Midians sell him in Egypt to Potiphar,
An officer of the Pharaoh, the captain of the guard.

Gen. 37.2–36

Joseph in Egypt Contends with Officer's Wayward Wife

Yosef is taken down to Egypt, and Potiphar,
An officer of Pharaoh, captain of the guard,
An Egyptian, brings him from the Ishmaelites,
Who have brought him there. And the lord
Is with Yosef, and he is a prosperous man,
And he is in the house of his Egyptian master.
And his master sees that the lord is with him,
And that the lord makes everything in his hands
Prosper. And Yosef finds favor in his sight,

15. The underworld.

And he serves him and he makes him overseer
In his house, and all that he places in his hands.
And from the time he makes him overseer

In his house and over everything he has.
The lord blesses the Egyptian's house for Yosef's
Sake, and the blessing of the lord is on
All that he has in the house and the field.
And he leaves all that he has in Yosef's hands,
And he is concerned with nothing but the bread
That he eats. And Yosef is handsome
And good-looking. After a while his master's wife
Casts her eyes on Yosef and she says, "Lie
With me." But he refuses. He says

To his master's wife, "Look, my master
Gives no thought to anything in the house
And all he has he has put in my hands.
There is none greater in this house than I.
He has withheld nothing from me
Except you, because you are his wife.
How could I do this evil act
And offend God?" And although
She speaks to Yosef day after day,
He did not consent to lie by her
Or be with her. However, one day
When he comes into the house

To perform his work, and while there is
No man of the men inside the house
She seizes him by his garment, and says,
"Lie with me," and he leaves his garment
In her hand and runs outside.
When she sees that he has left his garment
In her hand and has fled outside,
She calls out to people in the house

And speaks to them, saying, "See, my husband
Took a Jew into the house to play with us.

But when he came to lie with me,
I screamed loud and when he heard my scream,
He left his garment beside me and fled outside."
She keeps his garment by her until her master
Comes home. And she tells him the same story,
Saying, "The Jewish slave whom you brought
Among us came into the house to insult me
And I screamed and cried out and he left his garment
Beside me and fled outside." When his master
Hears the words that his wife spoke to him,

Saying, "This is the way Yosef your slave
Treated me," he is furious. And his master
Takes him and puts him in the prison
Where the king's prisoners are confined
And God is with Yosef in the prison,
And is kind to him, and disposes
Him favorably in the eyes of the chief jailer.

Gen. 39.1–21

Joseph Interprets the Pharaoh's Dreams

Yet the chief cupbearer does not think of Yosef.
He forgets him. After two years Pharaoh dreams,
While he is standing by the river. And, look,
There come up out of the river seven cows,
Sleek and fat, and they graze in the reed grass.
Then seven other cows come up from the Nile,
Ugly and lean. They stand beside the cows
On the bank of the Nile. The ugly and lean
Eat up the seven handsome cows. Pharaoh awakes.

Then he falls asleep and dreams a second time,
And, behold, seven ears of grain come up
On one stalk, plump and good, and look,
Seven thin ears blasted by the east wind
Spring up after them. The seven thin ears
Devour the seven plump and good ears.
And Pharaoh awakes. It is a dream.
In the morning his spirit is troubled,
And he sends and calls for all the magicians

Of Egypt and all its wise men. Pharaoh
Tells them his dream, but none can
Interpret them to Pharaoh. Then the chief
Cupbearer speaks to Pharaoh, saying,
"Today I remember my offenses. Pharaoh
Is angry with his servants, and puts me
And the chief baker in custody of the captain
Of the guard. Both me and the chief baker.
And we dream a dream on the same night,

He and I have a dream with its own meaning.
A young Jew is there with us, a servant
To the captain of the guard. When we tell him
Our dreams, he solves them for us, each dream.
Yes, he solves each of our dreams, and
I am restored to office and the baker is hanged."
Then Pharaoh sends and calls for Yosef,
And he is rushed out of the dungeon.
When he shaves himself and changes his clothes,

He appears before the Pharaoh. And Pharaoh
Says to Yosef, "I have dreamed a dream,
But no one can interpret it. I have heard
That you hear a dream and you understand."
Yosef answers Pharaoh, saying, "It is not I.

God will look to Pharaoh's welfare."
And Pharaoh says to Yosef, "In my dream,

I stand on the banks of the Nile, and look,
There come up out of the Nile seven cows,
Sleek and fat, and they graze in the reed grass.
Then seven other cows come up from the Nile,
Ugly and lean. They stand beside the cows
On the bank of the Nile. The ugly and lean cows
Eat up the handsome and fat cows, but they look
As ugly as before. And Pharaoh awakes
And falls asleep again and has a second dream.

Seven ears come up on one stalk, fat and good.
Then seven ears thin and blighted are blasted
By the east wind. The thin ears swallow
The fat and good ears, and Pharaoh awakes
And it is a dream. In the morning his spirit
Is troubled. He sends for the magicians in Egypt
But no one can interpret to it to him."
And Yosef says to Pharaoh, "The dream

Of Pharaoh is one and the same. God shows
Pharaoh what will happen. The seven good cows
Are seven years. And the seven good ears
Are seven years. The dream is one. And the
Seven lean and ugly cows that came up
After them are seven years, and the seven empty ears
Blasted by the east wind shall be seven years
Of famine. This is what I have revealed
To Pharaoh, and what will happen
He shows Pharaoh. See that there will come

Seven years of great plenty throughout all
The land of Egypt. And there shall arise

After them seven years of famine. And
All the plenty shall be forgotten in the land
Of Egypt and the famine shall consume
The land, and the plenty shall not be known
In the land by reason of that famine
Following. For it shall be very grievous.
And the doubling of Pharaoh's dream
Means that God has determined all this
And soon God will carry out his plans.

Now let Pharaoh look for and select a man
Discerning and wise, and set him over the land
Of Egypt. Let Pharaoh do this. Appoint
Overseers of the land who will store
One fifth of the produce of the land
During the seven years of plenty. And let them
Gather all the food of those good coming years
And lay up grain by authority of Pharaoh.
That food will be a reserve in the cities
Against the seven years of famine

That will come upon the land of Egypt
So that the land not perish through the famine."
The plan pleases Pharaoh and all his servants.
Pharaoh tells his servants, "Can we find
A man who has the spirit of God?"
And Pharaoh says to Yosef, "Since God
Has revealed all these things to you,
There is no one so discerning and wise as you.
Now you will be in charge of my house
And all my people shall follow your commands."

Gen. 40.23–41.40

Pharaoh Makes Joseph Master of Egypt

"Only by the throne will I be greater than you."
And Pharaoh tells Yosef, "See, I have
Placed you in charge of all the land of Egypt."
And Pharaoh takes his ring off his hand
And puts it on Yosef's hand, and arrays him
In robes of fine linen and hangs a gold
Chain around his neck. He has him ride

In the second chariot of his next-in-command.
They call out before him, *"Abrek! Make way!"*
So he sets him over all the land of Egypt.
And Pharaoh says to Yosef, "I am Pharaoh,
And without your wish no one shall raise his hand
Or foot in all the land of Egypt." And Pharaoh
Gives him the name "Zaphnath-Paneah," and gives

Him Asenath, the daughter of Potipherah,
priest of On, as his wife. So Yosef becomes
The governor of the whole land of Egypt. Yosef
Is thirty years old when he stands before Pharaoh,
King of Egypt. After Yosef leaves the presence
Of Pharaoh, he journeys throughout
All the land of Egypt. And in the seven

Years of plenty, the earth yields an abundance,
And he gathers all the grain of the seven years,
That are in the land of Egypt, and stores
The food in the cities. He gathers grain from
The countryside around. Joseph piles up
Grain like the sand of the sea and ceases
Counting since it goes beyond all measure.

Before the years of the famine came, Asenath,
Daughter of Potipherah Priest of On,
Bears Yosef two sons. He names the firstborn

Manasseh. He says, "God made me forget all
My hardships in my father's house."
He called the second Ephraim, "For God
Made me fruitful in the land of my misfortunes."

Gen. 41.40–52

Joseph Tells His Brothers to Go Home and Tell Jacob that He Is Alive

Yosef can no longer control himself before all
His attendants. "Clear out everyone." There is no
One there when he makes himself known
To his brothers. His sobs are so loud the Egyptians
And Pharaoh's household hear.
Yosef says to his brothers, "I am Yosef.

Is my father still alive?" His brothers dismayed
And dumbfounded cannot answer. "Come
Closer to me, I ask." They come closer.
He tells them, "I am your brother Yosef,
Whom you sold into Egypt. Do not despair
Or anger yourselves for selling me into Egypt.

God sent me here to save life. For two years
There has been famine in the land. There will be
Five more years of no plowing or harvest.
God sent me ahead to make you a survivor,
Both you and your offspring. So God sent me,
Not you. He made me a father to Pharaoh

And lord of his household and ruler of Egypt.
Hurry back to my father and say to him
That God has made me lord of all Egypt,
And come here without delay. You will live
In the land of Goshen, near me, you and your
Sons and their sons, your flocks and cattle

And everything yours. Despite five more years
Of famine, I will provide you and household
Against want. Now your eyes and the eyes of
My brother Benyamin know it is my mouth
Speaking to you. Tell my father everything
About my glory in Egypt and all you have seen,

And quickly bring my father here." Yosef
Hugs his brother Benyamin's neck and weeps
And Benyamin weeps on his neck. He kisses
All his brothers and weeps on them. Then,
His brothers can speak to him. The news reaches
Pharaoh's palace. "Yosef's brothers have come.

Tell your brothers to load up your beasts and go.
Do this. Go back to the land of Canaan. Return
With your father and your households and come
To me. I will give them the best land in Egypt
And you will live off the fat of the land.
More, take your wives and father here. Forget

Your belongings. The best land in Egypt
Will be yours." Yisrael's sons do so. Yosef
Gives them wagons as Pharaoh commanded
And supplies for the journey. To each he gives
A garment, three hundred pieces of silver
And five changes of clothes. To his father

He sends ten donkeys loaded with Egypt's
Best things, and ten female donkeys loaded
With grain, bread, and provisions for his father
For the trip. As he sends his brothers off,
He says, "Don't quarrel on the way."
So they go up out of Egypt and come to

Their father Yaakov in the land of Canaan.
They tell him, "Yosef is still alive! He is
Ruler of Egypt." His heart goes numb. Yaakov
Cannot believe them. But when they recount
All that Yosef said to them and he sees
The wagons that Yosef has ordered carried

To him, his spirit revives. "Enough!" says
Yisrael. "My son Yosef is still alive!
I must go and see him, before I die."

Gen. 45.1–28

God Speaks to Jacob Vowing to Make Him a Great Nation

"My son still alive! I must see him before I die."
And Yisrael takes his journey with all that
He has. He comes to Beersheba and offers
Sacrifices to the God of his father Yitzhak
And God speaks to Yisrael in the visions
Of the night, and says, "Yaakov, Yaakov."

And he says, "Here I am." And he says,
"I Am God, the God of your father.
Do not fear to go down to Egypt,
For I will go down with you and there
I will make you a great nation
And I myself will bring you back

And Yosef's hand will close your eyes."
Yaakov sets out from Beersheba
And the sons of Yisrael carry
Yaakov their father and their
Children and their wives in the wagons
That Pharaoh has sent to carry him.

They take their cattle, and their wealth
That they acquired in the land of Canaan,
And come into Egypt, Yaakov and all
His offspring with him: his sons, his sons' sons
With him; his daughters and his sons' daughters,
All his offspring he brings with him to Egypt.

Gen. 45.28–46.7

EXODUS

Ἔξοδος   Shimoth   שְׁמוֹת

The word "Exodus" in the Book of Exodus is a Latinized version of the Greek title "Exodos" (Ἔξοδος), meaning "the road out." In Torah it is Shemot (שְׁמוֹת), meaning "Names." As with Genesis, in the Hebrew Bible, the title derives from the first word of the book, which is Shemot. Exodus has been called the founding myth of Israel. On Mount Sinai Yahweh gives Moses a pact, called the Mosaic Covenant or the Sinaitic Covenant, by which Moses receives laws and the Ten Commandments and will lead his people from slavery, across Egypt and the Dead Sea, to freedom in Canaan. The covenant also prefigures a future event, when the Jews will reach Judah (Latinized as Judea) and found the southern kingdom of Israel. Throughout Exodus there are fragments of poems or complete ones, such as the heroic "Song of Moses," which may date back to the twelfth century and have somehow, fortunately, been preserved in the later compositions.

After the death of Jacob in Egypt the Jews are enslaved by Pharaoh. In this epic account, under Moses's leadership his people escape and survive, wandering in the wilderness for forty years until they reach the borders of Canaan. The early chapters tell the magic story of the baby Moses being discovered floating in the bull rushes of the Nile by Pharaoh's daughter, who loves the child. Moses grows up and becomes the leader of the Jews. Then there is a constancy of trouble as Pharaoh and Moses contend. Moses uses God's powers to inflict punishment on Pharaoh's Egypt of ten plagues, including ruination of crops, death of firstborns, and even of

Pharoh's own firstborn son. When nothing works to halt the persecution, with God's help Moses escapes in the night to begin the decades-long journey across the desert wilderness, accumulating new laws, a holy covenant from God, and promises of eternal support as the people persist in reaching the borders of Canaan.

Jews Oppressed in Egypt

Yosef dies and all his brothers and all that generation
But the Jews are fertile and prolific.
They multiply and increase greatly so the land
Is filled with them. A new king arises over Egypt
Who did not know Yosef.
He tells the people, "Look, the Jewish people

Are more numerous than we and more powerful.
Let us deal with them shrewdly
Or they will increase, or in event of war
Join our enemies and fight against us and escape
From the land." So they set task masters
Over them to oppress them into forced labor.

So for Pharaoh they build the garrison cities Pithom
And Raamses. The more they are oppressed,
The more they increase and spread about.
The Egyptians start to dread the Jews and ruthlessly impose
Burdens on them. Their lives are bitter,
Enslaved to mortar and brick and painful labor in the field.

Exod. 1.6–14

Murder of First Sons

The king of Egypt speaks to the Jewish midwives,
One of whom is named Shiprah,[1]
The other Pua,[2] and he says, "When you deliver
A child to a Jewish woman,
See them on the birth stool. If a boy, kill him.

If a girl, let her live." The midwives, fearing God,
Do not follow the king of Egypt's command

1. Shiphrah, meaning "beautiful."
2. Puah, meaning "splendid."

And let the boys live. The king of Egypt summons
The midwives, and says to them,
"Why have you done this? Allowing the boys to live?"

The midwives tell Pharaoh, "Jewish women
Are not like Egyptian women. They are
Strong and give birth before the midwife comes."
So God is good to the midwives,
And the people increase and become powerful.

The midwives fear God and he gives them families.
Then Pharaoh charges all his people,
Saying, "Every boy who is born,
You must cast into the river,
And every girl you must allow to live."

Exod. 1.15–22

A Jewish Baby Among the Bulrushes

A certain man from the house of Levi
Weds a Levite woman. She conceives and bears
Him a son. When she sees how beautiful he is,
She hides him for three months.
When she can no longer hide him,
She finds him a papyrus basket,
Coats it with bitumen and pitch,
Places the child inside and lays it among the reeds
By the bank of the Nile. His sister stands at
A distance to see what will happen to him.

The Pharaoh's daughter comes down to bathe
In the river while her maids walk

Along the Nile. When she spies
The basket among the reeds, she sends
Her maid to bring it. When she opens it,

She sees the child, a boy crying.
And she takes pity on him, and says,
"This must be a Jewish child."
Then his sister says to Pharaoh's daughter,
"Shall I go get you a Jewish nurse

From the Jewish women to nurse him
For you?" Pharaoh's daughter says,
"Yes." So the girl calls for the child's mother.
Pharaoh's daughter says, "Take this child
And nurse him for me. I will pay your wages."
The woman takes the child and nurses it,
When the child grows up, she brings him
To Pharaoh's daughter. She takes him as her son.
She names him Mosheh,[3] she explains,
"Because I drew him out of the water."

Exod. 2.1–10

Moses Kills an Egyptian, Flees, and Soon Finds a Wife

When Mosheh is grown, he goes to
His people and sees their forced labor.
He sees an Egyptian beating a Jew,
A kinsman. He looks all around,
And spotting no one near, he kills
The Egyptian and hides him in the sand.
When he goes out the next day,
He sees two Jews fighting. To one
In the wrong, he asks, "Why do you strike
Your own?" The man answers,
"Who made you chief and ruler over us?
Will you kill me like the Egyptian?"
Mosheh is afraid and thinks,

---

3. Mosheh from the מֹשֶׁה Hebrew (Mosheh), meaning "drawn from" the water.

"Surely they all know about it."
When Pharaoh hears of it, he tries
To kill Mosheh. He flees from Pharaoh
And settles in the land of Midian.[4]

Mosheh sits down by a well. Now
The priest of Midian has seven daughters.
They come and draw water. They fill
The troughs to water their father's flock,
When shepherds arrive and drive
Them away. Mosheh stands up
And defends them. He waters their flock.
And when they return to their father,
Reuel asks, "How can you be back
So soon today?" "An Egyptian rescued us
From the shepherds. He even drew water,
Enough for us to water the flock."
And he asks his daughters,
"Where is he? Why did you leave
The man? Call him to break bread."
Mosheh agrees to stay with them,
And Reuel gives Mosheh his daughter
Gipporah.[5] She bears him a son he names
Gershom, the stranger,[6] "For," he claims,
"I have been a stranger in a strange land."

Exod. 2.11–22

God Remembers Israel

After a long time, the king of Egypt dies,
And the Jews are groaning under their slavery.
And they cry out. Out of slavery, their cry
Reaches God. God hears their groaning,

---

4. Midian from Hebrew מִדְיָן (Midian). Midian was a son of Abraham.
5. Zipporah from Hebrew צִפּוֹרָה (Tsipora), meaning "small bird."
6. Goshem from Hebrew גֵּרְשֹׁם (gershom), meaning "stranger" and "sojourner."

And God remembers his covenant
With Avraham, Yitzhak, and Yaakov.
And God looks over the Jews
And God sees them with clarity.

Exod. 2.23–25

The Burning Bush

Now Mosheh tends the flock of Yethro,[7]
His father-in-law, the rabbi of Midian.
And he leads the flock into the wilderness,
And reaches Horeb, the mountain of God.[8]
And the angel of the lord appears

To him in a flame of fire in the middle
Of a bush. He gazes. The bush is blazing
With fire and the bush is not consumed.
And Mosheh says, "I must turn away to look
At this wondrous sight. Why is the bush

Not burning?" When the lord sees
Him turning to look, God calls to him from
The middle of the bush, and says, "Mosheh, Mosheh."
He says, "Here I am." He orders, "Do not
Come nearer. Remove the sandals from

Your feet. The place where you are standing
Is holy ground. Remember that I am
The God of your father, the God of Avraham,
The God of Yitzhak and the God of Yaakov,"
And Mosheh hides his face. He is

Frightened to look at God. The lord says,
"I have observed the misery of my people

7. Jethro from Hebrew יִתְרוֹ Yitro, meaning "Your excellency," and also "Rueul."
8. Mount Horeb may also be Mount Sinai.

In Egypt. I have heard their cry
Because of their taskmasters. Yes,
I know their sorrows, and I

Have come down to rescue them
From the Egyptians and to bring
Them up and out of that country to a good
And spacious country flowing
With milk and honey; to take them

To the home of the Canaanites,[9]
The Hittites, the Amorites, the Perizzites,
The Hivites and the Yevusees.[10]
The cry of the Yisraelis has reached me.
I have also observed the ways

The Egyptians enslave the people
With painful labor. Be prepared.
I shall send you to Pharaoh and you
Will bring my people, the Yisraelis,
Out of Egypt." Mosheh responds,

"Who am I to go to Pharaoh
And to undertake the job of bringing
The Jews out of Egypt?" God responds,
"I shall be with you and this will be
The sign for you that it is I

Who have sent you. When you have
Lifted the people to escape from Egypt,
You will worship God on this mountain."

---

9. Canaanites are from Canaan, from Hebrew כְּנַעַן (Kanaan). Canaan may be same as Phoenician, and in Greek appears so.
10. Jebusites from the Hebrew יְבוּסִי (Yevusee). A tribe from Canaan and uncertainly claimed as the first rulers of Jerusalem.

Mosheh asks God, "When I come to
The people of Yisrael, and tell them:

'The God of your fathers
Has sent me to you,' but if they ask me
'What is his name?' what shall I say?"
And God tells Mosheh, "*Ehyeh Asher Ehyeh*
I AM WHO I AM.[11] These are

The words you say to the Yisraelis.
'I AM has sent me to you.'" God says to Mosheh,
"Tell them, 'The God of your fathers, the God
Of Avraham, the God of Yitzhak,
The God of Yaakov has sent me to you.'

These words shall be my name
Forever and for all generations to come.
Go and gather the elders
Of Yisrael, and say to them,
'The lord God of your fathers,

The God of Avraham, of Yitzhak and Yaakov
Appeared to me, saying, "I have
Visited you. I have seen
You afflicted in Egypt. And I have said,
'I shall free you from your suffering in Egypt

To live in the land of the Canaanites and Hittites
Of the Amorites and Perizzites,
Of the Hivites and the Yevusites,
In lands flowing with milk and honey.'
And they will listen to your voice

---

11. I Am Who I Am, *Ehyeh Asher Ehyeh,* אֶהְיֶה אֲשֶׁר אֶהְיֶה.

And you and the elders of Yisrael
Will go to the king of Egypt.
Together you will tell him,
'The lord God of the Jews has met with us.'
Let us now go on a three day journey

Into the wilderness to sacrifice to the lord
Our God. Yet I know that the king of Egypt
Will not let you go unless
Compelled by a mighty hand.
I will stretch out my hand,

And strike Egypt with all my wonders
And miracles that I shall perform
Among them. After that they will let you go.
I will grant this people favor
In the eyes of the Egyptians

So that when you depart
You will not leave empty-handed.
Every woman will ask
Her neighbor or any lodger in her house
For jewelry of silver and ornaments of gold.

You will ask for robes,
And in these ways you will array
Your sons and array your daughters
And by these means you have a way
To despoil the Egyptians."

Exod. 3.1–22

Moses's Staff Becomes a Snake

Mosheh answers, saying, "What
If they do not believe me and do not
Listen to me and say the lord
Did not appear to him?"

The lord questions him, "What is in your hand?"
He answers, "A staff."
"Fling it on the ground." He flings it on the ground
And it becomes a snake.

Mosheh recoils. The lord says,
"Put out your hand and grasp its tail."
He seizes it and it becomes a staff
In his hand to make them believe the lord,

The God of their fathers. Then the lord
Tells Mosheh, "Place your hand
Inside your cloak." When he takes it out,
His hand is leprous white like snow.

God says, "Put your hand back in your cloak,"
And look, it comes back like all his flesh.
"If they will not believe you
Or these two signs or heed your voice,

You must take water out of the Nile
And pour it on the dry ground.
The water you take from the Nile
Will become blood on the dry earth."

Exod. 4.1–9

Plague of Death for Newborns

Mosheh is highly esteemed in Egypt
In the eyes of Pharaoh's officials
And in the eyes of the people. Mosheh says,

"God declares, 'Around midnight I shall go
Into the heart of Egypt and all firstborn
In Egypt will die, from the firstborn of Pharaoh

Who sits on his throne to the firstborn of the slave girl
Behind the mill, and all the firstborn of beasts.
There will be a great wailing through

All the land of Egypt never heard before
Nor ever will be heard again.
But no dog will snarl at the Jews, at man

Or beast, and you will see how God
Distinguishes between Egypt and Yisrael.
All your officials will bow low to me, saying,

"Go out, and all your people with you."
Then I shall go.'" In a flame of anger,
Mosheh leaves Pharaoh. God tells Mosheh

Pharaoh will not listen to you.
So that my miracles multiply in Egypt.
Then Mosheh and Aaron perform their wonders.

Exod. 11.3–10

Passover Matzot Feast

God says to Mosheh and Aaron in Egypt,
"This month will mark the beginning.
Tell the whole congregation of Yisrael
That on the tenth day of this month
They are to take a lamb for each family,
For each house. If the house be too small

For a lamb, let him share it with his neighbor
In proportion to the persons. One lamb
Take according to the number there.
Contribute one lamb for each house
Without blemish, a yearling male. You
May choose from the sheep or goat

And watch over it until the fourteenth day
Of the same month. The whole congregation
Of Yisrael will slaughter it at twilight.
They will take some blood and put it on
The two doorposts and on the lintels
Of the houses where they will eat it.

They will eat the lamb the same night,
Roasted over fire, with unleavened bread
And bitter herbs. Nothing raw or boiled in water,
But roasted, head, legs, and entrails,
Over the fire. Save nothing for the morning,
And what remains, burn. This is how you eat:

A belt around your waist, sandals on your feet,
Your staff in your hand. Eat quickly. It is
The Passover of the lord. On that night
I shall go through Egypt and kill all firstborns
In the land of Egypt, both man and beast,
And punish all the gods of Egypt. I am the lord.

Where you are when I see the blood, I will
Pass over you so no plague will destroy you
When I strike the land of Egypt. This day
Will be a remembrance. You will celebrate it
For a memorial, and you shall keep it a feast
To the lord throughout your generations."

Exod. 12.1–14

Death of the Firstborn

At midnight the lord strikes down
All the firstborn in Egypt from the firstborn
Of Pharaoh who sits on his throne
To the firstborn of the captive in the dungeon
And all the firstborn of cattle. Pharaoh rises
In the night along with all his officials

And all Egyptians. A loud cry covers Egypt.
There is no house without the dead.
He summons Mosheh and Aaron
In the night, and says, "Get up, depart
From my people, you and the Yisraelis!
Go worship your lord, as you have spoken.

Take your flocks and herds and be gone.
And bring me a blessing too." The people
Seize their dough before it is leavened,
Their kneading bowls wrapped in cloaks
On their shoulders. The Jews do as Mosheh
Told them. They ask Egyptians for jewels

Of silver and gold, and clothing. God disposes
Them favorably. They strip the Egyptians.
The Yisraelis journey from Rameses
To Succoth, six hundred thousand on foot,
Men and children, a motley crowd
Go with them, sheep and goats,

And vast livestock. They bake the cakes
Of unleavened dough they brought out
Of Egypt. It is not leavened
Since they are driven out of Egypt.
They cannot delay. They prepared
No provisions. Yisrael lived in Egypt

Four hundred thirty years. At four hundred
Thirty years to the day battalions of the lord
Depart from Egypt. It is a night of vigil
For the lord to bring them out of Egypt
And that same night is a vigil to be kept
By all Jews though every generation.

Exod. 12.29–42

God in a Pillar of Cloud Leads His People to the Sea of Reeds

When Pharaoh lets the people go,
God does not lead them through
The closer land of the Philistines,
Though it is nearer. God calculates,
"If people face war, they may regret
And return to Egypt." So God leads
The people around through the wilderness
Of the Sea of Reeds. The Jews are
Fully armed when they leave Egypt.
Mosheh takes with him the bones
Of Yosef, who has exacted an oath
From the Yisraelis, "God will surely
Visit you. You must carry my bones
With you from here on." They set out
From Succoth and encamp in Etham
And at the edge of the wilderness.
The lord goes before them by day
In a pillar of a cloud to guide them
Along the way, and by night in a pillar
Of fire to give them light to travel
Day and night. The pillar of cloud
And the pillar of fire by night he keeps
In place and never leaves his people.

Exod. 13.17–22

Pharaoh Will Chase Them with Chariots and Troops

The lord speaks to Mosheh, saying,
"Tell the Jews to turn back and camp
Before Pi Hahiroth, between Migdol
And the sea. You will camp facing Baal Zephon
By the sea. Pharaoh will think that the Jews

Are wandering lost in the wilderness
That has closed in on them. I will stiffen
Pharaoh's heart and he will pursue them
And so I will gain glory through Pharaoh
And his army. The Egyptians will know
That I am the lord." The Jews do so.
When the king of Egypt is told

That the people have fled, Pharaoh
And his officials have a change of heart,
And they say, "What have we done
By releasing Yisrael from our service?"
So he harnesses his chariot and takes
His men with him. He takes six hundred
Select chariots, and all other chariots
In Egypt, with officers in each. The lord
Stiffens the heart of Pharaoh king
Of Egypt, and he pursues the Yisraelis
Who are leaving defiantly. They
Overtake them camping by the sea

And all Pharaoh's horses and riders,
Chariots, and his troops overtake them
Camping by the sea, near Pi Hahiroth,
Before Baalzephon. As Pharaoh draws near,
The Jews look up terrified. They
Cry out to the lord. They tell Mosheh,
"Was it because there were no graves,
No graves in Egypt that you brought
Us here to die in the wilderness?
What have you done to us, taking us
Out of Egypt? Is this not what we
Told you in Egypt: to let us alone

And serve the Egyptians? It is better
To serve the Egyptians than to die

In the wilderness." But Mosheh says
To the people, "Have no fear, stand firm
And see your deliverance that the lord
Will accomplish today. The Egyptians
You see today, you will never see again.
God will battle for you. Keep your peace!"
Then the lord says to Mosheh, "Why
Do you cry out to me? Tell the Yisraelis
To go forward. Lift up your staff
And stretch your hand over the sea

And divide it so that the Jews can go
Into the sea on dry ground. Then
I will stiffen the hearts of the Egyptians
So they will go in after them. I will be
Glorious before the Pharaoh and before
His army, his chariots and chariot drivers.
The Egyptians shall know that I am
The lord when I am glorious before
His chariots and chariot drivers."
The angel of the God who went before
The Yisraeli army moves and goes
Behind them. The pillar of cloud

Shifts from in front to a place behind.
It comes between the Egyptian army
And the Yisraeli army. So there is a cloud
Of darkness and it lights the night.
No one comes near the other all night.
And Mosheh stretches his hand out
Over the sea and the lord drives
The sea with a strong east wind all
That night and turns the sea into dry
Ground. The waters form a wall
For them on their right and on the left
And the Jews march into the sea

On dry ground, and the waters
Are a wall to them on their right hand
And on their left. The Egyptians chase
After them, all Pharaoh's horses,
His chariots and his chariot drivers.
At the morning watch, the lord in
The pillar of fire and cloud looks down
On the Egyptian army and throws
His army into panic. He clogs
Their chariot wheels so they can hardly
Move and the Egyptians say, "Let us flee

From the Yisraelis, for the lord
Is fighting for them against Egypt."
Then the lord tells Mosheh,
"Stretch your hand over the sea
So the water may come back
Over their chariots and over the chariot
Drivers," and Mosheh stretches his hand
Over the sea, and at daybreak the sea returns
To its full flow as the Egyptians flee
Against it, and as the Egyptians
Flee against it, the lord throws
The Egyptians into the sea. The waters

Return and cover the chariots,
The chariot drivers, and Pharaoh's entire
Army that follows them into the sea.
Not one of them survives.
So the lord saves Yisrael that day
From the Egyptians. Yisrael sees
The Egyptians dead on the shore.
And when they see the wondrous power
That the lord wields against
The Egyptians, the people

Fear the lord and believe
The lord and in his servant Mosheh.

Exod. 14.1–31

Moses's Song of Deliverance

Then Mosheh and the Yisraelis
Sing this song to the lord.

"He triumphs gloriously.
He hurls horse and rider into the sea.

The lord is my strength and power
He is my salvation."

Exod. 15.1–3

The Song of Mary

The prophet Miryam, Aaron's sister,
Takes a timbrel in her hand.
All the women come out with her
In a dance with timbrels.
And Miryam chants:

"Let us sing to the lord
Who triumphs gloriously.
He hurls horse and rider into the sea."

Exod. 15.20–21

Cakes of Manna from Heaven

Mosheh leads Yisrael from the Sea of Reeds[12]
To the wilderness of Shur. They travel
Three days in the wilderness and find

12. The Red Sea.

No water. When they come to Marah, they
Cannot drink the water. It is bitter.
When they reach Marah, they cannot drink.

They call it Marah, meaning "bitter."
The people murmur against Mosheh, saying,
"What can we drink?" He shouts to the lord,

And God shows him a piece of wood. He throws
It into the water and the water turns sweet.
There he made a fixed rule and put them

To a test. He says, "If you hear your God
Carefully, do what is good in his sight
And obey his commandments and laws,

I will bring no disease I brought to Egyptians.
I am the lord who heals you." They reach Elim.
There are twelve springs of water and seventy

Palm trees, and they camp there by the water.
They lumber to Elim. The whole community
Of Yisrael comes to the wilderness of Sin that lies

Between Elim and Sinai. On the fifteenth day
Of the second month after leaving Egypt,
The whole congregation of Yisrael

Grumbles against Mosheh and Aaron in
The wilderness. "If only we had died in Egypt,"
The people say to them: "If only we had died

By the hand of the lord when we sat
By fleshpots in the land of Egypt,
When we ate our fill of bread! You have brought

Us out into the wilderness to kill us
With hunger." And the lord says to Mosheh,
"I shall rain bread from the sky to you,

And the people will go out each day and gather
Their portion they have brought in. So I
Shall test whether they follow my instructions

Or not. On the sixth day when they prepare
The portion that they bring in,
It will be twice what they gather

On other days." Mosheh and Aaron say
To all the Yisraelites, "By evening you
Will know that it was God who brought you out

Of Egypt, and in the morning you shall see
The glory of the lord, for God has heard
Your grumbling against him. But who are we

To grumble against him? And your complaint
Is not against us but the lord." Then Mosheh says,
"Draw near the lord. He has heard your grief."

And as Aaron speaks to the people, they look
And the glory of the lord appears in a cloud.
The lord spoke to Mosheh, saying, "I have heard

The grumbling of the Yisraelites. Speak
To them and say, 'By twilight you shall eat
Meat and in the morning you shall have your fill

Of bread. You will know I am your lord, your God.'"
That evening quail rises and chants over the camp,
In the morning there is a layer of dew around

The camp. When the layer of dew lifts,
Over the surface of the wilderness
Lies a fine flaky substance as fine as frost

On the ground. When the Jews see it, they ask
One another, "What is it?" They do not know.
Mosheh tells them, "This is the bread God

Has given you to eat. Gather as much
As each of you needs to eat, an *omer*
To a person. Each take enough for those

In tents." The Jews do so, some gathering
A lot, others little. They measure it by
The *omer*. "No one should leave any of it

Until morning." But they pay no attention
To Mosheh. Some leave it until morning.
It is infested by maggots and stinks.

Mosheh is angry. So each morning they
Gather. When the sun grows hot it melts.
On the sixth day they take twice the amount,

Two *omers* for each. When the leaders tell
Mosheh, he says, "What the lord commands
Is 'Tomorrow is a day of solemn leisure,

A holy sabbath to the lord. Bake what
You would bake and boil what you would boil.
What is left, put aside until morning.'"

So they put it aside until morning as Mosheh
Had ordered. It does not become foul.
No worms in it. Then Mosheh says,

"Eat it today for today is the sabbath
To the lord. Today you will not find it
In the field. Six days you gather.

On the seventh day, the sabbath,
There is none." On the seventh day some of
Them go out to gather, but there is none.

The lord says to Mosheh, "How long will you
Refuse to keep my commands and my
Instructions? The lord gives you the sabbath.

So on the sixth day he gives you bread for
Two days. Let all stay where you are.
Do not leave your place on the seventh day."

The people of Yisrael rest on the seventh day.
The house of Yisrael calls
It manna. It is like coriander seed

White and tasting like wafers in honey.
Mosheh says, "This is what the lord commands:
Let one *omer* of it be kept for generations.

As commanded by God so they may see bread
I fed you in the wilderness when I took
You out of Egypt." Mosheh says to Aaron,

"Take a jar, put one *omer* of manna
In it and place it before the lord to be held
For generations." As God commands Mosheh,

Aaron places it before the covenant for
Safety and the Jews eat manna for forty years
Until they come to the border of Canaan.

Exod. 15.22–16.35

Coming to Canaan

From the wilderness of Sin
The whole Jewish community
Journeys by stages as the lord commands
They camp at Rehidim, but there is no
Water for the people to drink.

The people quarrel with Mosheh
And say, "Give us water to drink."
Mosheh tells them, "Why do you
Quarrel with me? Why do you try
The lord?" But the people tormented

By thirst complain against Mosheh,
Saying, "Why bring us out of Egypt
To kill us and our children
And our livestock with thirst?"
And Mosheh cries out to God saying,

"What shall I do with this people?
They are about to stone me."
God tells Mosheh, "Go on ahead
Of the people, take the elders of Yisrael
With you, and the staff with which

You struck the Nile. I will stand there
Before you on the rock in Horeb.
Strike the rock and water will come out
So the people may drink." Mosheh
Does before the eyes of the elders of Yisrael.

Exod. 17.1–6

Moses's Hands and Joshua in Battle with Amalek

Then Amalek comes and fights with Yisrael
In Rephidim. Mosheh said to Yeshua,[13] "Choose men
To fight Amalek. Tomorrow I will stand on
The hilltop with the staff of God in my hand."
So Yeshua does as Mosheh tells him and fights Amalek.

Mosheh, Aaron, and Hur climb to the hilltop.
When Mosheh holds up his hand,
Yisrael prevails. When he lets his hands down
Amalek prevails. But Mosheh's hands are heavy.
They take a stone, place it below him, he sits on it,

And Aaron and Hur uphold his hands,
One on one side and one on the other.
His hands are firm until the sun sinks.
Yeshua overwhelms Amalek and his people
With the cut of his sword.

The lord tells Mosheh, "Record a memorial
In a book and read it loud to Yeshua's ears.
I will obliterate all memory of Amalek
Under heaven." Mosheh builds an altar,
And calls it *Adonai-nissi*, "God is my banner."

Exod. 17.8–15

Moses Goes Up the Mountain at Sinai and Speaks with God

On the third new moon of Yisrael's flight
From Egypt, on that day they come
To the wilderness of the Sinai. They leave Rephidim

---

13. Joshua. Yeshua in Hebrew and Aramaic for Joshua in Hebrew Bible translations and Jesus in New Testament translations. It remains the same original name.

And enter the wilderness of Sinai.
Yisrael camps there before the mountain
And Mosheh goes up to God.

The lord roars to him from the mountain,
Saying, "In this way you will speak
To the house of Yaakov and tell the Yisraelis,
'You have seen what I did to Egypt,
And how I bore you on eagle wings,
And brought you back to me.

If you will obey my voice and keep my
Covenant, you shall be my treasured
Possession among all peoples.
All the earth is mine. And you shall be
To me a rabbinic kingdom, a holy
Nation.' These are the words

You shall speak to the Jews." Mosheh
Arrives and summons the elders
Of the people, and sets before them
These words that God commands.
The people answer as one, saying,
"Everything God has spoken we will do."

And Mosheh returns the words of the people
To the lord. The lord tells Mosheh,
"I shall come to you in a thick cloud
So that people may hear when I speak
With you and believe you forever."
Then Mosheh tells the people's words

To the lord. And God says to Mosheh,
"Go to the people, sanctify them today
And tomorrow, and let them wash
Their clothes, and be ready for

The third day, for on the third day
The lord will descend on Mount Sinai

In the sight of everyone. You must limit
The people living nearby, saying,
Be careful not to go up the mountain
Or touch its edge. Whoever touches
The mountain shall be put to death.
Touch them and be stoned or shot

With arrows. Whether beast or man
He will die. When the ram's horn blasts
One may go up the mountain."
So Mosheh descends from the mountain
To the people. He blesses the people.
They wash their clothes, and he says

To them, "Prepare for the third day.
Do not go near a woman." On the morning
Of the third day there is lightning
And a thick cloud on the mountain,
And a blast of the ram's horn so loud
All the people in the camp tremble.

Mosheh leads the people out of the camp
To meet God. They stand at the foot
Of the mountain. Mount Sinai is wrapped
In smoke. The lord descends on it in fire.
The smoke rises like smoke of a kiln
While the whole mountain shakes
Violently. The blast of the ram's horn

Grows louder and louder. As Mosheh speaks,
God answers him in thunder. The lord
Descends on Mount Sinai, to its
Mountain top, and Mosheh ascends.

God tells Mosheh, "Go down.
And warn the people they cannot break

Through to gaze or many shall perish.
Even the high rabbis who come near must
Sanctify themselves or God will burst
Out against them." Mosheh says to God,
"The people cannot climb up Mount Sinai;
For you yourself warned us, saying,

'Set limits on the mountain, keep it holy.'"
God tells him, "Go down and come up
With Aaron. Do not let any rabbis
Or people break through to the lord
Or he will burst out against them."
So Mosheh descends to tell the people.

Exod. 19.1–25

The Ten Commandments (or The Decalogue)

God said these words,
1 I am the lord your God who brought you
Out of Egypt, out of the house of slaves.
You shall have no other gods before me.

2 You shall not make an idol[14]
Of what is in skies above or on the earth below,
Or in water under the earth. You shall not bow down
To them or worship them, for I am the lord your God.
I am a jealous God, punishing children
For the iniquity of the fathers down to the third
And fourth generation of those who reject me,
But showing mercy to the thousandth generation
Of those who love me and keep my commands.

14. Or sculptured or graven image.

Moses with the Ten Commandments by Rembrandt.

3 You will not misuse the name of the lord.
  God will not acquit those who misuse his name.

4 Remember the sabbath and keep it holy.
  You shall work for six days, doing all.
  The seventh day is the lord's sabbath.

You and your son and daughter must not work.
Nor your male or female slave, nor cattle,
Nor the foreigner living within your gate.
In six days God made heaven, earth,
The sea and all that is in them. He rested
On the seventh day. Thereby God blessed
The sabbath and hallowed that day.

5   Honor your father and your mother.
So your days be long on the land God gave you.

6   You shall not kill.

7   You shall not commit adultery.

8   You shall not steal.

9   You shall not give false evidence against your neighbor.

10   You shall not covet your neighbor's house.
You shall not covet your neighbor's wife
Or male or female slave or ox or donkey
Or anything that belongs to your neighbor.

Exod. 20.2–17

Smoking Mountain and Darkness

When the people see thunder and flashing sky,
Hear the ram's horn blast, and see
the smoking mountain, they are terrified.

They stand back, tremble, and tell Mosheh
"Speak to us and we will listen, but do not
Let God speak to us or we die."

Mosheh answers the people,
"Do not fear. God has come to test you
And make you fear and not go astray."

The people keep their distance
While Mosheh approaches
The dense darkness where God is.

Exod. 20.18–21

DEUTERONOMY

Δευτερονόμιον   Devarim   דְּבָרִים

The book of Deuteronomy is from the Greek Δευτερονόμιον, Deuteronomion, meaning "second law." The word for the fifth book in Torah is taken from the second century B.C.E. Septuagint translation of the Tanakh for the Greek-speaking Jews of Alexandria who could no longer read Torah in Hebrew.[1] The original name in Torah for the Septuagint is דְּבָרִים, Devarim, meaning "spoken words." The title reflects the early Jewish concern for Moses's additions to Jewish law.

In the literary world, T. S. Eliot, who knew his Bible and cats, chose Deuteronomy as the name of his favorite cat in *Old Possum's Book of Practical Cats*. Deuteronomy is also the hero and star of the musical *Cats* and fittingly acts as a magistrate of the law.

Traditionally, as for the other books in the Five Books of Moses, the author is Moses, but modern scholarship unanimously rejects a Mosaian authorship.

The Hebrew title of Book Five, "Spoken Words," reflects Moses's *telling* us the new set of Jewish laws. The book opens with "These are the words." At the end of the journey and the book, Moses gives a farewell address on the plains of Moav, consisting of three speeches before his people enter the Promised Land. He recounts the history of forty years of wilderness wanderings and exhorts them to observe the teachings, which later will be called "the Law of Moses."

A central moment in Jewish thought occurs in Deuteronomy 6.4: the

---

1. In *Letter to Aristeas*, Moses Hadas reveals that the Septuagint was translated into Greek in the late second century, not the third century as commonly believed.

Shema, which is the definitive statement of Jewish identity: "Hear, O Israel, the Lord our God, the Lord is one, Shema Yisrael Adonai Eloheinu Adonai Eḥad, שְׁמַע יִשְׂרָאֵל יהוה אֱלֹהֵינוּ יהוה אֶחָד."

Deuteronomy also promotes a social contract to help the poor and disadvantaged, which remains a central concept in Judaism to this day.

Judaism is a religion of written laws. But these now codified ideas were spoken to the people and recorded. Always along with the written law, there has been an oral law, much freer, often radical, and usually reformist. We associate later Hillel and the Pharisees, especially Paul, a Pharisee from the tribe of Benjamin, with oral law that rejects the conventional. This has permitted many voices in the Hebrew Bible, as there are many in the Greek scriptures, whose purpose is to change canonical thinking, to reform and float away from a tonnage of commands and restrictions. Oral law has been a liberation leading to a hundred possibilities of significant thought to change a person and a nation and a constant force in both Testaments.

Hear This, O Israel, Land Flowing with Milk and Honey

Hear, O Yisrael, the lord our God, the lord is one.
You shall love the lord your God with all your heart,
With all your soul and all your strength.
Keep in your heart these words I command you today.

Recite them to your children and your children's
Children, and speak them when you are at home
And when you go off on your way, when you lie down
And when you rise. You shall bind them on your hand.

Fix them as an emblem on your forehead, write them
On the doorposts of your house and on your gates.
It shall come about when the lord your God
Brings you into the land that he swore to your fathers,

Avraham, Yitzhak, and Yaakov to assign you
Great and flourishing cities you did not build,
Houses full of good things you did not fill,
Wells you did not dig, vineyards and olive groves

You did not plant. When you fill up with food,
Be sure you do not forget the lord,
Who brought you out of Egypt,
From the house of slaves.

Deut. 6.4–12

Land Flowing with Milk and Honey

"Keep the whole command I charge you
Today so you will be strong
And come to and possess the land
You are about to cross to and endure on her soil
That I God swore to your ancestors

To give them and their seed,
A land flowing with milk and honey.

The land you are about to enter and possess
Is not like the land of Egypt
Where you sow your seed
And water by foot like a vegetable garden.
The land you are crossing into
And will own is a land of mountains and valleys
That soaks up its water from rains of heaven,

A land your lord and God looks after
Perpetually. The eyes of your lord
And God are on it from the beginning
To the end of the year.
If you follow my commands today
And love the lord your God,
Serve him with all your heart and soul,

I will bring rain to you in season,
The early rain and late rain,
Of your land in due season, the early rain
And the late. You will gather
In your new grain, and wine and oil.
He will provide grass in the meadows
So you can eat and be fulfilled."

Deut. 11.8–15

Moses Sings about God Saving Israel

God finds her in a desert land,
 In a wasteland of howling wilderness.
  He shields her and guards her.
He keeps her as the pupil of his eye.

As an eagle rousing its nest,
 He hovers over its young,
  Spreads his wings, take them up
And carries them on his pinions,

So the lord alone guides her.
 There is no alien god by his side.
  He makes him ride on the high places of the land
And feeds him bounty of the fields.

He nurses her to suck honey
 Out of the crags
  With oil from flinty rock
Curds from the herd, and milk from sheep

With fat of lambs and rams
 Bashan bulls and goats,
  With fat kernels of wheat.
You drink fine wine from the blood of grapes.

Deut. 32.10–14

The Lord Speaks to Moses of His Death

On that very day the lord speaks to Mosheh,
Saying, "Climb the heights of Avarim
  To Mount Nevo,
 Which is in the land of Moav,
Facing Yeriho, and gaze
 At the land of Canaan
That I am giving to the Jews.

You will die on the mountain you are to ascend.
You will be gathered to your kin
  As your brother Aaron
 Died on Mount Hor
And was gathered to his people.

You both betrayed me
Among the Jews at the waters of

Meribah-Kadesh in the wilderness of Zin
Because you did not sanctify me
        Amid the children
    Of Yisrael.
You will see the land from far,
    But you will not enter
The land that I am giving to the Yisraelites."

Deut. 32.48–52

The Death of Moses

Mosheh climbs up from the plains of Moav
To the mountain of Nevo to the summit of Pisgah
Facing Yeriho. The lord shows him
The whole land, Gilead as far as Dan, all Naphtali,
The land of Ephraim and Manasseh,
All the land of Yehudah to the Western Sea,
The Negev and the plain—the valley of Yeriho,
The city of palm trees—up to Zoar, and God
Says to him, "This is the land which I swore
To Avraham, Yitshak and Yaakov, saying,
"I will give it to your seed. I have let you see it
With your eyes, but you shall not cross over."

So Mosheh, servant of the lord, dies there in the land
Of Moav, according to the word of the lord.
And he is buried in a glen in the land of Moav,
Opposite Beth–Peor, but no one knows his burial
Place to this day. Moses is a hundred and twenty
When he dies. His eyes are not bleary
And his vigor endless. The Jews of Yisrael weep
Thirty days for Mosheh in the plains of Moav.
The days of wailing and mourning for Mosheh ends.

Yehoshua son of Nun is filled with the spirit of wisdom.
Mosheh has laid his hands on him. The Jews obey him.
There has never risen a prophet in Yisrael like Mosheh,
Whom the lord singles out face to face.
He is unequaled for all signs and wonders that God sent him
To display in Egypt against Pharaoh and his officials
And the whole country, and for the great deeds
And terrifying display of power in the eyes of Yisrael.

Deut. 34.1–12

JUDGES

Shoftim   סֵפֶר שׁוֹפְטִים

The seventh book of the Hebrew and Christian Bibles is Judges. Its Hebrew name is Sefer Shoftim, סֵפֶר שׁוֹפְטִים, meaning "the book of judging." Like Deuteronomy, modern scholarship discounts Samuel as the author of Judges. It may be the oldest of the Deuteronomistic histories, redacted as early as the eighth century B.C.E.

Judges contains amid its histories the story of three strong women, Deborah (Devorah), Jael (Yael), and Delilah. Along with Ruth and Judith, these are among the truly memorable figures of the Bible. Deborah's fierce song is sonorous verse. Jael is a ferocious warrior, supplanting commander Barak, to destroy the Canaanite king Sisera. She is a precursor of Judith in using her sexuality to seduce and crush her enemy. As a warrior leader, Delilah is a figure approaching Eve in her dissidence and Joan of Arc in her heroic leadership. Although she betrays Samson, Samson is initially responsible for loving an enemy woman, though modernly we might admire his novelistic act and passion. Delilah's betrayal is virtually identical to that of Judith's, who poses as a smitten lover of the Assyrian general Holofernes, but whose real and fulfilled intention is to seduce and ultimately behead Holofernes after her "sacrificial" act of yielding him her physical love.

The Hebrew Bible, in contrast to the Christian Bible, has strong representations of many women figures. We are scarcely acquainted with the voice of Mary, mother of Jesus. Mary of Magdala (Mary Magdalene) emerges with major significance in the Gospels.

DEBORAH דְּבוֹרָה

Deborah, דְּבוֹרָה, meaning "bee," is a prophet, warrior, and the only female judge in the Bible.

Song of Warrior Deborah

On that day Devorah and Barak, son of Avinoam, sing:

"When people loosen their hair in Yisrael,
When people gladly labor, bless the lord!
Hear, O kings, give ear, O princes.
    To God I will sing a song.
    I will sing a song to God of Yisrael.

Lord, when you come out of Seir,
When you march from the meadows of Edom,
The earth shakes, the heavens pour rain,
Clouds melt rain. Mountains melt
    Before the lord of Sinai,
    Before the God of Yisrael.

In the days of Shamgar son of Anath,
In the days of Yael the caravans cease
And wayfarers keep to the byways.
The unwalled villages are disappearing
    Until you arise, O Devorah,
    As our mother in Yisrael.

They choose new gods. War comes
To their gates. Is there one shield or spear
Among forty thousand in Yisrael? My heart
    Is with the leaders who
    Labor gladly for Yisrael.

Bless the lord! You who ride white donkeys.

Who sit on regal saddle rugs
And wayfarers who walk on paths
Speak louder than the noise of archers
    By the watering places,
    Extol the bounties of God

Who saves the unwalled villages,
Who saves the peasantry.
Sing the triumph of God's acts
When God's people march to the gates.
    Awake, awake, O Devorah!
    Awake, awake, sing your song!"

Judg. 5.1–12

Song of Woman Warrior Jael

Most blessed above women is Yael,
Wife of Heber the Kenite. Among women
In their tents, she is most blessed.
Sisera[1] asks for water. She gives him milk
    And butter curds
    In a lordly dish.

Her left hand reaches for the tent pin,
Her right hand for the workman's hammer.
She hammers Sisera, she crushes his head.
    Between her legs he kneels, falls.
    He falls, lies still at her feet.

At her window she peers. Sisera's mother
Gazes through her lattice. Why are his chariots
So long in coming? Where are the chariots'
Hoof beats? The wisest of her ladies replies,

---

1. Commander of nine hundred chariots opposing Israel's possession of northern Esdraelon. Sisera's mother supposes he has won and is delayed dividing the spoils.

"They are dividing the spoil.
A virgin or two for each man.

The spoil of dyed cloth. The spoil of embroidered
Needlework and one for my neck."
"Perish all your enemies, O lord! But may
Your friends be like the sun rising with strength."
And the land remains
Quiet for forty years.

Judg. 5.24–31

SAMSON   SHIMSHON   שִׁמְשׁוֹן

Samson in Hebrew is Shimshon, שִׁמְשׁוֹן, and means "man of the sun." God endows Samson with supernatural strength. With the jawbone of an ass he destroys an army and a pagan temple. When attacked by a lion, he tears the lion apart. His strength lies in his hair. His weakness is his love for Delilah and his vulnerability, should his hair be cut off. One night Delilah orders her servant to shave off Samson's hair. Thereupon, Samson is captured, his eyes are dug out, and he is tied to two pillars of the enemy stadium. He prays for God to return him his strength. He exclaims, "Let me die with the Philistines," whereupon he pulls the pillars down and all are crushed to death, including himself.

Samson Offers to Help Fight to Save Israel But Falls in Love with Delilah

After that Shimshon loves a woman in
The Valley Of Sorek. Her name is Delilah.
The Philistine lords come to her, saying,
"Cajole him and discover where his power lies
And how we can overpower him. Bind him
and afflict him. We will each give you

Eleven hundred shekels to learn his secret."
So Delilah asks Shimshon,
"Tell me, what makes you so strong?
What would it take to bind and torture you?"
Shimshon tells her, "Bind me with seven
Green bowstrings not yet dried out.

Then I should be weak like any man."
The Philistine lords bring her seven
Green bowstrings not yet dried out.
She binds him with them while
An ambush lingers in her room. She tells him,
"The Philistines are upon you, Shimshon!"

He breaks them as a thread of tow comes apart
When it touches a fire. The secret of his strength
Remains unknown. Delilah tells Shimshon,
"You have been laughing at me, telling me lies.
Tell me, how can you be bound?" "You can rope me
With new ropes, I would be weak like any man."

Delilah takes new ropes and binds him with seven
Tresses and as she pegs him to the wall
She cries, "The Philistines are upon you,
Shimshon!" He wakes from sleep and snaps
The ropes around his arms like thread.
She says to him, "You say you love me,

But your heart is not with me. You laugh
Three times at me three times, yet have not told
Me what makes your strength so great." She nags
Him constantly. He is tired to death. Finally
He tells her the whole secret. He confides, saying,
"No razor has ever touched my head. I have been

A Nazirite to God from my mother's womb.
If my hair is cut, my strength leaves me
And I should be weak like any man."
When Delilah hears him confide his secret,
She sends for the Philistine lords to come
And bring the money in their hands.

The Philistine lords come to her and bring
The money in their hands. She lulls him
To sleep on her lap. Then she calls a man
Who shaves his seven locks of his head.
She weakens him. He is helpless. His strength
Leaves him. Then she says, "The Philistines are

Upon you, Shimshon!" And he wakes from sleep,
Thinking he will break loose as in other times.
He does not know that God has left him.
The Philistines seize him and gouge out
His eyes. They bring him down to Gaza
And shackle him in bronze fetters. He becomes

A mill slave grinding in the prison. After
His hair is cut, it begins to grow back.
Now the Philistine lords gather to offer
A great sacrifice to their god Dagon
And to celebrate. They chant, "Our god
Has delivered our enemy Shimshon into

Our hands." When the people see him, they
Sing praises to their god, "Our God delivered
Him into our hands, ravager of our country,
Who killed many of us. When their spirits rise,
They say, "Call Shimshon. Let him dance for us."
They call Shimshon from prison and he

Dances for them. They put him between the pillars.
Shimshon tells a boy who is leading them,
"Let go of me and let me feel the pillars
On which the temple rests." The temple is filled
With men and women. All the Philistine princes
Are there. On the roof there are about

Three thousand men and women who look on
While Shimshon dances. Then Shimshon calls
To the lord, "O lord God! Remember me
And strengthen me just this time, O God,
So with this single act of revenge I may pay back
The Philistines in one blow for my two eyes."

Shimshon grasps the two center pillars
On which the temple stands. He leans his weight
Against them, with the right hand on one,
The left hand on the other. Shimshon says,
"Let me die with the Philistines." He pulls
With all his might and the temple falls,

On the princes and all the peoples who are inside.
Those whom he slays are more than all he has slain
In his lifetime. His brothers and father's household
Come down and carries him out and buries him
In the tomb of his father Manoah between
Zoah and Eshtaol. He led Yisrael for twenty years.

Judg. 16.4–31

SAMUEL

Shmuel שְׁמוּאֵל

In the opening lines of 1 Samuel (or "Samuel" in the Hebrew Bible), we have the Song or Prayer of Hannah, mother of Samuel. Hannah in Hebrew is Hanah, חַנָּה. The song is a powerful prayer for her forthcoming son Samuel, for a possible future king of the Jews. She refers to her earlier barrenness and how prayer to God gave her her son. Outstanding is her evocation of the need to feed and help rise the poorest of the nation:

> He casts low and he exalts.
> He raises the poor from the dust.
> He raises beggars from the dunghill.
> And seats them among princes.

Hannah's Song is a model for how to pray and is read in the synagogues on the first day of Rosh Hashanah as the "haftarah." The haftarah, הַפְטָרָה, meaning "taking leave," refers to a passage read from the books of Nevim, the Prophets.

Like the Song of Deborah, Hannah's song takes its place as the work of a strong woman poet.

Song of Hannah

My heart exults in the lord,
My strength is exalted in the lord.

I gloat over my enemies.
I rejoice in your salvation.

There is none holy as the lord.
There is none but you.

There is no rock like our God.
No one speaks so proudly.

Let no arrogance leave your mouth.
The lord is God of knowledge.

By him actions are measured.
The warriors' bows are broken.

The tottering now have strength.
Men once full hire out for bread.

Men hungry are fat with spoil.
The barren bears seven children.

The mother of many is forlorn.
God kills and brings to life.

He casts down to Sheol and raises up.
The lord impoverishes and makes rich.

He casts low and he exalts.
He raises the poor from the dust.

He raises beggars from the dunghill.
And seats them among princes.

They inherit seats of honor.
The pillars of the earth are the lord's.

On them he balances the world.
He safeguards the steps of the faithful.

But the wicked will vanish in darkness.
By strength no man shall prevail.

The enemies of God shall be shattered.
The most high will thunder from heaven.

The lord shall judge the ends of the earth,
Strengthen his king and empower his messiah.

1 Sam. 2.1–10

STORY OF DAVID AND JONATHAN IN SAMUEL

David in Hebrew is David, דָּוִיד. In the Books of Samuel, David is the second King of the United Kingdom of Israel.

In the New Testament genealogies, Jesus is central. Jesus's ancestry goes back through his father Joseph, despite problems of paternity, directly to David, and then back through Noah and Adam to God, yielding Jesus son of God.

David is equally known as a poet and musician and the author of the Book of Psalms. The Psalms actually date from diverse periods. Although Psalms remains one of the giant accomplishments of the Bible, we do not know its authorship, but, as with most of the books, the authorship is multifold.

In Islam David is a prophet.

In the Biblical narrative David kills the Philistine giant Goliath, who has been attacking the Jews (2 Samuel 21.19). David, who has killed a lion and a bear, offers to go out in single combat with Goliath. Goliath laughs. With five clean stones from a brook for his slingshot, David strikes Goliath in the forehead, and he dies. David seizes Goliath's sword and beheads him, and the Philistines flee.

In the Bible, God selects Saul as the first king of Israel. But Saul loses favor with God and chooses the prophet Samuel to find his replacement. Samuel finds David, the son of Jesse, to be that king. Initially, Saul makes David commander of his armies. But he has great distrust for the young warrior, and David is warned by Jonathan that Saul intends to murder him (Samuel 1.25–26). There follows a tremendous Hollywood chase for David, who at the last moment always escapes. Eventually, both Saul and his son Jonathan are killed in battle. David is distraught. But soon David himself will become king. David rules Jerusalem for 33 years, and all Israel for 40 years.

When David is king, he brings the Ark of the Covenant to Jerusalem.

David and Goliath

David says to Shaul, "Let no man's heart fail
Because of him. Your servant will go
And fight with this Philistine!" Shaul tells David,
"You cannot take on this Philistine
To battle him. You are only a boy.
He is a man of war from his youth."

David says to Shaul, "Your servant tended
His father's sheep. If a lion or a bear
Came and took a lamb from the flock,
I went after it, clubbed it, and rescued
It from his mouth. If it turned on me
I caught it by the jaw, bashed it down

And killed it. Your servant killed lion and bear,
And this uncircumcised Philistine
Shall end up like the others. He has defied
The armies of the living God."
David goes on, "The lord who delivered
Me from the paw of the lion

And the paw of the bear will save me
From the hand of this Philistine."

Shaul tells David, "Go and God be with you."
Shaul arms David with his armor.
He places a brass helmet on his head
And clothes him with a coat of mail.

David buckles his own sword. He tries to walk,
But cannot. "Shaul, I cannot walk.
I am not used to them." He picks
Up a stick and chooses five smooth
Stones, smooth out of the creek, and drops them
In the pouch of his shepherd bag.

Sling in hand, he draws near the Philistine
And the Philistine comes on
And draws near David, his shield bearer in front.
When the Philistine sees David,
He scorns him. He is a boy, ruddy
And handsome. The Philistine shouts

To David, "Am I a dog that you come against me
With a stick?" The Philistine curses
David by his gods. The Philistine taunts
David, "Come to me, and I will give

Your flesh to the birds of the air and to the beasts
Of the field." David answers the Philistine,
"You come at me with a sword, javelin and shield
But I come at you in the name
Of the lord of Armies, the God of the Soldiers
Of Yisrael, whom you defy.

This day God will deliver you into my hand.
I shall kill you and cut off your head
And give your corpse and the corpses
Of the Philistine camp to the birds
Of the air and to the wild beasts of the earth
That all the earth may know

That Yisrael has a God! All this assembly will know
That the lord can give victory
Without sword or javelin. This is God's battle
And he will give you into our hand."
When the Philistine moves to meet David,
David races to the battle line

To face the Philistine. David reaches in his bag.
He takes out a stone and slings it.
It strikes the Philistine in the forehead. It sinks in
And he falls on his face to the ground.
David prevails over the Philistine with a sling and stone.
He strikes him and he kills him.

He has no sword in his hand, but David runs
And stands over the Philistine,
Grasps his sword, pulls it from its sheath,
Slays him and cuts his head off.
When the Philistines see their champion dead
They flee. The troops of Yisrael

And Yehudah rise up with a shout and pursue
The Philistines all the way
To Gath and up to the gates of Ekron.
The Philistines fall mortally
Wounded all along the road of Shaaraim
Up to Gath and Ekron.

Then the Yisraelites return from chasing
The Philistines. They plunder
Their camp. David takes the head of the Philistine
And brings it to Yerushalayim,
And he places his own weapons in his tent.

1 Sam. 17.32–54

The Souls of David and Jonathan Are Knit

When David finishes speaking to Shaul,
The very being of Yonatan is bound
To David's being. Yonatan loves him
As himself. That day Shaul takes him to serve
In his house. He would not let him return
To his father's house. Yonatan and David
Make a covenant, because he loves him
As himself. Yonatan strips himself

Of his cloak and tunic and gives them
To David along with battle garb and even
His sword and bow, and even his belt.
Whenever he is sent out to fight
He is successful in every mission.
Paul puts him in command of fighting forces,
And his own servants. Everyone approves.

1 Sam. 18.1–5

Saul Gives David His Daughter Michal to Wife But Is Jealous and Fearful and Plans to Slay Him

David returns from killing the Philistine.
Women come out of the towns of Yisrael,
Singing and dancing, to greet King Shaul
With timbrels, shouting and sistrums.
The women call out as they dance:
"Shaul has slain his thousands.
David his tens of thousands."
Shaul is furious. He mutters, "They ascribe

Ten thousands to David, and only thousands
To me. All he lacks now is to become king."

From that day on he eyes David with jealousy.
Then a mad spirit of God possesses him.
He raves through the house while David
Is playing his lyre. He does so daily.
Shaul is carrying a spear in his hand.
He hurls his javelin at David to pin him

Against the wall. David eludes him twice.
Shaul fears David, because the lord
Is with him and turns away from him.
Shaul removes him from his presence
By making him commander of a thousand.
He marches at the head of his troops.
David is victorious. When Shaul sees him
Victorious, he dreads him. All Yisrael and Yehudah

Love David. He marches them in and out.
Shaul tells David, "Here is my eldest daughter
Merav. I will give her to you as your wife.
In return, be my warrior. Fight the battles
Of the lord." Shaul thinks, "Let my hand
Not strike him. Let the Philistine hand
Strike him." David replies, "Who am I
To be your kin? My father's family lives

In Yisrael. Why should I become the son-
in-law to the king?" Now Shaul's daughter
Merav[1] was promised to Adriel the Meholathite.
But she has fallen in love with David.
Shaul is pleased. "I will give her to him
As a snare so the Philistines can kill him.
And Shaul says, "I will give him her so
She will be a snare and Philistines slay him."

1 Sam. 18.6–21

---

1. Also called Mihah from the Hebrew מִיכָה.

David's Marriage to Michal

Shaul tells David, "Be my son-in-law."
Shaul instructs his servants to tell David
Privately, "The king is fond of you.
All his officials esteem you. Become
His son-in-law." David replies, "Do you
Think being the son-in-law of a king
Means little? I am a poor man, of no
Consequence." The servants tell Shaul

David's words. "Tell David," Shaul says,
"Tell David the king wants no bride price
Except the foreskins of one hundred
Philistines, a vengeance on my enemies."
Shaul devises this plan so David will fall
To the Philistines. David is pleased by
The idea of becoming the king's son-in-law.
And there is still time. Then David rises

And slays two hundred Philistines and brings
In their foreskins which they count so he
Can be the king's son-in-law. Shaul gives him
His daughter Mihal as a wife. When Shaul
Realizes that the lord is with David
And that his daughter loves him, he becomes
More terrified. From then on David is
His enemy. The Philistines come out

To battle. They sally and David defeats
Them. He is wiser than any commander
Of Shaul and so his reputation soars.

1 Sam. 18.22–30

Saul Plans to Kill David

Shaul tells his son Yonatan and all
His officials to put David to death.
But Yonatan is very fond of David.
He tells David, "My father Shaul is trying
To kill you. Be careful tomorrow morning.
Go to a secret place and hide. I will stand
In the field where you are, and I will speak
To my father about you. If I learn anything,

I will tell you." Yonatan speaks well to Shaul
His father, saying, "Let the king not harm
His servant David. He has not wronged you.
He has served you well. He risks his life, killing
The Philistine and brings a victory
To all Yisrael. You see it and rejoice.
Why sin against his innocent blood
By taking David's life for no reason?"

1 Sam. 19.1–5

Saul Promises Jonathan He Will Not Kill David

Shaul heeds Yonatan's plea and swears
As the lord lives he shall not be put to death.
Yonatan goes to David and relates what
Was said. They bring David to Shaul
And he serves him as before. Again new war.
David goes out and fights the Philistines.
He launches a heavy attack on them.
They flee. An evil spirit of the lord

Comes over Shaul. He is sitting in his house
With his spear in his hand while David plays
The harp. Shaul tries to pin David to

The wall, but David eludes him. The spear
Drives into the wood. David flees that night.
Shaul sends agents to David's house to watch
Him and he plans to kill him in the morning.
His wife Mihah warns him, "If you do not

Flee tonight, tomorrow you will be dead."
Mihah takes a household idol, lays it on
The bed and covers it with a cloth.
On the pillow with a twist of goat hair
As his head. Shaul sends his agents to seize
David, but she says, "He is sick." Then Shaul
Sends back the agents to see for themselves.
"Bring him to me in the bed so I can

Kill him." Shaul says to Mihah, "Why did you
Trick me and let my enemy escape?"
Mihah answers, "He said to me, 'Let me
Go or I will kill you.'" David makes good
His escape. He comes to Smuel at Ramah

And tells him all that Shaul has done to him.
He and Smuel leave and stay at Naioth.
Shaul discovers and sends a band of agents
To capture David. They see a band
Of prophets speaking in ecstasy and Smuel
Is the leader. The spirit of God comes
Upon Shaul's agents and they too speak
In ecstasy. When Shaul hears about this,
He sends other agents. They too speak
In ecstasy. Shaul sends a third band
Of agents and they speak in ecstasy.

Then he himself goes to Ramah. When he
Comes to the great well at Secu, he asks,
"Where are Smuel and David?" Someone says

"They are at Naioth in Ramah." He is
On his way there to Naioth in Ramah
When the spirit of God comes upon him
Too and he walks on, speaking in ecstasy
Until he reaches Naoith in Ramah. He too

Strips off his clothes. He speaks in ecstasy
Before Smuel. He lies naked all that day
And through the night. That is the reason
People say, "Is Shaul also with the prophets?"

1 Sam. 19.6–24

Jonathan Goes to David's Hiding Place; They Weep, Kiss, and Pledge Allegiance to Each Other

In the morning Yanatan goes to the fields
To meet David, with a young boy. He tells
The boy, "Run ahead and find the arrows
I shoot." As the boy runs he shoots an arrow
Beyond him. The boy reaches the place where
The arrows fall. Yanatan calls, "Is the arrow
Beyond you?" Yanatan calls, "Do not delay."
Yanatan's boy gathers up the arrows

And brings them back to his master. The boy
Knows nothing. Only Yanatan and David know.
They know the arrangement. Yanatan gives the boy
His gear. "Take them to the city." The boy
Gone, David rises from concealment, flings
Himself to the ground. He bows three times
And they kiss each other and weep. David
Weeps most. Yanatan tells David, "Go in peace.

We have sworn ourselves together in
The name of the lord, saying, 'The lord

Is our witness between us and between
My descendants and your descendants,
Now and forever!'" David gets up and leaves.
Yanatan arises and goes into the city.

1 Sam. 20.35–42

David Spares Saul

David is in the wilderness of Ein Gedi.
Shaul takes three thousand chosen men from all
Yisrael, and goes to find David and his men
On the rocks of the wild goats. He comes to
The sheepfolds by the way, where is a cave.
Shaul goes in to urinate. David
And his men are sitting in the back of
The cave. David and his men say to him,

"On this day God states. 'I will deliver
Your enemy into your hands. Do with him
As you please.'" David cunningly cuts off
A corner of Shaul's cloak. Later, he feels
Remorse for cutting a corner of Shaul's cloak.
"Forbid this act to my master, God's anointed."
David orders his men not to attack Shaul.
Shaul leaves the cave and goes on his way.

David leaves the cave and calls after Shaul.
"My lord king!" Shaul sees David bowing low
In homage, his face to the ground. David
Tells Shaul, "Why do you listen to those
Who say, 'David is out to harm you?' Today
You see how God delivered you into my hands.
I was urged to kill you. I showed pity. I will
Not raise my hand against the lord's anointed.

Look at the corner of your cloak in my hand.
I cut it off. I did not kill you. In me
There is no treason. I have not rebelled
Or wronged you, but you mean to kill me.
I had pity for you. Let God judge between
You and me. He may take vengeance on you,
But my hand will never touch you. Who is
The king of Yisrael after? Whom are you hunting?

A dead dog, a single flea. Let the lord be
Arbiter. May he uphold my cause against you."
When David ends his words, Shaul says,
"Is that your voice, my son David?" Shaul raises
His voice and weeps. He says, "You are right, not I.
You treated me generously. I treated
You badly. You reveal how generously when
God delivered me into your hands and you

Did not kill me. You find an enemy
And you let him go. God will reward you
For what you did this day. Now I know
You will become king and the kingship of
Yisrael will remain in your hands. Swear
Before the lord you will not destroy
My descendants, nor wipe my name from
My father's house." David swears this to Shaul.

1 Sam. 24.1–21

At the Battle of Mount Gilboa and Death of Saul and His Three Sons

The Philistines attack Yisrael. The men
Of Yisrael flee before the Philistines. Many
Fall on Mount Gilboa. The Philistines
Bear down on Shaul and his sons. They kill

Yonatan, Abinadav, and Malhishua.
The battle rages around Shaul. The archers
Hit him. He is severely wounded. Shaul
Tells his arms bearer, "Draw your sword and run

Me through so the uncircumcised may not
Stab me and make sport of me." The arms bearer
Is unwilling and terrified. Shaul seizes
His own sword and falls on it. When his
Arms bearer sees Shaul dead, he falls on his sword
And dies with him. So Shaul, his three sons,
His arms bearer and all his men die together
On the same day. When the men of Yisrael

On the other side of the valley and those
Beyond the Yarden[2] see that the men of
Yisrael has been routed and that Shaul
And his three sons are dead, they abandon
Their towns and flee. Then the Philistines come
And occupy them. Next day the Philistines
Come to strip the dead. They find Shaul
And his three sons fallen on Mount Gilboa.

They cut off his head and strip him of armor
And send messengers throughout the land of
The Philistines to spread the good news
In the temple of Astarte and among
The people. They place his armor in the
Temple of Ashtaroth and fasten his body
To the wall of Beth-Shan. They come
To Yabesh and burn them there. The bones

They take and burn under the tamarisk tree
In Yabesh and they feast for seven days.

1 Sam. 31.1–13

2. Jordan.

SOLOMON

Shlomoh   שְׁלֹמֹה

Solomon in Hebrew is Shlomoh, שְׁלֹמֹה. His rule is conventionally set at circa 970–931 B.C.E., but the date is uncertain, as are all events in Solomon's fabulous life. The biblical account has Solomon, a son of David, born in Jerusalem, the second born child to David and his wife Bathsheba, widow of Uriah the Hittite. Solomon comes easily into power in the first lines of Kings, but that quickly becomes a pipe dream. There are intrigue and killings, and finally Solomon emerges the victor who will punish his still threatening rivals. He rules as the third king of the United Monarchy. After his death the kingdom will split into the Northern Kingdom of Israel and the southern Kingdom of Judah. The Kingdom of Israel will eventu-

Russian icon of Solomon holding
a model of the Temple.

ally be overrun and disappear. After Solomon's death, Solomon's patrilineal descendants rule over the Kingdom of Judah (Yehudah), which will remain thereafter the country of the Jews. Solomon figures in the Talmud as one of the 49 prophets. He also is said to have built the first Temple. In this endeavor, he accomplishes miraculous feats of architecture and fills the immense structure with priceless furnishings of ivory, gold, and precious stones out of a Persian dream.

Solomon's reputation is huge and a mixture of wisdom, virtue, wealth, deceit, and turning away from Yahweh (the Jewish God), which leads him to idolatry and dissolution of greater Israel in the era of his son Rehoboam. In later times he is even accused of being an exorcist and a magician. All the accusations are legendary. At the same time, his name is also attached to the most beautiful lyric poetry in the Bible, the Song of Songs, Shir ha-Shirim, which is a haunting, evenly amazing cycle of dramatic moments in the life of the princess and the suitor king. The Song of Songs is not by Solomon but a collection gathered many centuries later, just as David is not the author of the Psalms, which, with the Book of Revelation in the New Testament, comprise three insuperable masterpieces that have seminally influenced world poetry and thought.

According to the Bible, Solomon has 700 wives and 300 concubines. The wives are foreign princesses and include the Pharaoh's daughter. A major wife is the Queen of Sheba. Her arrival in Jerusalem and all the events that follow comprise one of the great romantic myths.

Solomon and the Queen of Sheba

When the Queen of Sheva hears
Of Shlomoh's fame due to the name of the lord,
    She comes to test him with hard questions.
    She comes to Yerushalayim
With a very great retinue, with camels bearing spices,
    And very much gold, and precious stones

    There is nothing so obscure
That the king cannot tell her. When the queen
    Sees Shlomoh's deep wisdom
    And the palace he built,
The food of his table, the sitting of his officials,
    The service and attire

    Of his attendants, his cupbearers,
And the burnt offerings that he offers at
    The House of the Lord,
    She is breathless. She tells
The king, "The report I heard in my own land of your
    Accomplished wisdom is true.

    I did not believe until I saw
With my eyes. Not half was told me. Your sagacity
    And wealth surpass rumors.
    Happy are your wives, happy
Your servants and courtiers who attend and hear
    Your wisdom! Blessed be the lord

    Your God who delights in you
And sets you on the throne of Yisrael. Everlasting love
    For Yisrael makes you king
    To grant righteousness and justice."
Sheva gives the king one hundred twenty gold talents,
    A large variety of spices

And precious stones. Never is
There such a vast quantity of spices of the kind
That Sheva gives Shlomoh.
Hiram's fleet carrying gold
From Ophir brought in an abundance of sandalwood
And precious stones. The king

Uses sandalwood to decorate
The House of the Lord, the royal palace, and for
Musicians' harps and lyres.
Such a quantity of sandalwood
Was never before seen. In turn King Shlomoh gives
The Queen of Sheva everything

She desires and Shlomo endows her
With goods from his royal bounty. So she turns,
And she and her servants
Leave for her own country.

1 Kings 10.1–13

Solomon's Opulence in Building the Temple

The weight of gold that Shlomoh receives each year
Is six hundred sixty-six talents of gold, besides
What pours in from tradesmen, merchants,
And all the kings of Arabia, and regional governors.
King Shlomoh makes two hundred large shields
Of beaten gold. Six hundred shekels of gold
Go into each large shield. He makes three hundred
Shields of beaten gold. Three minas of gold

Go into each large shield. Three hundred bucklers
Of beaten gold. Three minas of gold for each buckler.
The king places them in the House of the Forest of
Lebanon. The king also makes a large ivory throne

And overlays it with refined gold. The throne has six
Steps and is rounded at the top. On each side of the seat
Are two lions standing by the arm rests while twelve
Lions stand on the sides of the six descending steps.

No equal throne has ever been made for any kingdom.
King Shlomoh's drinking cups are gold. All vessels
From the House of the Forest in Lebanon
Are solid gold, none of silver. No equal in
The kingdom. Silver is nothing in Shlomoh's days.
The king has a Tarshish fleet and a Hiram fleet
At sea, bearing gold and silver, ivory, apes and
Parrots. King Shlomoh exceeds all kings on earth.

Everyone seeks his wisdom, seeks his presence
To hear his wisdom that God fixes in heart. They
Bring gifts of silver and gold objects, cloaks,
Weapons and spices, horses and mules each year.
Shlomoh assembles chariots and horses. He has
Fourteen hundred chariots and twelve thousand
Horses that he stations in the chariot cities
And with the king in Yerushalayim. The king

Makes silver as plentiful in Yerushalayim as stones.
Cedars are as plentiful as sycamores in Shephelaw.[1]
Shlomoh imports horses from Egypt and Kue,
The king's dealers take them from Kue at a fixed
Price. A chariot from imported Mizraim costs six
Hundred silver shekels and a horse for one hundred
Fifty. And these in turn are exported to all the kings
Of the Hittites and the kings of the Aramaeans.

1 Kings 10.14–29

1. Lowlands.

KINGS

Mlahim   מְלָכִים   Elijah Eliyahu   אֵלִיָּהוּ

Elijah in Hebrew is Eliyahu, אֵלִיָּהוּ. It means "My God is Yahu or the lord." The authorship is unknown. Elijah is frequently considered the most significant and distinctive of the prophets, and unusual in that he came from a wealthy city family. He was a prophet and miracle maker from the Northern Kingdom during the reign of Ahab in the ninth century B.C.E. He could raise the dead, bring fire out of the sky down on the earth, and also be translated himself in a whirlwind into the heavens. In short, he has many of the powers of Yahweh, whom he defends against Canaanite Baal. Jesus Christ (Yeshua ben Yosef) will enjoy some of Elijah's supernatural feats and is in part based on the earlier prophet.

The prophet is quoted in the New Testament. In the four canonical gospels he is cited with reverence as a precursor of the Christian Messiah, Mark, Talmud, and Mishnah, and is also singular in the Qur'an. His name is evoked in prayers for the main Jewish holidays, at Passover and as the ending of Shabbat, and in the Synoptic Gospels (Mark 9.4, Matthew 17.3, and Luke 9.3). He along with Moses appears at Jesus's transfiguration, suggesting two messianic precursors.

When Elijah is with the prophet Elisha and must leave him, as they near the Jordan, Elijah strikes the land they pass over. And then we read the most apocalyptic lines in the Hebrew Bible about Elijah's departure in chariots of fire. Elijah is a major Hebrew poet. As with all the poets, his work is surely a combinatory selection from other poets at different periods. Nevertheless, there is a fine unity to his work. He does not bring the customary wrath and punishment on a sacrilegious people who have betrayed the faith. That angry repertoire is often repeated in other major prophets. With the exception here of the great poems "Ahab and Jezebel" and "Elijah's Epiphany," Elijah is often a meadow of his own.

Ahab and Jezebel[1] Threaten to Kill Elijah So Elijah Sits Forty Days Below a Juniper Tree

Ahab tells Izevel everything Eliyahu has done,
How he slays all the Baalist prophets with a sword.
Izevel sends a messenger to Eliyahu, saying,
"Let the gods bring me unnamable horror,
And worse, if by tomorrow I have not made
Your life like theirs!" Eliyahu is afraid.
He rises and goes down to Ber Sheva,[2]
Part of Yehudah, and leaves his servant there.
He goes on a day's journey into the wilderness.
He comes to a broom tree. He sits under it.
He prays and asks to die. He cries, "Enough,
O lord! Take my life. I am not better than my fathers."

He lies down and sleeps under the broom tree.
Suddenly, an angel[3] touches him, and says,
"Get up and eat." He looks about. There at his head
Is a cake baked on hot stones, and a jar of water.
He drinks and lies down again. The angel
Of the lord comes again and touches him
And says, "Get up and eat or the journey will be
Too much for you." He gets up and eats and drinks.
Then with strength from the meal,
He walks forty days and nights
As far as Horev, the Mountain of God.
There he finds a cave and spends the night.

1 Kings 19.1–9

---

1. Jezebel from the Hebrew Izevel אִיזֶבֶל.
2. Beersheba from the Hebrew שֶׁבַע בְּאֵר.
3. A holy messenger of God.

Elijah's Theophany

Comes the word of God, "Why are you here, Eliyahu?"
"I am moved by zeal for the lord, God of armies.
Yisraelites have broken your covenant, torn down
Your altars, killed your prophets with a sword.
I alone am left and they are out to take my life."
God says, "Come out, stand on the mountain
Before the lord." The lord passes by. There is
A great wind splitting mountains and shattering
Rocks in pieces before the lord. The lord is not
In the wind. After the wind, an earthquake.
But the lord is not in the earthquake. After
The earthquake, fire. The lord is not in the fire.
After the fire, the sound of absolute silence.

When Eliyahu hears, he wraps his mantle
Around his face and stands at the entrance
To the cave. Then a voice comes to him.
"Why are you here, Eliyahu?" "I am moved
By zeal for the lord, God of armies."
God says, "Go back by way of Dammesek.
When you arrive, anoint Hazael as King of Aram.
Anoint Yehu son of Nimshi as King of Yisrael.
Anoint Elisha son of Shaphat of Abel Meholah
As prophet to succeed you. Whoever escapes
Hazael's sword Yehu shall kill. Whoever escapes
Yehu's sword, Elisha shall kill. I will leave seven
Thousand in Yisrael, every knee that has not bowed
To Baal. Every mouth that has not kissed him."

1 Kings 19.9–18

Elijah Departs in a Chariot of Fire;
Elisha Follows

When the lord is ready to raise Eliyahu up to heaven
In a whirlwind, Eliyahu and Elisha are leaving Gilgal.
                    "As the lord lives
And as long as you live, I will not abandon you."
Elisha says. So they go down to Bethel.

Fifty of the company of the acolyte prophets follow.
They stand at a distance from them as the two stop
                    At the river Yarden
Eliyahu takes his mantle, rolls it up and strikes the water.
The water changes from one side to the other. The two

Cross over on dry land. While crossing, Eliyahu says
To Elisha, "Tell me what I can do for you before I am
                    Taken from you."
Elisha says, "Please pass on a double portion of your spirit
To me." "That is hard to do. Yet if you see me as I am

Being taken up, this will be granted you. If not, it will not be."
As they are walking along suddenly there appears
                    A chariot of fire
With fiery horses. They separate one from the other
And Eliyahu ascends to heaven in a whirlwind.

Elisha sees it. He shouts, "My father, My father!
Yisrael's chariot and its horsemen!" When he can
                    No longer see,
He grasps his own cloak, tears it in two, arrays himself
In Eliayahu's mantle, and stands on the bank of the Yarden.

                                    2 Kings 2.1, 2, 7–13

Proverbs of Solomon

Mishle Shlomoh מִשְׁלֵי שְׁלֹמֹה

The Book of Proverbs, Mashai, מִשְׁלֵי, was attributed incorrectly to Solomon, but is no longer so. It was a common practice to bring dignity and authority to a text by attributing it to a well-known personage.

Proverbs is an anthology of oral wisdom poetry of the Jewish people in the postexilic period. Gnomic in nature and popular in origin, it sticks to pragmatic experience rather than law. It was passed-down wisdom poetry composed in discrete periods and resembles the early Egyptian instruction book Amenemope, read by children to learn to read and write. Wisdom proverbs have been found in Persian and other wisdom collections through-out Mesopotamia. We see the wisdom word and spirit incorporated in the Gospel of Matthew.

The majority of this binary verse reflects the memorable sayings of a people aimed at the young. Varying in quality, as does the great Book of Psalms, the best survive as pithy wisdom observations. If you laugh, you are reading it or hearing it just fine. At the same time, many are classic poems whose lines have entered our culture.

Mystery Teacher

A villainous scoundrel
Cruises with crooked speech.

He winks his eyes,
He shuffles his feet.

He teaches with his fingers.
His heart is duplicitous,

Beating discord.
Disaster will break him.

Prov. 6.12–14

How I Came into Being

God shapes me at the beginning of his work
In ancient days when the earth is made,

When there is no watery abyss, no springs
Abundant with water, before mountains

Are settled. Before hills I am born.
God has not yet made earth and meadows

Or fashioned the first clumps of clay.
When he makes skies I am there.

When he fixes horizons of the skies
And draws a circle on the fountains of the sea,

When he strengthens the fountains of the deep,
So waters will never transgress his command,

When he sets the foundations of the earth,
I am his confidant. It makes me happy every day,

Ever playing before him in his inhabited world,
Enraptured by the presence of human beings!

Prov. 8.22–31

Inherit the Wind

Who trusts in his riches will fall
But a just person blossoms like foliage.

A trouble maker in her family
Will inherit the wind.

The fool will be slave to the wise.
The fruit of the good is a tree of life.

Prov. 11.28–30

Blow-Hard

Guard your mouth and keep your life.
Open your lips and welcome ruin.

Prov. 13.3

The House

A wise woman builds her house.
A foolish one tears it down with her own hands.

Prov. 14.1

Beware of Dumbbells

Watch out for a dumbbell.
You find no words of knowledge.

The clever are wise, know where they go.
The dumbbell lives in delusion.

Prov. 14.7–8

Modest Proposals

Better to be poor with the lowly
Than share loot with the proud.

The pauper is hated by his neighbor,
The rich man has many friends.

Scorning a neighbor is wrong.
Care for the poor and be happy.

Prov. 16.19–21

The Heart of the Wise

The wise in heart discerns
And sweet speech persuades.

Good sense is a fountain
To one who has it.

Folly is the punishment
Of the fool.

Kind words are honeycomb.
Sweet to soul, health to body.

Prov. 16.21–24

Paradoxes

Confidence in a scoundrel in time of trouble
Is like a poison tooth and a broken foot

Or taking off your coat in freezing weather
Or pouring vinegar on a wound.

Do not sing songs to a sorrowful heart.
If your enemy is starving, give him bread.

Prov. 25.19–21

JOB

Yov אִיּוֹב

Job in Hebrew is Yov or Yob, אִיּוֹב. It is philosophical drama and belongs to the poetical books, Writings (Ketuvim), composed by diverse authors between the seventh and fourth centuries B.C.E. The story covers a much earlier period. The frame of the book is a prose prologue and epilogue, and between them poetic dialogues, not dissimilar to Ancient Greek and Elizabethan dramas.

The Biblical story follows the changes in Job's life commanded by God as recounted in speeches. Job strongly reacts to his unjust situation and God's commanding authority to impose and then justify his actions. Neither side gives in easily. The main actors are Job, friends including the difficult Elihu, and the lord. As a book of dissident theology, it ranks with Ecclesiastes as being original, profound, and of unequaled poetry. Job ranks with Homer, Sappho, and Shakespeare.

Job is a good man, but God takes away everything in his life that he has worked for: family, land, wealth, and health. God awards with wealth and position the evil, the invidious, and the avaricious while the good poor suffer. Job will hear no moral explanation to justify the injustice of punishment for the righteous and award for the bad one. God's answer is to show his great powers conveyed in magnificent speech. God made the world, the sharks, and the rainbows. He causes hurricanes and equipoise in the seasons. God is an inventor. "What have you done like me," he asks Job. Job is a dissident, tortured in mind, and shouts to the heavens like Lear on the cliffs, cursing the day of his birth. The vast book remains a wisdom book and a metaphysical discourse on being. It is an enduring centerpiece of world literature.

Prologue: God Tests Job Who Tumbles and Is Aggrieved

There is a man in the land of Uz named Yov.
That man is blameless and upright
He fears God and shuns evil.
He has seven sons and three daughters.
He owns seven thousand sheep, three thousand camels,
Five hundred yoke of oxen, five hundred donkeys,
And many slave servants.

His sons feast in one another's houses.
Each on a set day in his own home.
They invite three sisters to eat and drink with them,
When a round of feasts is over,
He sends word and purifies them.
He rises at dawn the next day
To make burnt offering for each of them.

Yov thinks, "Perhaps my sons have sinned
And curse God in their hearts."
This is how Yov used to act.
One day the holy sons of God come before the lord,
With Satan[1] who is God's adversary.
The lord asks Satan, "Where have you been?"
Satan answers, "I have been roaming all over the earth."

The lord tells Satan, "Did you notice my servant Yov?
There is no one like him on the earth,
A blameless and upright man who fears God,
Who turns away from evil?"
Then Satan answers the lord,

---

1. Satan in Hebrew is God's legal adversary, not the New Testament devil, a perversion of the title. Here, however, Satan urges God to test Job's loyalty as earlier he tested Abraham's willingness to sacrifice his first son, Isaac. For Job, the test signifies catastrophe.

"Has Yov not good reason to fear God?
Have you not put a wall around him and his slaves?

You have blessed the work of his hands,
His broad lands, the flocks that fill the countryside,
But lay your hand on all he owns and strike it down
And he will curse you to your face."
Satan leaves God's presence.
One day as his sons and daughters are eating
And drinking wine in the eldest brother's house,

A messenger comes to Yov, saying,
"The oxen were plowing and donkeys feeding near them.
The Sabeans attacked and carried them off
And killed the servants by the edge of the sword.
I alone have escaped to tell you."
He is speaking when another comes and says,
"The fire of God fell from heaven,

Burned up the sheep and the servants.
I alone have escaped to tell you."
He is speaking when another comes and says,
"A Chaldean formation of three columns
Raided the camels and carried them off
And killed the servant with the sword.
I alone have escaped to tell you."

He is speaking when another comes and says,
"The fire of God has fallen from heaven,
Burnt up the sheep and the servants.
I alone have escaped to tell you."
He is still speaking when another comes and says,
"Your sons and daughters were eating and drinking wine
In the house of their eldest brother

When suddenly a great wind came from the wilderness.
It struck the four corners of the house.

It collapsed on the young people and they died.
I alone have escaped to tell you."
Then Yov stands up, he tears his robe, shaves his head,
Falls to the ground, bows his head and says,

"Naked I came out of my mother's womb
And naked I shall return there.
The lord has given. The lord has taken.
Blessed be the name of the lord!"

Job 1.1–21

Job Sore with Boils

God says, "There is no one like him on earth,
A sound and honorable man. He fears God.
He shuns evil and maintains his integrity
Though you provoke and ruin him without reason."
Satan answers the lord, "Skin for skin!
A man will give everything away to save his life.
But stretch out your hand now
And touch his bone and flesh
And he will curse you to your face!"
God says to Satan, "He is in your power. But spare his life!"

Satan leaves the presence of God and inflicts Yov
With sore boils from the sole of his foot
To the crown of his head.
Yov takes a potsherd to scrape himself
And sits among the ashes.
His wife tells him, "Do you still have your dignity?
Curse God and die."
Job says, "You speak like any foolish woman.
Shall we receive the good from God and not the bad?"
Despite these things, Yov does not sin with his lips.

Job 2.3–10

Let the Day Perish When I Was Born

Afterward Yov begins to speak and curses the day of his birth.

Perish the day when I am born,
    And the night it was said,
        "A male has been conceived."

Let that day be darkness.
    Let God not observe it.
        May no light shine on it.

May darkness and death's shadow stain it.
    Let a mass of clouds hover over it.
        Let obscurity of day terrify it.

On that day let murk seize it.
    Let it not be counted as a day in the year,
        Let it not appear in a month.

O let that night be barren.
    Let no sound of joy be heard.
        Let the spell caster curse the day,

Let those ready to rouse the Leviathan
    And its twilight stars go dark.
        Let it hope for light and see nothing.

Let it not see the eyelids of the dawn
    And hide misery from my eyes.
        Why did I not die in the womb

And breathe no more at birth?
    Why were there knees to welcome me,
        And breasts for me to suck?

Now I would lie still and repose
    With kings and councilors of earth
        Who rebuild ruins for themselves

Or with princes who possess gold
    And fill their houses with silver
        Or why am I not a buried stillborn

An infant who never sees light?
    There the wicked cease their troubles
        And the weary repose.

The prisoners are tranquil.
    They hear no oppressor's voice.
        The small and the great are there.

Slaves from the master are free.
    Why give light to the sufferer
        And light to the embittered spirit

Who waits for death in vain,
    Dig for it like a treasure
        And are filled with happiness

To reach the grave?
    To the man who loses his way
        Whom God has shuffled around?

My groaning is my bread,
    My roaring pours out like water.
        What I fear has overtaken me.

What I dread comes upon me.
    I have no tranquility, not quiet, no rest
        And my troubles mount.

Job 3.1–26

Shaddai's Arrows Are in Me

But Yov answers and says,

"Were my anguish weighed and disaster laid on scales,
They would be heavier than sand of the sea.
My words are choked. Shaddai's arrows are in me
And my spirit drinks their venom.
The terrors of God gather and attack me.
Does the wild ass bray when he has grass?
Does a bull bellow over his fodder?
Can tasteless food be eaten without salt?
Does the oozing of mallow juice have flavor?[2]

My throat refuses to touch them.
Loathsome they resemble my sickening flesh.
If only my wish were fulfilled,
And God might grant my longings.
Let God consent to crush me,
Loosen his hand and tear me apart.
That would be my consolation.
I writhe and exult in pain. He does not spare me.
I would not contend with God's decrees.

What is my strength that I should hope,
How long do I have for me to be patient?
Is my strength the strength of stone?
Is my flesh made of bronze?
Yes, I cannot help myself.
I am deprived of resourcefulness.
A friend owes kindness to his blighted companion
Though he abandon fear for Shaddai.
My comrades are treacherous like a wadi,

2. Others conjecture "Does the egg white have flavor?"

Like the sand beds of brooks that run dry.
They darken with ice. Snow obscures them.
When they thaw, they vanish.
In the heat they melt from their place.
Their course twists and turns.
The caravans of Tema observe.
The convoys from Sheva depend on them.
They are morose when they were confident.
They return confounded, their hopes aghast.

As such you have become to me.
You see calamity, you fear.
Have I asked you for a gift,
Ransom me out of your wealth,
Redeem me from an oppressor's hand?
Teach me and I will be silent
And instruct me where I go wrong.
Honest words are trenchant.
But what is your reproof?

Can you reprove words as if speech
Of the desperate were wind?
Would you cast lots over an orphan
And haggle over your friend?
Look at me. I will not lie to your face.
Relent! I am still in the right.
Is there injustice on my tongue?
Does my palate not discern disaster?

Job 6.1–30

Am I the Sea or a Sea Dragon Beast?

Does a man not have an appointed time on earth?
His days are like those of a worker,
Like a slave who longs for evening shadow,
Like a laborer waiting for his pay.

I have been allotted my months of emptiness.
I have been assigned my nights of misery.

When I lie down, I think, "When shall I wake?"
The night is long. I toss until dawn.
My flesh is coated with worms and clods of earth.
My skin is broken and festering.

My days are swifter than a weaver's shuttle,
And come to their end without hope.
Consider that my life is but wind.
I shall never see happiness again.

Your eyes are gazing toward me.
Your eyes are seeking me.
But I shall not be there.
As a cloud disappears into nothing,
Whoever goes down deep into Sheol
Will not come up.
They return no more to their houses.
His house knows him no more.

I will speak for my tormented spirit.
I will complain in the bitterness of my soul.
Am I the sea or a sea dragon beast
Whom you shadow for danger?
When I think my bed will comfort me,
When I say, "My couch will share my sorrow,"
You terrify me with visions
Until I prefer strangulation and death

To my wasting body. I loathe my life.
I will not live forever. Leave me alone.
My days are a breath.
What are beings that you magnify us,
That you set your mind on us,

That you visit us every morning,
That you test us every moment?
How long will you turn away from me?

Ignore me until I swallow my spittle?
If I have done wrong, what have I done
To you who are our inspector?
Why have you made me your target?
Why have I become a burden to you?
Why do you not pardon my transgression
And remove me from the iniquitous?

Job 7.1–21

God Commands the Sun to Rise and Fall

How can a man win a trial with God
    If he essays a grievance against him?
        He cannot answer one charge in a thousand.

God is wise in heart and of colossal strength
    Who can challenge him and come out whole?
        He moves mountains. They are unaware.

He overturns them in his anger,
    He trembles the earth out of its place
        And its pillars shudder.

He commands the sun and it does not rise.
    He seals up stars.
        No one can fathom his numberless miracles.

Look. Overhead he is floating by. I see nothing.
    He slips by me. I do not perceive him.
        He secrets away. Who can stop him?

Job 9.1–12

My Soul Is Weary of My Life

My soul is weary of my life.
I will free my lament
I will speak in the bitterness of my soul.
I say to God, "Do not condemn me.
Let me know what you charge me with.
Is it good to oppress and despise
The work of your hands
And favor the schemes of the wicked?

God, do you have eyes of flesh?
Is your vision of a man?
Do you see as woman sees?
Your years the years of a man,
That you seek to find my crime?
You know I am not evil
Yet no one can rescue me from your grasp.

Your hands fashion and make me
And now you turn and destroy me.
Remember how you fashioned me like clay.
Will you turn me back into dust?
Did you not pour me out like milk
And congeal me like cheese?
You clothed me with skin and flesh
And knit me together with bones and sinews.

You gave me life and love.
Your providence cared for my spirit,
Yet these things you hide in your heart.
I know this was your purpose.
When I am in error, you watch me
And do not clear me of my iniquity.
When I am guilty of wrong, poor me!
When I am generous, I cannot lift my head.

For I am filled with shame
And drenched in misery.
You are a triumphant lion hunting me
And wondrously you keep striking me.
You keep sending witnesses against me
And your vexation with me increases.
Why did you let me emerge from the womb?
Better had I died before an eye saw me

And were as if I had not been,
As if I were carried from the womb to the grave.
Are my days not few? Leave me alone,
Let me find happiness before I go,
Never to return, to the land of gloom,
A land whose light is darkness,
Where light exists as the dark.

Job 10.1–22

Coming Forth as a Flower and Soon Cut Down

A man is born of a woman for few days and full of trouble.
   He blossoms like a flower and withers.
      He flees like a shadow. He will not stay.

Do you fix your gaze on him?
   Do you bring judgment with you?
      Can you make the unclean clean?

No one can. Our days you have measured.
   The number of our months you know
      And you have fixed the borders

We cannot pass. Turn away from us and cease
   Until we can like workers enjoy our days.
      There is hope for a tree.

It is cut down and it will sprout again.
    Its shoots will not halt
        Though its root grows old in earth

And its stump dies in the ground,
    At the scent of water it will bud,
        Shoot out branches like a sapling

But mortals languish and die.
    We breathe our last and where are we?
        As waters of the sea fail

And a river dries up and is parched
    So we lie down and will not arise.
        Only when skies are gone will we awake.

Only then are we aroused from sleep.
    O hide me Sheol! Conceal me until your anger
        Passes. Set a time and remember me!

Job 14.1–13

The Poor of the Earth Hide Together

The starving are forced off the road.
    The poor of the earth hide together.
Look. Like wild asses in the wilderness
    They are scavenging for food for their young
In the wasteland. They harvest fodder in the field
    And grapes in vineyards of wicked rich.
They lie all night naked, no garment in the cold.
    The mountain rain soaks them.

Lacking shelter, they huddle against rock.
    Some steal an orphan from the breast,
Or a child from the poor exacted as security.

They force the unclothed
And starving to carry sheaves of grain.
    In the groves they make olive oil.
They tread the winepresses and suffer thirst.
    From the towns the dying groan.

The throats of the wounded cry for help.
    God ignores their prayer.
They join the rebels against the light,
    These strangers ignorant of way
Ramble futilely away from the right path.
    The murderer appears at dusk
To murder the miserable and indigent.
    And in the night he is a thief.

The adulterer's eye waits until twilight, saying,
    "No eye will spot me in my mask."
In the dark the thief tunnels into houses.
    By day they seal themselves.
They know no light. For them morning
    Becomes death's shadow,
And they are now friends with the terrors
    Of the deep shadow of deat h.

Job 24.4–17

Brother of Jackals

When I seek good fortune, evil comes.
I hope for light and darkness comes.
My bowels are relentlessly in turmoil.
Days of affliction are my company.
I walk about in sunless gloom.
I am a brother of jackals,
A companion to ostriches.
My skin turns black on me
And my bones burn in the heat.

My lyre has turned into mourning.
My flute is the voice of the weepers.

Job 30.26–31

God Recounts His Miracles

God answers Yov out of the whirlwind, saying

"Who is this who darkens counsel and speaks ignorantly?
    Brace yourself like a man. I question
And you respond. Where were you when I created
    The earth and its foundations?
Speak if you understand. Do you know who fixes
    Its dimensions? Who stretches a line
Across it, and on what are its bases sunk?
    Who sets its cornerstone
When the morning stars sing together
    And all God's beings scream in joy?
Who closes the sea behind doors
    When it gushes wildly from the womb

And I make clouds to garment the earth
    And black clouds for its swaddling bands?
I prescribe breakers that are my limit
    And set up gates and their bolts.
I say you can come this far and no farther.
    Here your surging waves will stop.
Have you ever commanded morning to come
    And assigned dawn its place
So it seizes the corners of the earth
    And shakes the wickedness out of it?
It changes like sealing clay
    And its hues fixed like a garment

And light withheld from the wicked
    And their raised arm broken.

Have you entered the springs of the sea
    Or walked in the abyss of the deep?
Have the gates of death been disclosed to you?
    Have you seen the gates of death's shadow?
Have you surveyed the expanse of the earth?
    Tell me if you know all this.
Where is the path to where light lives
    And where the habitat of darkness
So you can take them to their domain
    And know their way home?

Surely you know when you were born
    And the number of your days is huge.
Have you entered the storehouse of snow
    Or seen the storehouse of hail,
Which I reserve for times of adversity,
    For the day of war and battle.
Where is the west wind dispersed from
    And the east wind scattered on the earth?
Who has cut a channel for torrents of rain
    And a path for the thunderbolts
To drench a land where no one lives,
    To soak a desolate wasteland?

Waters grow hard like stone
    And the face of the deep is frozen.
Can you tie the cords of the Pleiades
    Or loosen the reins of Orion?
Can you lead constellations[3] out of their season,
    Guide the Bear with her cubs?
Do you know celestial laws
    And impose their authority on earth?
Can your voice carry to a cloud
    So a flood of water cover you?

3. Or Mazzaroth.

Can you dispatch blasts of lightning on a mission
 And hear them say, 'We are ready?'

Who puts wisdom in our inner parts,
 Or gives understanding to mind?
Who has the wisdom to count the clouds
 Or tilts the water skins of the sky
When wet dust solidifies
 And clogs cling together?
Can you hunt prey for the lion
 Or appease the hunger of young lions
When they crouch in dens to ambush covert?
 Who provides food for the raven
When its young cry out to God
 And roam without food?"

Job 38.1–41

SOLOMON'S SONG OF SONGS

Shir Hashirim   שִׁיר הַשִּׁירִים

The Song of Songs or The Songs of Solomon is the fifth book in the Ketuvim. In Hebrew it is "Shir Hashirim," שִׁיר הַשִּׁירִים. The book takes its name from the opening phrase, "It is also equally placed, which is of Solomon." Songs has been traditionally attributed to Solomon in the tenth century B.C.E., but again the attribution to a king is to secure a place in the canon. Its date of composition may be between the fourth and the second centuries B.C.E. Its sources are frequently thought to derive from much earlier Egyptian love poetry from the thirteenth to eleventh centuries B.C.E., skillfully translated by Ezra Pound and others. The Egyptian erotic love songs are not sacred, nor is Song of Songs.

The Song of Songs celebrates sexual love and is the only extended love sequence in the Bible. So to keep this most beautiful and dramatic sequence safely in Scripture, it was held to be an allegory of the relation between God and his people. In the Christian Bible it is an allegory of Christ the groom and his church the bride. The Spanish mystic St. John of the Cross read the Song of Songs as a physical union of the soul with God, represented as the Shulamite princess with her lover prince. Songs is a broken drama in stunning scenes of pastoral beauty and sensuality.

The Song of Songs is sometimes called a wedding idyll. It is actually a fragmentary collage of dramatic events of a singular woman and her princely lover in sublimely erotic lyrical moments. Its setting is Israel with a view to the beauty of Lebanese gardens beyond the mountains. The characters speak in plain, lucid defiance of their elders' authority in an escape to erotic freedom and humanity. Love is better than wine and triumphs over death.

The woman, the hero in one of the Songs, is beaten by the city watchmen as she looks for her love who has abandoned her; then she welcomes him back to her so they can spend the night together. In the morning they wander unknown villages. It ends as it begins, with the affirmation that love is better than all else, better than wine, stronger than death. The Song of Songs is the love poem of love poems. Poets of the West as well as Sufi Persian poets have looked to it as their model. The three major poems of St. John of the Cross retell the Canticles.

Your Love Is Better than Wine

Kiss me with kisses from your mouth.
Your love is better than wine.
Your ointments have a good fragrance!
Your name is spread far like fragrance of oils
Poured on the body
And so young women love you.
Take my hand.
We will run together.

You the king takes me to his rooms.
I am happy, happy in you,
And say your love at night is better than wine.
It is right for me to love you.

Song. 1.1–4

I Am Black

I am black yet beautiful,
O daughters of Yerushalayim,
As black as the tents of Kedar
As lovely as Solomon's tapestries.
Don't look at me with scorn
Because I am black,
Because the sun has scorched me.

My mother's sons hate me.
They make me guardian of the vineyards
Yet I fail to guard my own vineyard.
You whom my soul loves, tell me
Where you graze your sheep,
Where they lie down at noon.
Why should I wander veiled
Among the flocks of your companions?

Song. 1.5–7

Like My Glowing Mare

O beautiful one, if you do not know,
Go and follow the flocks
And feed your lambs and small goats
By the shepherd's tents.
I compare you to my mare
Glowing among the Pharaoh's stallions.
Your cheeks tease me with ornaments,
Your neck with strings of jewels.
I will make gold loops for your ears,
With studs of silver.

Song. 1.8–11

My Love Lies Between My Breasts

While the king lies on his couch
The spikenard aroma of my body fills the air.
My love is a sachet of myrrh
As he lies at night between my breasts.
My love is a cluster of henna blossoms
In the desert orchard of Ein Gedi.

Song. 1.12–14

King and Woman

You are beautiful, my darling.
You are beautiful,
Your eyes are doves.

You are beautiful, my lover.
You are beautiful,
Our couch is the fresh grass,
The beams of our house are cedar,
Our rafters are the cypress.

Song. 1.15–17

Rose

> I am a rose of Sharon,
> A lily of the valleys.

Song. 2.1

Lily

> A lily among thorns
> Is my love among women.

Song. 2.2

In the Rooms

> An apple tree in the forest
> Is my love among young men.
>
> I love sitting in his shade,
> His fruit is sweet to my tongue.
>
> He leads me to his banquet room
> And his banner of love is over me.
>
> Feed me your raisins,
> Comfort me with apples,
>
> For I am sick with love.
> His left hand is under my head,
>
> His right hand caresses my body.
> O daughters of Yerushalayim,
>
> Swear by the gazelles
> And deer of the fields

Not to wake us until
After we have merged in love.

Song. 2.3–7

My Lover's Voice

My lover's voice is coming.
Hear him! O hear

Him bounding on mountains,
Skipping over hills.

My lover is a gazelle
Or a young stag.

He is standing
Behind our wall,

Gazing in through the window.
Peering through the lattice.

My lover answers
And speaks to me:

"Rise, my love, my beauty.
And come away.

Winter is past,
The rains are over and gone.

Wild flowers appear on the earth,
The time of the nightingale has come.

The voice of the turtledove
Is heard in our land.

The fig tree is grown heavy
With small green figs,

And grapevines are in bloom,
Pouring out fragrance.

Rise, my love, my beauty,
And come away.

My dove, you are in the crevices of the rock,
In the recess of the cliffs.

Let me look at your face,
Let me hear you.

Your voice is delicious
And your face is clear beauty.

Song. 2.8–14

The Foxes

We must catch the foxes,
The little foxes,
Who are ravaging the grapes.
Our vineyards are in blossom.

Song. 2.15

In Lilies and Mountains

My lover is mine
And I am his.

He feeds his sheep
Among the lilies.

Till day cools
And shadows tumble,

Come stay with me.
Be a gazelle

Or a young stag bounding
On jagged mountains.

Song. 2.16–17

In My Bed at Night

In my bed at night
I look for him whom my soul loves
And cannot find him.

I'll rise and wander in the city
Through streets and markets,
Looking for him whom my soul loves.

Yet I cannot find him.
The watchmen who go about the city
Find me. I ask them:

"Have you seen him whom my soul loves?"
I barely leave them
When I find him whom my soul loves.

I seize him. I won't let him go
Until I've taken him to my mother's room
And he is lying in the bed

Of her who conceived me.
O daughters of Yerushalayim,
Swear by the gazelles

And the deer of the hills
Not to wake us
Till after we have merged in love.

Song. 3.1–5

Solomon Is Coming

Who is coming up from the sand and wilderness
Like a pillar of smoke
From burning myrrh and frankincense
And all the powders of the merchant?

Look. It is the carriage of Shlomoh
And around it sixty brave men,
Sixty brave men from Yisrael.
They carry swords and are expert in war.

Swords are strapped to their thighs
Against the terror in the night.
King Shlomoh makes a carriage
From the cedars of Lebanon.

He makes the posts of silver, its back
Of gold, its seat purple
And the interior inlaid with love
By the daughters of Yerushalayim.

Come outdoors, daughters of Zion. Gaze
On the king with the crown
His mother gives him on his wedding day,
The day his heart was happy.

Song. 3.6–11

Your Lips Are a Thread of Scarlet

You are beauty, my love,
You are the beautiful.
Your eyes are doves

Behind your veil.
Your hair is a flock
Of black goats weaving

Down the hills of Gilead.
Your teeth are flocks
Of lambs newly shorn

Fresh from the watering
Trough, perfect,
With no flaw in them.

Your lips are a thread
Of scarlet and your voice
Is a cloth of softness.

Your cheeks are halves
Of a fresh pomegranate
Cut open and gleaming

Behind your veil.
Your neck is a straight
Tower of David

Built with turrets
And a thousand shields,
Armor of brave men.

Your breasts are twin
Fawns, twins of a gazelle
Feeding among the lilies.

Song. 4.1–5

Before Twilight

Until afternoon is cold
And its shadows blur,

I will climb over
The mountains of myrrh

And wander across a hill
Of spices.

Song. 4.6

Perfection

In you is beauty,
My lover, with
No stain in you.

Song. 4.7

Come Away with Me

Come away with me. Let us leave Lebanon.
Let us leave the hills, my bride.
Come down from the peak of Amana.
Let us descend the peaks of Senir
And Hermon. We will abandon
The dens of lions
And walk down the mountain of leopards.

Song. 4.8

Love Better than Wine

You have ravished my heart, my sister, my bride,
You ravished my heart with one of your eyes,
With a single jewel from your necklace.
How tasty are your breasts, my sister, my bride!
How much better is your love than wine.
Your ointments are richer than any spice,
Your lips drip like the honeycomb, my bride,
And under your tongue as pure honey and milk.
Your clothing tastes of Lebanon's meadows.

Song. 4.9–11

My Sister, My Bride

My sister, my bride, you are a garden
Enclosed and hidden,
A spring locked up, a fountain sealed.

Your cheeks
Are an orchard of pomegranates
With rare fruits,

Henna, spikenard, spikenard and saffron.
Calamus and cinnamon
And every tree bearing incense.

From you drip aloes
And all choice spices.
You are a fountain

Of gardens, a well
Of living waters
And bubbling springs from Lebanon.

Song. 4.12–15

Winds

Awake north wind and come south wind!
Blow on my garden, let the spices
Be tossed about. Let my love come into
His garden and eat his precious fruits.

Song. 4.16

Gardener

My sister and bride, I enter the orchard and gather
Wild herbs and condiments.
I eat my honeycomb with honey, drink wine with milk.

Friends and lovers, imitate me. Drink deep.

Song. 5.1

My Hair Is Wet with Drops of Night

I'm sleeping but my heart is awake.
My lover's voice is knocking:
"Open, let me in, my sister and darling,
My dove and perfect one.
My head is soaked with dew,
My hair is wet with drops of night."

I have taken off my garments.
How can I put them on?
I have washed my feet.
How can I dirty them now?

My lover's hand shows at the door
And in me I burn for him.
I rise to open to my love,
My hands drip with liquid myrrh,

My fingers drench perfume
Over the handle of the bolt.

I open to my love
But my love has turned and gone.
He has vanished.

When he spoke my soul vanished.
I look for him and can't find him.
I call. He doesn't answer.
The watchmen who go about the city find me.
They beat me, they wound me,
They strip me of my mantle,
Those guardians of the walls!

I beg you, daughters of Yerushalayim,
If you find my love
You will say that I am sick with love.

Song. 5.2–8

Her Companions

How is your friend the prince of lovers,
O beautiful woman?
How is your friend the prince of lovers?
Why do you swear us to an oath?

Song. 5.9

Doves by the Small Rivers

My love is radiant. He is ruddy,
One in ten thousand.
His head is fine gold,
His locks are palm leaves in the wind,
Black like ravens.
His eyes are doves by the small rivers.
They are bathed in milk

And deeply set.
His cheeks are a bed of spices
Blowing in fragrance.
His lips are lilies,
Moist with tastes.
His arms are rounded gold
Inset with beryl.
His belly is luminous ivory
Starred with sapphires.
His legs are pillars of marble
Set on sockets of fine gold.
His appearance is the tall city of Lebanon,
Excellent with cedars.
His mouth is luscious, made of desire,
All of him is pleasant.
This is my lover and friend,
O daughters of Yerushalayim.

Song. 5.10–16

Companions

Beautiful woman,
Where has your lover gone?
He has disappeared.
We will help you find him.

Song. 6.1

Lilies

My love has gone down to his garden
To the beds of spices,
To feed his sheep in the orchards,
To gather lilies.
I am my lover's and my lover is mine.
He feeds his flock among the lilies.

Song. 6.2–3

A City with Banners

Your beauty is Tirzah
Or even Yerushalayim
And frightening as an army with banners.

Look away from me.
You make me tremble.
Your hair is a flock of black goats weaving

Down the hills of Gilead.
Your teeth are flocks of lambs newly shorn
Fresh from the watering trough, perfect,

With no flaw in them.
Your cheeks are halves of a fresh pomegranate
Cut open and gleaming behind your veil.

Sixty queens and eighty concubines
And countless virgins are nothing like my dove,
Undefiled love and unique choice

Of her mother who bore her.
Women look at her and call her happy.
Concubines and queens praise her.

Who is she? Her gaze is daybreak,
Her beauty the moon,
And she is the transparent sun,
Yet frightening as an army with banners.

Song. 6.4–10

Walking Around

I go down to the orchard of nut trees
To see the green plants of the valley,

To see if the vines are in bud,
Whether the pomegranates have blossomed.
Unaware, my soul leads me
Into a chariot beside my prince.

Song. 6.11–12

Dancer

Come back, come back, O Shulamite,
And we shall look at you.
Will you look at the Shulamite
As at a dancer before two armies?

Song. 6.13

Your Navel a Moon-Hollow Goblet

Your sandaled feet define grace,
O queenly woman!

Your round thighs are jewels,
Handiwork of a cunning craftsman,

Your navel a moon-hollow goblet
Filled with mixed wines.

Your belly is a bed of wheat
Laced with daffodils.

Your two breasts are two fawns,
Twins of a gazelle.

Your neck is a tower of ivory,
Your eyes are pools in Heshbon

By the gate of Beth-rabbim.
Your nose is a tower of Lebanon

Facing the city of Damascus.
Your head is like Carmel,

And purple is your flowing hair
In which a king lies captive.

How calm and beautiful you are,
My happy love.

You are stately like a palm tree
And your breasts a cluster of grapes.

Song. 7.1–7

I Will Climb

I will climb the palm tree
And take hold of the bough.
Let your breasts be the grapes of the vine,
Your breath the taste of apples.
For the roof of your mouth
The choice wine for my love
Goes down smoothly and makes
Your lips tremble in sleep.

Song. 7.8–9

Let Us Go Out into the Fields

I am my lover's and he desires me.

Come, my darling,
Let us go out into the fields
And spend the night in villages.
Let us wake early and go to the vineyards
And see if the vine is in blossom,
If the new grape bud is open
And the pomegranates are in bloom.

There I will give you my love.
The mandrakes will spray aroma,
And over our door will be precious fruits,
All the old and new
That I have saved for you, my darling.

Song. 7.10–13

If You Were My Brother

Oh, if you were my brother
Who sucked my mother's breasts!
When I find you in the streets
Or country, unashamed I will kiss you
And no one will despise me.

I'll take you to my mother's home
And into her room
Where she conceived me
And there you'll instruct me.

I'll give you spiced wine to drink,
The juice of my pomegranates,
Your left hand lies under my head,
Your right hand caresses my body.

O daughters of Yerushalayim,
Swear by the deer of the hills
Not to wake us till after we have merged in love.

Song. 8.1–4

Companions

Who is coming out of the desert wilderness,
Leaning on her lover?

Song. 8.5

Under the Apple Tree

Under the apple tree I aroused you
And you woke to me,
Where your mother was in labor,
Where she who bore you was in labor.

Song. 8.5

A Seal on Your Heart

Set me as a seal on your heart,
As a seal on your arm,
For love is strong as death.
Jealousy is cruel as the grave.
Its flashes are flashes of fire,
A flame of God.
Many waters cannot quench love,
Rivers cannot drown it.
If a man measured love
By all the wealth of his house,
He would be utterly scorned.

Song. 8.6–7

The Brothers

We have a young sister
And she has no breasts.
What will we do for our sister
When they ask for her hand?
If she is a wall
We will build turrets of silver on her.
If she is a door
We will enclose her with boards of cedar.

Song. 8.8–9

My Towers

I am a wall
And my breasts are towers,
And in his eyes
I bring peace.

Song. 8.10

Her Vineyard

Shlomoh has a vineyard at Baal-hamon.
He let out the vines to the guardians,
Each bringing a thousand pieces of silver
For the good fruit.
My own vineyard is about me.
You may keep the thousand, my king,
And use two hundred to pay off the guardians.

Song. 8.11–12

The King Begs

You who live in the gardens,
Your companions are listening for your voice.
Let me hear it too.

Song. 8.13

Come, Young Stag

Hurry, my darling!
And be like a gazelle
Or a young stag
Upon the mountain of spices.

Song. 8.14

RUTH

רוּת

The Book of Ruth, or literally the Scroll of Ruth, is in Hebrew Megilah Ruth, מגילת רות. In the Jewish canon Ruth is in Writings (Ketuvim), the third division of the Bible. The hero Ruth is a Moabitess, that is, not a Jew until her conversion. She is also the great grandmother of David. The story ends with a mixed marriage of Jew and Gentile. It is an ideal example of acceptance of conversion.

More, Ruth is a beautiful figure, heroic in her ideals. The book represents a great kindness and a high point of Hebrew poetry. Ruth says unforgettably, "Do not urge me to leave you, to turn back, / Not to follow wherever you may be. / Where you go, I shall go. Where you lodge, I shall lodge. / Your people are my people, / And your God is my God." Not only does Judaism make the outsider convert a hero, but her direct descendent is David, the foremost king of Israel, going back to Adam and God and forward to Jesus the Christ.

Ruth Speaks Her Loyalty to Naomi and to Her God

Naomi tells her two daughters–in–law,
"Go back each of you to your mother's house.
May God treat you kindly as you have been kind

To the dead and to me. May the lord grant
You to find safety in the house of a husband!"

She kisses them and they weep. They tell her,

"No, we will return with you to your people."
Naomi said, "Turn back, my daughters. Why
Should you go with me? Do I have more sons

In my womb to be your husbands? I am too old
To have a husband. Even if there was hope
For me to have a husband tonight and bear sons,

Would you wait until they are grown? Why not
Marry now. My daughters, it has been more bitter
For me than for you. The hand of the lord has turned

Against me." They weep again. Orpah kisses
Her mother–in–law farewell. But Ruth clings to her.
"See, your sister–in–law has gone back to her people

And her gods. Follow her." Ruth replies to her,
"Do not urge me to leave you, to turn back,
Not to follow wherever you may be.

Where you go, I shall go. Where you lodge,
I shall lodge. Your people are my people,
And your God is my God. Where you die,

I will die and there I will be buried. Let the lord
Do to me what he must do and more,
For only death will part you and me!"

Ruth 1.8–17

Naomi and Ruth Remain in the Country of Hunger and Ruth Becomes a Gleaner of the Fields Belonging to Naomi's Kinsman

When Naomi sees that Ruth is determined
To go with her, she no longer argues.
They walk until they reach Beth Lehem.[1]
The city is stirred up about them.
They ask, "Can this be Naomi?"
"Do not call me Naomi," she says.
"Call me Mara. Shaddai has made my life bitter.
I go away full. God brings me back empty.

Why call me Naomi when the lord
Witnesses me so harshly?
The almighty brings calamity upon me."
Naomi and Ruth the Moavite come back
With her from the meadow plains of Moav.
They reach Beth Lehem for the harvest.

Naomi has a kinsman through her husband,
A man of wealth and the wealthy family
Of Elimelech. His name is Boaz.
Ruth the Moavite told Naomi, "I want to go
To the fields and glean among the ears of grain
Behind someone who may show me kindness."
"Yes, daughter, go," said Naomi. She goes
And gleans in the field behind the reapers.

1. Bethlehem.

She chances on the field belonging to Boaz
Who is of the family of Elimelech.

Just then Boaz arrives from Beth Lehem.
He tells the reapers, "The lord is with you!"
They respond, "Lord bless you!"
He asks the servant in charge of the reapers,
"Whose girl is that?" The servant replies,
"She is a Moavite who came back with Naomi
From the meadow plain of Moav."
"Please let me glean and gather among the sheaves
Behind the reapers," Ruth asks. So she is on her feet
From early morning, scarcely resting.

Boaz tells Ruth, "Listen, my daughter,
Do not go to glean in another field.
Do not leave this one. Stay here close
To my young women. Follow them.
I have ordered the men not to molest you.
When you are thirsty, go to the jars to drink
What the young men have drawn."

She falls to the ground, her face on the earth,
And says, "Why are you so kind to me? I am
A foreigner." Boaz, "I know all you did from Naomi
After the death of your husband. You leave
Your mother, father, and native land
And come to an unknown people. May God
Reward your deeds. A full reward from God
Of Yisrael under whose wings you sought refuge!"

Ruth said, "You are kind, my lord, to comfort me
Though I am not one of your slave maids.
At mealtime Boaz says to her, "Come over here.
Join the meal. Dip the bread crust in

The sour wine." So she sits by the reaper.
He hands her roasted grain. She has her fill
And has some leftover. She gets up to glean.
Boaz orders his young workers, "You are
Not only to allow her glean among the sheaves

And do not harass her, you must also pull out
Sheaves from the bundles and leave them
For her to glean, and do not rebuke her."
She gleans in the field until evening.
Then she beats out what she has gleaned.
It comes to an *epah* of barley. She carries it
Back to town, shows Naomi what she gleans.

Ruth 1.18–2.18

Lie Down at Night with Boaz on the Threshing Floor

Naomi tells Ruth, "My daughter, I must seek
A home for you where you will be happy.
Boaz is our kin, with whose young women
He will winnow barley on the threshing floor
Tonight. So bathe and perfume yourself, put
A cloak on and go down to the threshing
Floor. Do not disclose who you are to the man
Until he has finished eating and drinking.

When he lies down, note the place. Then go,
Uncover his feet and lie down. He will tell
You what to do." Ruth tells her, "I will do
All you tell me to do." She goes down to
The threshing floor and does what Naomi
Tells her. Boaz eats and drinks. Cheerfully
He lies down by the heap of barley.

Stealthily she comes, uncovers his feet and lies
Down. At midnight he wakes with a shock,
Turns over and there, lying at his side, is a woman!
"Who are you?" "I am Ruth,
Your servant. Spread your cloak over your servant,
For you are a redeeming kin." "God bless you,
My daughter. Your deed of love is better
Than your first. You have not gone after
Younger men, poor or rich. Daughter, do
Not fear. I will do for you what you ask.

The people in my town know you are worthy.
Though I am your kin, there is kin closer
Than I. Stay for the night. In the morning.
If he redeems you, it is well. If he does not
Want to be your redeemer, then as God is
Alive, I shall redeem you. Lie down until
Morning." She lies at his feet until morning.

She lies at his feet until dawn. She rises
Before one might recognize one another.
He thinks it must be unknown that Ruth came
To the threshing floor. He says, "Hold out
The shawl you are wearing." She holds it while
He measures out six measures of barley,
Puts it on her back, and she goes to the town.

Ruth 3.1–15

Boaz Acquires Land for Naomi and Ruth and He Gains a Wife

Boaz takes Ruth and she becomes his wife.
When he goes to bed with her, God lets her
Conceive and she bears a son. The women
Say to Naomi, "Blessed be God who today

Has left you a redeemer. May his name be
Proclaimed in Yisrael! He will restore your life
And comfort you in old age. He is born
To your daughter-in-law Ruth who has been
Better to you than seven sons." And Naomi
Takes the child to her breast to nurse him.
The women of the neighborhood give him
A name. "A son has been born to Naomi
And his name is Obed." He is the father
Of Jesse who is the father of David.

Ruth 4.13–17

THE PSALMS (OF DAVID)

Praises   Tehillim   תְּהִלִּים

The Psalms in Hebrew is Tehillim, תְּהִלִּים. They appear in the first book of the Ketuvim ("Writings"), the third section of the Hebrew Bible. The word "psalms" comes from the Greek *Psalmoi,* Ψαλμοι, which means "instrumental music." This anthology of psalms is traditionally linked in part or fully to King David, though modern scholarship rejects any connection.

The prosody of Psalms follows biblical practice: parallelism of phrases, where in the Greco-Roman and modern practice we would use meter, and beginning with medieval verse rhyme to hold stanzas together. Saint Augustine claimed they had a secret meaning, which he had not been able to decipher.

The Psalms have been alive for almost 3000 years and have profoundly influenced persons, religious sects, and innumerable poets. The 150 psalms resemble the cumulatively magnificent 152 sonnets that William Shakespeare will compose. Or perhaps the psalmists themselves devised Shakespeare's sonnets, lending his love poems a personal divinity and eternity.

The themes are of the good and the wicked, the plea for protection and salvation of self and of Israel. They speak of the escape from Egypt, of pilgrims on the way to Jerusalem, praise for Israel and for the divine God. There are psalms of pure song that were written to be sung. In synagogue and church they are chanted and sung.

The imagery of the Psalms varies as the themes and moods change. There is a majesty in language at every rhetorical level. An exquisite example of beauty and feeling for the earth's and ocean's imagery is Psalm 139:

If I take the wings of the morning,
And dwell in the uttermost parts of the sea,
Even there shall thy hand lead me
And thy right hand shall hold me.

The psalms have been set to music by Monteverdi, Bach, Mozart, Brahms, and countless others, including major composers of the twentieth century.

A Little Lower Than the Angels?

Lord my God, your name is majestic through the world!
You have covered the heavens with splendor.
Even in the mouth of sucklings and infants
You are a fortress against enemies,
Against your silent enemy and the avenger.
I gaze at the heavens you shaped with your fingers,
The moon and the stars you set in place.
What are we beings that you observe,
We mortals whom you take care of?
You have made us a little lower than God
And adorn us with glory and majesty,
Laying the world at our feet,
Every sheep and ox and wild beast,
The birds of the sky, the fish of the sea,
Whoever voyages on the paths of the seas.
Your name is majestic through the world!

Ps. 8

The Lord Is My Shepherd

The lord is my shepherd, I have no needs.
He makes me lie down in green meadows.
He leads me by peaceful waters.
He restores my soul.
He leads me on pathways of the just
As becomes his name.
Though I walk through a valley of gloom and darkness,
I fear no harm. You are with me.
Your rod and your staff comfort me.
You prepare a table before me
Below the eyes of my enemies.
You anoint my head with oil
And my cup overflows.
Surely goodness and mercy will follow me

All the days of my life,
And I shall live in the temple of my lord
My whole life long.

Ps. 23

The Lord Is My Light

The lord is my light and my shelter.
Whom shall I fear?
The lord is the fortress of my life.
Whom shall I dread?

When evil men advance to devour me,
My opponents and enemies,
Though an army besieges me,
My heart will not fear.

Though a war engulfs me,
I will be confident.
One favor I ask the lord.
Only that I remain constant:

That I may live in the house of my lord
All the days of my life
To gaze at the beauty of the lord
And always be in his temple.

He will conceal me in his refuge
On days of trouble.
He will hide me in the recess of his tent,
Raise me high on a rock.

Now my head is lofty
Over my enemies who surround me.
I will sacrifice in his tent and scream with joy.
I will sing and chant a tune to the lord.

Hear me, O lord, when I call.
Grant me grace and respond!
My heart says, "Come. Look at my face."
O lord, I seek your face.

Do not hide your face from me.
Do not in anger cast out your servant.
You are always my helper.
Do not thrust me aside.

Do not abandon me.
O God, my shelter.
Though my father and mother forsake me,
The lord will take me in.

Teach me your way, O lord, and lead me
On an even path because of enemies.
Do not cast me to the will of foes,
For false witnesses and unfair accusers

Breathe violence. I shall know the goodness
Of the lord in the land of the living.
Wait for the lord, be strong and courageous.
O wait for the lord!

Ps. 27

As a Deer Longs for Brooks of Water

As a deer longs for brooks of water,
My soul calls for you, O God.
My soul thirsts for God, the living God
When shall I come and see the face of God?
Night and day, my tears are my bread.
People hound me all day long,

Saying, Where is your God?
I remember these things and pour out my soul—
How I joined the crowd, the happy crowd.
I would parade festive to the house of God
Joyfully shouting praise and thanksgiving.
O my God, my soul is cast down!

Why do you live disquieted inside me?
My hope is in God. I keep praising my rescuer.
I think of you in the land of Yarden and Hermon
And from Mount Mizar where waters call to waters
In the roar of your cataracts.
All your waves and breakers sweep over me.

By day the lord disperses kindness,
And at night his song is within me,
I pray to the God of my life.
I say to God, who is my rock,
"Why have you forgotten me when I walk
In gloom, hunted by my enemy?"

They kill me in my bones. They hate me,
Ever taunting me, "Where is your God?"
O my soul, why am I cast down?
Why am I disquieted within me?
My hope is God. l acclaim him,
My deliverer and my God.

Ps. 42

God Is Our Refuge and Our Strength

God is our refuge and stronghold,
A help when troubles surround.
So we will not fear when the earth breaks,
When mountains tremble in the heart of the sea,
Though sea waters roar and foam
And swollen mountains totter and heave.

There is a river whose outlets gladden God's city,
The holy habitat of Elyon, of lofty God.
God is in its midst. It will not be toppled.
At daybreak God will help it not collapse.
Nations rage, kingdoms tumble.
His voice thunders and earth crumbles.

The lord of armies is with us.
The God of Yaakov is our haven.
Come see the miracles of the lord,
How he slaps desolation on the earth,
How he terminates war everywhere.
He breaks the bow, snaps the spear

And burns the chariot in fire.
"Be quiet and know that I am God!
I am exalted among nations.
I will dominate the earth."
The lord of the armies is with us.
The God of Yaakov is our haven.

Ps. 46

My Throat Thirsts for You

O God, my God, I search for you. My throat
Thirsts for you. My body longs for you
Like a waterless and famished wasteland
I observe you in your sanctuary
And gaze on your strength and glory.
Your constant kindness is better than life.
My lips declare your praise.
I shall be blessing you all days of my life.

I raise my hands and call your name. Full
As after a sumptuous feast,
With happy song on my lips and in mouth,

I sing your praise. I think of you
When I am alone in my bed.
I recall you in the watches of the night.
You are my helper. I clamor with joy
In the shadow of your wings.

My soul embraces you. Your right hand sustains me.
Those who seek to destroy my life
Will plunge into the crevices of the earth.
May they feel the blade of my sword
And become the jackal's prey.
The king will rejoice in God.
While the mouths of liars will be gagged.
All who swear by him will exult.

Ps. 63

You Will Be Like the Wings of the Dove

Let God arise and his enemies scatter.
Let those who hate him flee before him.
Disperse them as smoke is dispersed.
As wax melts near fire

So the evil will perish before God.
Let the good be happy.
They will exult in the presence of God.
They will be jubilant.

Sing to God. Chant hymns to his name.
Sing to the Cloud Rider.
Yah[1] is his name.
His name is the lord.

Feel joy in his presence
Father of orphans, defender of widows,

1. God.

God in his holy habitation,
God restores the lonely to their homes,

Frees prisoners, leads them to prosperity
But rebels live on parched land.
God when you lead your people's army,
When you march through the wilderness

The earth shakes, the sky pours before God,
God of the Sinai, God of Yisrael.
You release a bountiful rain, O God,
You restore your earthly land when it languishes.

Your flock lives there. In your goodness, God,
You provide for the poor. God commands.
Women who bring the news are a great host:
"Kings and their armies are in headlong flight.

Even you who lie in the sheepfold
Share the spoils. You are like
The wings of a dove inlaid with silver,
Her pinions in fine gold.

When Shaddai scatters the kings
Snow falls on Zalmon.
O enormous mountain, Mount Bashan,
O majestic mountain, Mount Bashan.

Jagged mountain, Mount Bashan,
Many-peaked mountain why are you hostile
To the mountain God wished as his dwelling?
The lord will live there forever."

God's chariots are countless thousands,
Thousands on thousands.
As in Sinai—O holiness!—the lord is among them.
You ascend the summit, with your captives.

They are gifts of people, even from those
Who rebel against lord God living there.
Blessed is the lord. Day by day
He sustains us. God rescues us.

Our God is a God who gives us haven.
God our lord has the ways to escape from death.
God will smash the heads of enemies,
The hairy pate of the criminals parading around.

The lord says I shall retrieve them from Bashan,
I shall retrieve them from the depths of the sea
So you can bathe your feet in their blood,
So the tongues of your dogs share your foes.

Your processions, O God, the processions
Of my God, my King, into the sanctuary,
Singers in front, musicians last
Amid virgins who beat drums.

Great choruses bless God the lord,
O you who come from the fountain of Yisrael.
There is little Benyamin in the lead,
Princes of Yehudah in bright-colored robes,

Princes of Zebulun and Naphtali.
Your God ordains strength in you,
Strength, O God, you reveal to us.
Because of your temple above Yerushalayim

Kings bring you gifts
And rebuke the wild Beast of the Reeds,
The herd of bulls with calves among people
Cringing with offerings of silver.

He scatters those who delight in wars!
Tribute bearers will come from Egypt,
Cush[2] will quicken its gifts to God.
O kingdoms of the earth,

Sing to God, chant hymns to the lord,
To the rider in the ancient heavens
Hear his voice thunder, the voice of strength.
Ascribe strength to God,

Whose majesty is over Yisrael,
Whose power is in the skies.
You are awesome in your holy sanctuary
God of Yisrael gives huge power to the people.

Ps. 68

God Is Love

O my soul and being, bless the lord and his name.
Bless the lord, O my soul,
And do not forget his kindness.
He forgives all our wrongs, heals diseases.
He redeems your life from the abyss,
Surrounds you with constant love and compassion.

Early in life he pleases you with good things.
He renews your youth like the eagle's.
The lord works in fine ways.
He brings justice to the oppressed.
He made his ways known to Mosheh,
To the people of Yisrael.

The lord is compassionate and gracious,
Slow to anger, abounding in constant love.

2. Also Kush. Black Nubians in southern Egypt or a tribe in Ethiopia.

He will not always contend.
He ignores our wrongdoings,
He does not make us pay for offences.
As high as the skies are over the earth,

So great is his compassion for those who fear him.
As far as the east is from the west,
So far he removes our wrongdoings from us.
As a father he loves his children,
So he loves those who fear him.
He knows how we are formed.

He is mindful that we are dust.
Our days are like those of grass.
We bloom like a flower in the field.
A wind passes by and it is gone.
Its own place no longer knows it.
But the lord's kindness is forever

And ever to those who fear him.
His benevolence goes to children's children,
To those who keep his covenant
And remember to observe his precepts.
The lord has made his throne in heaven
Where his kingdom rules over all.

Bless the lord, O you angels who do his word,
Who keep his word.
Bless the lord and all his armies,
His servants who perform his will.
Bless the lord, all his works,
Up and down his dominion.
Bless the lord, O my soul.

Ps. 103

You Water the Hills from Your Chambers

Bless the lord, O my soul,
O lord my God, you are very great!
You are clothed in glory and majesty
And wrapped in light like a cloak.
You stretch the heavens like a tent,
You lay beams of your chambers on waters
And turn clouds into your chariot.
You ride on the wings of the wind.
You make the winds your angels.
Your servants are a bloom of flame.

You fix the earth on its foundations
So they will never rumble down.
You cover sea depths with a garment.
The waters stand above the mountains.
At your reproof the waters roar away.
At the sound of your thunder they flee.
Mountains rise and valleys sink
To their appointed place.
You set a border they cannot pass.
Never again will they cover the earth.

You loosen springs to gush in torrents.
They meander among the hills,
Giving drink to all wild beasts.
The wild donkeys content their thirst.
Birds of the air find domain by streams
And sing amid the foliage.
You water mountains from your chambers
And earth is glad with fruit of your labor.
You make grass grow for cattle
And plants that people need.

From earth come grain and bread
And wines to cheer the heart

And oil to make their faces shine.
The trees of the lord are generously watered.
You plant the cedars of Lebanon
Where birds make their nests.
Storks have their home in the cypresses.
High mountains are for wild goats.
Crags are a refuge for badgers.
You make the moon to mark the seasons

And the sun to know when to go down.
You invite darkness in and it is night
When all beasts of the forest stir.
The young lion roars for prey
Asking food from God.
When sun rises, he steals
Back to his lair and lies down.
A man or woman goes out to work.
And labors till the evening comes.
How manifold is your work, O lord!

You make them all with wisdom.
Earth teems with your creations.
There is the sea vast and wide,
With creatures floating beyond number.
You make little beasts and large. There go the ships,
The Leviathan you made to play with.
They all look to you to offer food in season.
You furnish it and they gather it.
You open your hand and take in the good.
You hide your face and they are terrified.

You take away their breath, they die
And turn again to dust.
You send out spirit and they live
And you renew the face of the earth.
May the glory of God endure forever.

May the lord be glad in his works!
He looks at earth and it trembles.
He touches mountains and they smoke.
May wrongdoers and evil disappear from the earth,
Bless the lord, O my soul. Halleluyah.

Ps. 104

Mountains Skip Like Rams

When Yisrael escapes from Egypt,
The house of Yaakov leaves an alien tongue,
Yehudah becomes his sanctuary
And Yisrael his dominion.

The sea looks and flees.
The Yarden runs backward.
Mountains skip like rams,
Hills dance like lambs.

Sea, what alarms you to flee?
Yarden, you run backward.
Mountains you skip like rams
Hills you dance like lambs.

Earth, tremble before the lord,
Before the house of Yaakov.
Who turns rock into a pool of water,
Flinty rock into a fountain?

Ps. 114

I Will Raise My Eyes to the Mountains

I will raise my eyes to the mountains.
Where will my help come from?
My help comes from the lord,
Who made the sky and earth.

He will not let your foot be moved.
He who keeps you will not slumber.
He who keeps Yisrael
Will not slumber or sleep.

The lord is your keeper.
The lord is your shade on your right hand.
The sun will not strike you by day,
Nor the moon by night.

The lord will keep you from all evil.
He will keep your life.
He will guard your going out and your coming in
From this time and forevermore.

Ps. 121

When Brothers and Sisters Live as One

Look how good and pleasant it is
When brothers and sisters live as one.
It is precious olive oil on the head,
Running down on the beard,
On the beard of Aaron,
Running down on the collar of his robes.
It is dew on Mount Hermon,
Which falls on the mountains of Zion,
For there the lord commands
His blessing of life forever more.

Ps. 133

By the Rivers of Babylon

By the rivers of Babylon, there we sit down and weep
When we remember Zion.
On the willow trees, there we hang our harps,

For there our captors ask us for songs,
And our tormentors ask us for mirth,
Saying, "Sing us a song of Zion."

How can we sing the lord's song in a foreign land?
If I forget you, O Yerushalayim,
Let my right hand wither,
Let my tongue cling to the roof of my mouth
If I do not remember you,
If I do not set Yerushalayim above my highest joy.

Remember, O lord, the ways of Edomites
On the day Yerushalayim fell,
How they shouted, "Tear it down! Tear it down!
Down to the foundations!"
O daughter of Babylon, you devastator!
Happy will be those who pay you back
For how you treat us.
Happy will be those who take your little ones
And dash them against the rock.

Ps. 137

If I Take the Wings of the Morning and Dwell in the Uttermost Parts of the Sea

Lord, you have examined me and know me.
When I sit down and when I stand up,
You also know it and discern my thought from far.
You observe me when I walk and lie down.
You are acquainted with all my ways.
A word is on my tongue.
O lord, you know it.
You know it before I do.

You fence me in, before and behind.
You lay your hand on me.

Your knowledge is mystery,
A wonder impossible for me to fathom.
Where can I go to escape your spirit?
How can I race away from your presence?
If I soar to heaven, you are there.
If I make my bed in Sheol, you are also there.

If I take the wings of morning
And settle at the farthest limits of the sea,
Even there your hand is guiding me.
Your right hand holds me fast.
If I tell you, "Surely darkness will conceal me
And night will be light for me,"
For you darkness is not dark
And night is light as the day.

Darkness and light are one.
You formed my inner parts.
You knit me together in my mother's womb.
I praise you. I am awesome, wondrously made.
Your labor is wonder.
I know my being profoundly.
My frame is not hidden from you
Which I make in a secret place,

Knit together in the depths of the earth.
Your eyes see my unformed limbs.
In your book you record
Every day that you form me.
No day is missing from your log.
How weighty are your thoughts, O God.
How great their number!
If I count, they exceed sands in the sea.

I wake to life and I am still with you.
O God, I wish you to slay the wicked.

Blood murderers stay away!
They say your name and falsify.
Lord, I hate those who hate you.
I despise your enemies. Probe me, O God,
Know my heart and thought. If vexatious,
Guide me on the eternal way.

Ps. 139

ECCLESIASTES

Koheleth קֹהֶלֶת

קֹהֶלֶת In Hebrew the name means the "Gatherer" as here it refers to one who makes this compendium of wisdom literature or gathers people for a meeting. In English we read the Latin transliteration of its beautiful-sounding but inappropriate Greek title, Ekklesiasttes, Ἐκκλησιαστής, meaning "Of the Church."

The "Gatherer" appears in the book mainly under the pseudonym "Preacher" or "Teacher." Because the author is a true philosopher, "Philosopher" would be an excellent name for the book, since like the Book of Job, Ecclesiastes is a philosophical discourse in poetic form.

Composed in the postexilic period and anonymous, surely by several authors, its message is consistent in presenting the vanity of life. Composing wisdom philosophy in verse and in aphoristic poems is typical of ancient Hebrew, Greek, and Latin letters. We hear it in Hebrew in Job and Koheleth, in Greek in the Presocratics Parmenides and Heraclitus; in Latin authors Cicero and Marcus Aurelius as well as in Lucretius, who composed the epic wisdom poem, "De Rerum Mundi" ("Things of This World"). The first line presents Koheleth as the son of David. In reality the Preacher is neither prince nor king but a keen unknown outsider to royal privilege, who bequeaths us his audaciously elegant philosophical messages. Though later we die, now let us enjoy, drink, and throw ourselves into all things that are the gift of God who gives us glorious existence but no promise of eternal afterlife.

Writers have seized upon Ecclesiastes' revolutionary thought and beauty of expression. Generations of artists have sung its verses verbatim from the King James Version of Ecclesiastes, including Peter Seeger's "Turn, Turn, Turn" and Judy Collins's "To Everything There is a Season." In 1967 Marlene Dietrich recorded Collins's adaptation of Ecclesiastes in German translation: "Für alles kommt die Zeit."

The Sun Also Rises[1]

Words of Koheleth the teacher, son of David king in Jerusalem
"Mere futility!" utters Koheleth.
"Mere futility! Everything is futile!
What profit is there from all our labors
When toiling under the sun?
A generation goes, another comes
But the earth remains forever.
The sun rises and the sun goes down
And glides back to where it rises.

It blows around north,
It blows round and round
And circles around and returns.
All rivers run to the sea
And the sea is never full.
Rivers keep flowing seaward
And float back again.

All things are a weariness.
No one can explain it.
The eye is not satisfied with seeing,
Nor the ear with hearing.
What happened will happen again.
What was done will be done again.
There is nothing new below the sun.

Can one say of something,
'Consider. This is new?'
That happened eons ago.

---

1. Ernest Hemingway found his striking title *The Sun Also Rises* in the King James Version of Eccle-siastes 1.5, though the KJV actually says, "The Sun Also Ariseth."

There is no memory of first things
And of last things that will be.
There is nothing new below the sun."

Eccles. 1.1–11

Chasing the Wind

I Koheleth am king of Yisrael in Yerushalayim.
I set my heart on knowing wisdom
In everything done below the sun.
God gives his children a dark job of keeping busy.
I see everything done below the sun.
All is futile like chasing the wind.

What is crooked cannot be made straight.
What is not there cannot be counted.

I think I have gained a wisdom
Surpassing the earlier kings of Yerushalayim.
My mind knows wisdom and knowledge.
I try to use them wisely
To understand the mad and insane.
I learn that too is chasing the wind.

Eccles. 1.12–17

To Everything There Is a Season

To everything there is a season,
A time to be born and a time to die,
A time to plant and a time to pluck up what is planted,
A time to kill and a time to heal,
A time to break down and a time to build up,
A time to weep and a time to laugh,
A time to mourn and a time to dance,
A time to cast stones and a time to gather them.

A time to embrace and a time to stop embracing.
A time to seek and a time to lose,
A time to keep and a time to throw away,
A time to tear and a time to sew,
A time to keep silent and a time to speak,
A time to love and a time to hate,
A time of war and a time for peace.

Eccles. 3.1–8

Sorrow of the Solitary Man

I see the futility below the sun of a man
Who is alone and has no companion.

He has no brother, sister or child.
There is no end to his work.

His eye is not happy with riches.
Why do I work, become wealthy,

Wanting and denying myself pleasure?
Mine is the vanity of unhappy work.

Two are better than one.
They share their good reward.

If one falls, one lifts the other.
It is sad and hurtful

When one falls alone
And has no one to help.

If two sleep together they keep warm.
How can one be warm alone?

Eccles. 4.7–11

Gigolos

Where goods abound
The parasites come round.

Eccles. 5.11

Money

Sweet is the sleep of a worker.
He may have little to eat
But the surfeit of the rich
Will not let them sleep.

Eccles. 5.12

A Living Dog Is Better than a Dead Lion

If you have joined the living you have hope.
Even a live dog is better than a dead lion.
If you are alive you know that you will die
But the dead know nothing. They have no reward.
Even the memory of them dies. Their loves,
Hates, their jealousies are already lost.
They share nothing till the end of time
In everything that happens below the sun.
Go eat your bread and enjoy. Drink your wine
Happily. God long ago approved your acts.
Let your clothes always be freshly washed.
Keep your hair scented with good oil.
Enjoy life with the woman you love
During all the shining days you are given
Below the sun. Your unique purpose is
To bellow a good life below the sun.
Use all your powers while you are here.
There is no action, reason, learning,
Wisdom in Sheol where you are going.

Eccles. 9.4–10

Wisdom Is Better than War

I return to observe below the sun
That races are not won by the swift,
Nor battle won by the courageous,
Nor bread earned by the wise,
Nor wealth found by the sharp.
Nor favor by the discerning.
A time of mishap comes to all.
You cannot know your name.
As fishes are caught in a fatal net,
As birds are trapped in a snare,
So you are caught in a time of
Calamity striking with no warning.
I have observed below the sun
Ways of wisdom deep in my eyes.

There is a small city and a few
People in it. A major king arises
And builds a huge bulwark around it.
In the city there is a poor man who
Might have saved it with wisdom.
So I observe: Wisdom is better
Than valor. His wisdom is despised
And his words are ignored, but
Quiet words of the wise are heard
Above a screaming lord amid fools.
Wisdom is better than weapons of war,
Yet one bungler destroys the good.

Eccles. 9.11–18

Cast Your Bread on the Waters

Cast your bread on the water. After many days
You will find it. Give a share to seven or eight.
You cannot know what disaster may happen

On the earth. When clouds are full they pour rain
On the earth. A tree falls to the south or the north.
There it will lie. If you observe the wind,
You will not plant. If you observe the clouds,
You will not harvest. You know how life breath
Enters the limbs of a mother's womb,
So you cannot foretell the deeds of God,
Who does all things. Cast your seed in the morning
And do not slow your hand until evening.
You do not know which hand will succeed,
One or the other or both are equally good.

How sweet is light! Your eyes delight
When they see sun. If you live many years
Enjoy each one. Remember how many days
Of darkness will come. Futility awaits you.
Young woman and man be happy while
You are young. Enjoy the days of your youth.
Let your heart demand and your eyes desire
And know that God will be there to judge.
Banish worry from mind, clear pain from flesh.
The morning of youth makes way for futility.

Eccles. 11.1–10

The Golden Bowl Be Broken

Remember your creator when you are young
Before the bad days. They arrive and you say,
"I find no pleasure in them, before sun and moon
And stars are shadow, and clouds come after rain."
When your watchman is shaky and strong men
Are bent, women who grind are few and idle.
The doors on the street are closed. The noise
From the mill low. Birdsong wakes you
But these daughters of song are weak.
You become afraid of high places

And there is terror on the road.
The almond tree blossoms, the grasshopper
Drags rather than hop. Capers fall apart
And desire fails. A man leaves for his eternal
House and his mourners mill the streets.
Before the silver cord snaps and golden bowl
Is smashed, the pitcher broken against the well,
And the wheel is broken at the cistern,
And dust returns ground to how it was
And a lifespan returns to God who gave it,
Utter vanity, says Koheleth, sheer futility!

Eccles. 12.1–8

ISAIAH

Yeshayahu   יְשַׁעְיָהוּ

saiah is from Hebrew Yeshayahu, יְשַׁעְיָהוּ. Isaiah begins with its description of "The Vision of Isaiah" (1.1). And Isaiah is identified as Isaiah ben Amos, a prophet who lived in the latter part of the eighth century B.C.E. However, the internal evidence suggests that the work was composed centuries later during the Assyrian invasion, Babylonian captivity, and Persian domination. It is widely assumed that there are three Isaiahs, First Isaiah (1–39), Second Isaiah (40–55), and Third Isaiah (56–66). Nevertheless, Isaiah remains a great source of knowledge from all these periods, providing us oral or lost textual information that the successive authors possessed.

Again, the final version of the book was composed to convey one prophet with a vision, and that vision, whatever the authorship and ways of getting there, have produced one of the great prophets in history, often the most esteemed. There are poems of social critique of person and city. Very early Isaiah speaks of vision and blindness again and again. Other passages describe Jerusalem's destruction and its restoration. More than any biblical figure, Isaiah speaks with the voice of God in the act of creating a new world and how to govern it and always waiting for the son, for the Jewish messiah, who will turn all wrong to right. Of course Isaiah is especially significant to Christians, and it is common to speak of Jesus as Isaiah's foretold Messiah.

Isaiah has breadth, enormous breadth in volume and range. His poems form an anthology of discrete poems of great diversity. Among the many poets of the Bible, Isaiah is a key figure, who should have anthologies of his poems as we do of Sappho, George Herbert, William Shakespeare, and Robert Frost.

I Do Not Delight in the Blood of Bulls, Says the Lord

I have had enough burnt offerings of rams
And the fat of well-fed beasts.
I do not delight in the blood of bulls or of lambs and goats.
You come before me.
Who told you to come? These presents trample my courts.
Bringing donations is a waste.
The smell of incense is an abomination.
I cannot endure your new moon and Shabbat solemnity.
They burden me. I am weary of them.
When you stretch out your hands, I turn my eyes away.

You offer countless prayers. I do not listen.
Your hands are stained with crime.
Wash them clean.
Put your wrongful acts aside out of my sight.
Do no evil. Learn to be good.
Devote yourself to justice and rescue the oppressed.
Defend the orphan. Plead for the rights of the widow.
Come here and let us reason together.
Your wrongs are crimson. They shall be white fleece.
If you agree, you will eat the good of the earth.

Isa. 1.11–19

Behold, a Virgin Shall Conceive

Once again the lord speaks to King Ahaz,
"Ask a sign from me your lord your God.
Make it deep as Sheol or as high as the skies."
Ahaz replies, "I will not ask. I will not test our lord."
Yeshayahu retorts, "Hear this, House of David.
Is it not enough that you treat mortals as helpless.
You also weary my God.
He will give you a sign of his own accord.

Consider the young woman who is with child
And about to give birth to a son.[1]
And she will name him 'Immanuel.'
He will eat curds and honey by the time
He learns to refute bad and choose good.
The land before you, whose two kings you abhor,
Will be deserted. The lord will inflict on you,
Your people and your ancestral house, days

Unseen since Ephraim turned away from Yehudah.
Unseen even by the King of Assyria.
On that day the lord will hiss to mosquitoes
From remote channels of Egypt
And bees from the land of Assyria.
They will settle in streams down in the gullies,
In holes of the rocks, in the thorn bushes
And across all the watering places.

In that day the lord will shave the King of Assyria
With a razor hired from beyond the Euphrates.
God will shave the hair off his head, the hair
On his legs, and clip off his beard as well."
In that day everyone will keep alive a young cow
And two sheep of the flock. There will be
An abundance of milk and all will eat curds.
Everyone will feed on curds and honey.

Isa. 7.10–22

A Child Is Born in a City of Light

The people who walk in darkness
    Have seen a brilliant light.
    Those who live in a land of shadow
See the dawn blaze.

---

1. The King James and other Christian versions interpret this Isaian prophecy as the coming of the Christ child. The KJV translation is "Behold, a virgin shall conceive and bear a son, and shall call His name Immanuel."

You magnify the country.
    You have given her joy.
    They are happy before you
As they celebrate

At harvest time when they divide the spoil.
    The yoke that they bear,
    The wood on their shoulders,
The rod of the oppressor

You break apart as on the day of Midian.
    The boots of tramping soldiers,
    Their outfits soaked in blood
Have been fed to flames,

Devoured by fire.
    Now a child has been born to us.
    A son given to us.
Dominion settles on his shoulders.

He has been named
    "The wonderful counselor of mighty God,
    The eternal father of abundant
Strength and limitless peace

For David's throne and his kingdom."
    He will establish and uphold it
    In justice and in goodness.
Now and forever more.

Isa. 9.2–6

Paradise

A shoot will grow from the stump of Jesse.[2]
A branch will grow from its roots.

2. Father of David.

The spirit of the lord will rest on him.
A spirit of wisdom and insight.
A spirit of council and power
A spirit of knowledge.

His inspiration is the lord.
He delights in revering the lord.
He will not judge by appearance,
Nor reprove on hearsay.
With quietude he will judge the poor
And the weak with no land.

He will strike earth with the rod of his mouth,
And slay the wicked with the breath of his lips.
His rectitude is the belt around his waist.
His constancy the belt around his hips.
The wolf will live with the lamb
And the leopard lie down with the kid.

The calf and lion and fatling are together
With a little boy to herd them.
The cow and the bear will graze.
Their young will lie together.
And a lion will eat straw like the ox.
A baby play over the hole of the asp.

An infant will extend his hand
Over an adder's den.
No one will wound or destroy
On my holy mountain.
Earth will lie below the knowledge of the lord
As waters cover the sea.

Isa. 11.1–9

Sing to the Lord!

O lord, I thank you!

You were angry with me.
Your anger is gone. You comfort me.
God is my salvation.
I am confident and unafraid.

The lord is my strength and my song.
He is my salvation.
Happy you draw water
From the well of salvation.

On that day you will say,
"Thank you, O lord. I call your name.
May your deeds be known among nations.
Exalt your name.

Sing the lord. You work in glory.
Let everyone on earth know.
Shout joy you who live in Zion!
Great and near is holy Yisrael."

Isa. 12.1–6

Resurrection of Dust into Morning Dew

My soul yearns for you in the night.
All the spirit in me seeks you.
I wait for you as a woman with child,
Writhing in pain, screaming pangs
When she is near the birth.
So because of you, O lord, we writhe
But give birth only to wind.
We win no victories on earth.
No one is born for this world.

Your living dead are merely corpses.
But dead awake and corpses rise.
You living in dust, wake. Sing joy.
Your dew is radiant dew
And the lands of shadows come to life.

Isa. 26.9, 17–19

In "No Kingdom" Wild Beasts Will Prosper

Wildcats will meet hyenas.
Goat satyrs will greet goat satyrs.
There too Lilith will repose.
She will find somewhere to rest.
The screech owl will build its nest,
And brood and hatch in shadow.
There too vultures will gather,
Each with its mate.

Search through the book of the lord.
Not one of these will be absent.
The mouth of the lord commands.
His spirit has assembled them.
His hand has given each one a lot
And they will possess it forever.
From generation to generation
There they will live.

The wilderness and dry land are glad.
The desert will rejoice
And blossom like a rose.
It will blossom abundantly.
It will also exult and sing.
It receives the glory of Lebanon;
The splendor of Carmel and Sharon.
They see the glory of the lord,

Strengthen your weary arms.
Make feeble knees strong.
Tell the fearful heart,
"Be strong and do not fear!"
Here is your God.
Vengeance is on its way
And the recompense of God.
He is coming to bring you triumph.

Then the blind will open their eyes,
The ears of the deaf will open.
The lame will leap like a deer
And the tongue of the dumb will sing.
Waters will invade dry wilderness.
Streams pass through the desert.
The torrid sand will be a pool
And thirsty ground fountains of water.

The haunt of jackals is a pasture.
The home of ostriches reeds and rushes
And a highway will be there
And be called the Holy Way.
The unclean will not journey it.
They will not be seen there.
No traveler nor fool will go astray.
No lion will lounge about.

No ferocious beast be upon it.
None of them will be found.
The redeemed will walk there.
Those ransomed by God return
And come to Zion with song.
Everlasting joy is on their face
And they possess eternal joy.
Sorrow and sigh have fled.

Isa. 34.14–35.10

God Who Measures Waters in the Hollow of His Hand

Climb an enormous mountain,
Zion, messenger of the good word.
Lift your voice. Do not fear,
Yerushalayim of good deeds.

Say to the cities of Yehudah, Here is your God.
See how God comes with a powerful hand.
Your reward is with you.
Your recommence before you.

You will feed your flock like a shepherd.
Gather lambs into your arms,
Hold them on your chest.
And gently lead the mother sheep.

Who has measured the waters of the sea
In the hollow of his hand,
And calculated the skies
With a simple span,

And measured the dust of the earth,
Weighed the mountains on scales
And hills in a balance?
Who has directed the spirit of the lord?

Isa. 40.9–13

God Cares for the Poor and Needy

When the poor and needy seek water,
And there is none,
And their tongue is dry with thirst,
I the lord listen to them.
I the God of Yisrael answer them.
I will not abandon them.

I will open rivers on bare heights
And fountains in the valleys.
I will make the wilderness a pool of water
And deserts into springs.
I will fill the wilderness with cedars,
Acacias and myrtles and oleasters.

The wasteland will be cypress
And place plane and pine together
So everyone will see and know,
Consider and comprehend
That the lord's hand accomplishes.
The Holy One of Yisrael has authored it.

Isa. 41.17–20

The Carpenter

The carpenter measures with a line,
And makes an outline with a marker.
He roughs it out with chisels and marks it with compasses.
He gives it a human form and a human beauty
To be established as a shrine.
He chops down cedars but chooses a holm or an oak
And lets them grow strong among the trees of the forest.
He plants a cedar and rain nourishes it.
It can be used for fuel.
Part of it he saves to warm himself.
He builds a fire and bakes bread.

Isa. 44.13–15

The Suffering Servant of Isaiah

Look, my servant will prosper.
You shall be exalted and elevated.
You will be raised to heights
As many were astonished by him,

Your appearance is disfigured,
Your form not of a man
And you will startle many nations.
Kings will be silenced by you.

They will see what you have been told.
What is not told they will see.
Who believed what we have heard?
To whom has the arm of God been revealed?

You grow up before him like a sapling,
No beauty to win our hearts.
No form of majesty to make him pleasant.
You despised as the lowest man,

A man of suffering, acquainted with disease,
One from whom others hide their faces.
You are reviled as a no one.
Yet it is our sickness that you bear.

But we think you are stricken,
Struck down by God and afflicted,
You are wounded by our wrongdoings.
You bear the punishment that makes us whole,

And by your bruises we are healed.
We are all sheep led to slaughter.
We have all gone our own way
And the lord hits you with our transgressions.

You are maltreated and wounded
And do not open your mouth
Like a lamb led to slaughter,
Like a ewe silent before her shearers

And you do not open your mouth.
By distorted justice you are led away.
Who might imagine your future?
You are cut off from the land of the living,

Attacked for transgressions of my people.
They make your grave with the bad
And your tomb with the rich
And there is no deception in your mouth.

Yet it is the lord's will to crush you with pain.
You make your life an offering for sin.
He sees your offspring and prolongs your days.
Through you the lord's purpose prospers.

Out of anguish you will see light
And be happy in your knowledge.
You my virtuous servant
Will make a multitude know virtue

And you will bear their punishments.
So I place you with the great.
You will share spoil with the strong.
You have poured out your soul to death

And are numbered with the transgressors
You bear the sin of many.
With all your heart
You intercede to help wrongdoers.

Isa. 52.13–53.12

I Will Make Your Gates of Sapphire

For a quick moment I abandon you
But with vast compassion
I draw you back to me.
In a flash of anger I hide my face from you.
With eternal kindness
I take you back to love,

Says your lord, your redeemer. I swear
That the floods of Noah
Will never again flood the earth.
I swear not to be angry or rebuke you.
Mountains may move
And hills be shaken

But my constant love will not depart,
Nor my covenant of peace
Disappear, says the lord. He cares.
If you are storm-blasted, discomforted,
I will make your stone foundations
Of sapphire, your gates of gems.

The surrounding wall of precious jewels.
Your children will be students
Of the lord in great happiness.
You will be established in goodness,
Free of oppression
And will not know terror.

Isa. 54.7–13

Give Your Soul to the Hungry

Share your bread with the hungry
And bring the homeless poor into your house.
If you see them naked, clothe them.
Do not hide from your kin.
Then your light will burst like daybreak.
Give your heart to the famished,
Help the starving creature.
Your light will shine in darkness.
Your gloom be like the noon.

Isa. 58.7–8

Heaven on Earth

Look, I am creating a new heaven on a new earth.
The former world will not be remembered,
Will never come to mind. Enjoy my creation.
I am making a new Yerushalayim
Of joy in my people, joy in Yerushalayim
And delight in the people of the city.
The voice of weeping will not be heard.
No more sound of weeping. No cry of distress.
There will be no infant or old person
Not living out a lifetime. Dying at one hundred
Will be like dying in youth. Those who fail
To reach a hundred will be the cursed.
The people will build and live in houses.
They who plant vineyards will eat the fruit.
My chosen will long enjoy the work
Of their hands. They will not labor in vain.

Isa. 65.17–23

JEREMIAH

Yirmiyahu　יִרְמְיָהוּ

Jeremiah in Hebrew is Yirmiyahu, יִרְמְיָהוּ. He is the second among the prophets in the Jewish Bible. He is identified as a son of Hilikiah and a descendant of a family of priests devoted to Yahweh and opposing the drift of the monarchy to flirtations with Canaanite Baal. Compared to other Biblical figures, his dates are more accurate and we know more facts of his life. He was born in the last years of the tyranny of King Maneeseh and began preaching in 627 B.C.E. during the golden age of reform under King Josiah (640–609 B.C.E.). He continued his prophecy in Babylon after he and fellow Jews were deported there in 586 B.C.E. from the destroyed Temple and city of Jerusalem. Like all major Bible figures, his life and his historic time are wholly entwined. The essence of this sorrow is contained in the always moving Psalm 137, which may have its source in Jeremiah's writing:

> How can we sing the lord's song in a foreign land?
> If I forget you, O Yerushalayim,
> Let my right hand wither,
> Let my tongue cling to the roof of my mouth
> If I do not remember you,
> If I do not set Yerushalayim above my highest joy.

Jeremiah is also famous for his despairing complaints, his "jeremiads," which gave him a gloom-and-doom reputation, yet there is equal material to call him a prophet of hope and love, which he expresses with fresh metaphor. Jeremiah is most famous for his poems of hope to the Jews in Babylonian exile. Jeremiah was deported with the exiles and shared and sang their sorrows and hopes in his poems.

God Touches Jeremiah's Face, Placing His Words in His Mouth

Now the word of the lord comes to me, saying,
"Before I create you in the womb, I know you.

Before you are born, I consecrate you
And ordain you a prophet to nations."

"Ah lord God. I do not know how to speak.
I am only a boy." But the lord tells me,

"Do not say, 'I am only a youth.' You will go
To all to whom I send you. You will speak

Whatever I command you. Have no fear of them.
I am here to rescue you," says the lord.

God extends his hand and touches my mouth.
The lord tells me, "I place my words in your mouth.

On this day I appoint you over nations and kingdoms
To uproot and tear down, to destroy and to build."

Jer. 1.5–10

The Stork in Heaven Knows Her Appointed Times

Even the stork in the sky
Knows her appointed season,
And the turtledove, swallow and crane
Observe the time of migration.
But my people pay no heed
To the law of the lord.
How can you say, "We are wise
And the law of the lord is with us
And possess the lord's instructions

When a false pen of the scribes
Turns edicts into a lie?"

Jer. 8.7–8

Arise, and Go Down to the Potter's House

Word comes to Yirmiyahu from the lord.
"Go down to the potter.
There you can hear my words."
So I go down to the potter's house
And find him working at the wheel.
If the vessel he is working is spoiled
As happens in a potter's hands,
He reworks it into another vessel
That the potter thinks good to make.
Then word from the lord comes to me,
"O house of Yisrael, can I not deal with you
Like the clay in the hands of the potter,
And at any time decree that a nation
Or kingdom, O house of Yisrael, might be
Uprooted, pulled down, and destroyed?"

Jer. 18.1–7

LAMENTATIONS

Eikhah אֵיכָה

The Book of Lamentations, אֵיכָה, is a collection of poems that mourn the destruction and fall of Jerusalem, the most tragic event in Jewish history.

It appears in the Ketuvim (Writings) along with the other poetry books in the Bible. It was attributed to Jeremiah. It is no longer so, but Lamentations still incorporates his deepest spirit of regret and longing for their city. The short book consists of five sorrowful poems, among the finest in the Bible. The dirges are short and the poems unique with their experimental prosody, recalling acrostic experimentation in medieval poetry and even modern concrete poetry.

Like Ostriches in the Wilderness

How the gold has darkened!
How its pure gold has changed!
The sacred gems are scattered
At every street corner.
The children of Zion,
As precious as finest gold
Are seen as earthen pitchers
From the hands of a potter!
Even jackals offer a nipple
And suckle their young
But my people now are cruel
Like ostriches in the wilderness.

The tongue of the suckling sticks
To its palate for thirst.
Little children beg for bread.
None gives them a morsel.
They who feasted on delicacies
Lie dying in the street.
They who were reared in purple
Embrace garbage heaps.
The chastisement of my people
Exceeds punishment in Sodom
That is overthrown in a moment
Without a hand striking it.

Her princes are purer than snow
And whiter than milk.
Their limbs are ruddier than coral,
Their bodies are sapphire.
Now their faces are black soot,
Unrecognized in the streets.
Their skin shrivels on the bones.
The skin is dry as wood.

Happier are those pierced by a sword
Than those slain by famine.
They long and waste away
With no food from the fields.

Lam. 4.1–9

EZEKIEL

Ehezkel יְחֶזְקֵאל

Ezekiel is from Hebrew Ehezkel, יְחֶזְקֵאל, and is the third of the major prophets, following Isaiah and Jeremiah. He was said to be the son of a priest named Buzi. Ezekiel writes as one from Babylon during the sixth century B.C.E. period of the Jewish captivity, and it is possible that the seven visions of Ezekiel were composed by the priest among the Jews deported to Babylon in 596 B.C.E. Paradoxically, while he is prolix in condemnations, Ezekiel appears stoically under control. His use of the phrase "son of man" more than a hundred times has not been ignored by Christianity.

While Ezekiel is over the top in raging against abominations of the three whores, daughters of whore mothers, Jerusalem, Samaria, and Sodom, which James Joyce calls Ezekiel's "Whorerusalim," and a fury against the Prince Gog of Magog, in whose jaw God will put hooks (38.4), after despair comes the homeland of peace. He rebounds with the encouraging metaphor of Jerusalem as YHWH's wife whom he will love and protect. The literary upside of the prophet poet, who is always a man of letters, is his wildly imaginative surrealism and apocalyptic imagery that infuse his work and will be heard in Daniel and Revelation, and also in Dante, Milton's *Paradise Lost*, and William Blake's visionary and mystical writing. His work is replete with allegories and parables. There is the "wheel with the wheel" (1.4). God is seen in a battle chariot drawn by a man, a lion, an ox and an eagle.

Four Faces of Angels in the Flaming Wheels of the Throne Chariot (the Merkabah) Carrying God

I look. A windstorm comes out of the north,
A great cloud and flashing fire encircled
By a radiance, and in its center, the center
Of flame, a gleaming amber. In its center
Are the figures of four living creatures.
They have the appearance of a human form.
Each has four faces and each four wings.
Their feet are straight. The soles of their feet
Are like the soles of a calf's foot. They sparkle
With the color of burnished bronze.

Under the wings on their four sides
They have human hands. The four of them
Have faces and wings on all four sides.
As for the appearance of their faces,
The four have the face of a human being:
The face of a lion on the right, the face
Of an ox on the left, and the face of an eagle.
Each one's wings touches each other,
And two wings cover their bodies.

Each can move in the direction of any face.
They move wherever the spirit impels them
And move straight ahead without turning.
In the middle of the living creatures
Something looks like burning coals of fire,
Like torches meandering among the creatures.
The bright fire has lightning at the center.
Whirling among creatures are lightning flares.
As I gaze at creatures I see a wheel on earth

Next to each of the four-faced creatures
In a structure of glittering beryl.

All four have same form of two wheels
Whirling and cutting through each other.
They move in four directions of any quarter
And do not veer off as they dart about.
The rims are tall, hugely tall and dreadful
Since all four rims are full of eyes all around.
When the creatures move forward, the wheels

Move at their sides. When the creatures float
Above the earth, the wheels float too.
The spirits are in the wheels. They move as one.
When spirits stand still, wheels stand still.
When floating high above the earth, the wheels
Float by them. Creatures' spirits are in wheels.
A likeness of the firmament over the heads
Of the living creatures is a dome shining
Like crystal and stretching over their heads.

Below the expanse pairs of wings extend straight,
One toward the other. Each has another pair
Of wings covering its body. When they move,
I can hear the sound of wings like the sound
Of mighty waters, like thunder of Shaddai,
A tumult like the roar of an army.
When they stop they let their wings droop.
Over the dome over their heads is a semblance
Of a throne of sapphire. High above on the throne,

The throne is the semblance of a human form.
Above what appear to be the loins, I see a gleam
Of amber and fire enclosed upward in a frame
And down from the waist I see an image of fire
With splendor all around like a bow in a cloud,
Burning through on a rainy day. Then the semblance
Of the presence of the lord. When I see I fling
Myself on my face. I hear a voice of someone talking.

Ezek. 1.4–28

End of Prince Gog in the Country of Magog Who Threatens to Invade Israel

God says, "I am coming against you, O Gog,
Chief prince of Meshech and Tubal. I shall turn
You around and put hooks in your jaws
And bring you out with all your army,
Horses and horsemen, all of them clothed
In full armor, a vast assembly, all with bucklers
And shield and wielding swords. Among you
Will be Persia, Nubia and Put, everyone with shield
and buckler and helmet. Gomer and all its cohorts,
Beth Togarmah in the remotest parts of the north.

"On the day when Gog sets foot on the soil
Of Yisrael," God declares, "my furious anger
Will boil up, I have declared my indignation.
In my anger and in the heat of fury, I say:
'On that day a terrible earthquake will strike
The land of Yisrael. The fish of the sea, the birds
Of the sky, the beasts of the field, all creeping things
That move on the ground, and every person on earth
Will quake before me. Mountains will tumble,
Cliffs will topple and every wall crumble to earth.'

"I shall then summon the sword against Gog
In every mountain," says lord God. "Every man's sword
Will pierce your comrades. I will punish you
With plague and bloodshed, and pour torrential
Rains and hailstone, fire and sulfur on you
And on your troops and the many people with you.

I shall break the bow in your left hand, and dash
The arrows out of your right. You will fall
On the mountains of Yisrael, you and nations
With you. I will make you food for birds of prey

And every animal will devour you lying in
The open fields. You will collapse in the wilds,"
God declares. "I will send down fire on Magog
And those living tranquilly on the coastlines
And then you shall know that I am the lord."

Ezek. 38.3–6, 18–22

DANIEL
דָּנִיֵּאל

D aniel is in Hebrew Daniel, דָּנִיֵּאל. In the Hebrew Bible it is found in the Ketuvim (Writings). In the Christian Bible it appears among the Prophets. While it is ascribed to Daniel and takes place during the sixth century B.C.E. of the Babylonian Captivity, the anonymous writers actually compiled the book in the second century from the time of the Maccabean resistance to the Greek tyrant Antiochus IV Epiphanes (c. 167–164 B.C.E.), who attempted to eradicate the Jewish religion.

Daniel is also a dream book, in which Daniel correctly interprets Nebuchadnezzar's dream of four kingdoms, and as a result is promoted to a high position of leadership. Daniel enters the lion's den and survives as the tamer of lions, and performs numerous miraculous acts. There is the bravery and possible martyrdom of Shadrach, Meshach, Abednego, who walk into the fiery furnace, protected by God's shield. Daniel himself faces death rather than conforming to the worship of idols. There are so many wondrous tales in the volume. We might say it contains a Belshazzar's feast of amazing tales. From a political point of view Nebuchadnezzar's madness and "the writing on the wall" (today a common phrase in most languages) now spells the end of the Babylonian regime. The conquering Persian troops of Cyrus the Great enter the scene, as in a Napoleonic moment, bring an end to Babylonia hegemony, and liberate the Jews in 539 B.C.E.

A great many returned to what is now Israel and rebuilt the city and the Temple. However, a great many remained in the Near East, and the majority of Jews from Iraq, Syria, Lebanon, and Iran have all been there as residents since the sixth century B.C.E., almost fifteen hundred years before

Islam and an Arab presence. In terms of fable, dream, adventure, apocalyptic vision, and pure storytelling, there is no volume in the Bible of enduring epic poetry that is more exciting to read. His dream scenes of fantastic beasts coming up from the seas (along with Ezekiel's equally wild animal imagery) have been the subject of many later works, including *Belshazzar's Feast*, one of Pedro Calderón de la Barca's most famous *autos sacramentales* (short sacred plays called "curtain raisers"). Critically, they account for a large proportion of the fantasy images in John's Book of Revelation (Apocalypse), the last book in the New Testament.

God Gives Daniel Secrets for Reading Dreams

King Nebuchadnezzar in the second year of his reign
Dreams a disturbing dream and loses his dream.
He orders his magicians, exorcists, sorcerers
And Chaldeans summons to explain his dream.
The Chaldeans say to the king in Aramaic,
"O king, live forever! Tell your servants your dream
And we will tell you its meaning." The king replies,
"I decree, if you do not tell me the dream

And what it means, you shall be torn limb from limb
And your houses made a dunghill. If you tell me
The dream and its interpretation, you will receive
My gifts, rewards and great honor. Tell me the dream."
Again they say, "Tell your servants your dream
And we will tell you its meaning." The king replies,
"Clearly you are playing for time. You know my decree.
Relate the dream to me and I will know its meaning."

The Chaldeans reply, "There is no one on earth
Who can satisfy the king's demand. No great king
Or ruler has asked such a thing from magician,
Exorcist or Chaldean. What the king asks
Is difficult. No one can tell the king except the gods
Whose habitat is not among the mortals."
The king flies into a rage. The decree condemning
The wise men of Babylon is issued and they look

For Daniel and his companions who are also set
To be put to death. So Daniel goes to see Arioch,
The king's chief executioner, who was appointed
To execute the wise men of Babylon.
He tells him, "Do not execute the wise men
Of Babylon. Bring me to the king.
I will tell the meaning to the king."
Then Daniel goes to his home and asks his companions,

Hananiah, Mishael, and Azariah, to implore
God for help about the mystery so Daniel
And his companions and the wise men not
Be put to death. The mystery is revealed
To Daniel in a night vision. Daniel blesses God
In Heaven and he says:
"Let the name of God be blessed forever.
He alone has wisdom and power.

He changes times and seasons,
He makes and unmakes kings.
He confers wisdom on the wise.
And knowledge to those who know.
He uncovers depths and mysteries.
He knows what is in darkness
And light resides with him.
I acknowledge and praise you.

O God of my fathers,
You have given me wisdom and power,
You have explained the problem of the king."
So Daniel goes to see Arioch. The king
Ordered him to execute the wise men
Of Babylon. When he comes he tells him,
"Do not kill the wise men of Babylon.
Bring me to the king and I will reveal

The meaning to the king." So Arioch
Rushes Daniel into the presence of the king.
He tells him, "Among the exiles from Yehudah,
I know someone who can tell you the meaning.
King Nebuchadnezzar asks Daniel, "Can you
Reveal its meaning?" Daniel answers, "King,
The mystery you ask about, the wise men,
Exorcists and diviners cannot explain.

Dan. 2.1–27

Daniel Tells the King His Gold and Iron Dream

"There is a God in heaven who reveals mysteries."
Daniel makes known to King Nebuchadnezzar
What will happen to him in his last days.
"This is the dream and visions in your head
When you lay in your bed. O king the thoughts
And vision that came into your mind when you
Lay in your bed are about future events.
The revealer of mystery disclosed to you what will be.

The mystery has not been revealed to me because
My wisdom is greater than other creatures
But so I can reveal them to the king
And you might know the thoughts in your mind.
You are looking, O king. Suddenly at a great statue.
The statue is huge and extraordinarily brilliant.
It is standing before you and it looks fearful.
The head of the statue is made of fine gold,

Its chest and arms of silver, its middle and thighs
Of bronze. Its legs are iron, part iron and clay.
Look. A stone is cut out, untouched by human hands.
It strikes the statue on its feet of iron and clay
And crushes them. Then iron, clay, bronze, silver,
Gold are broken up like chaff on threshing floors
In summer. Wind carries them away. No trace left.
But the stone hitting the statue is a great mountain

And fills the earth. This was your dream. Now we tell
Its interpretation. You O king, the king of kings,
God in heaven has given you kingdom, power,
Might and glory. You have been given it in your hands.
You have dominion over people wherever they live,
Wild beasts, animals on field and birds in air.

You are the head of gold. After you will rise
Another kingdom inferior to yours, and a third

Kingdom of bronze which will rule the whole earth.
There will be a fourth kingdom strong as iron.
As iron crushes and shatters everything,
It will crush and shatter all these. Since the kingdom
Is part iron, part clay, so it will in part be strong,
In part brittle. You see iron mixed with clay.
So they will mix with one another in marriage.
They will not hold. Iron does not mix with clay.

In days of those kings, the God in Heaven will set up
A kingdom that will never be destroyed. A kingdom
Not transferred to another people. It will crush
And annihilate all these kingdoms, end them
And it will stand forever. As you see how a stone
Hewn from the mountain, not by human hands,
Will crush iron, bronze, clay, silver and gold
To powder. The great God tells the king the future,

The dream is real and its interpretation certain."
King Nebuchadnezzar falls prostrate. He orders
A homage to Daniel. He commands meals
And fragrant sacrifices. Your God is the God
Of gods, master of kings, a revealer of mysteries.
The king elevates Daniel to governor of Babylon
And head of the wise men. Daniel asks the king
To appoint Shadrach, Meshach, and Abednego
To administer the provinces. Daniel stays with the king.

Dan. 2.28–49

Shadrach, Meschach, and Abednego
Walking in the Fiery Furnace

King Nebuchadnezzar makes a golden statue
Sixty cubits high and seventy cubits wide.
He sets it up on the plain of Dura
In the province of Babylon.

Then King Nebuchadnezzar dispatches satraps,
Prefects, governors, counselors, treasurers, justices,
Magistrates, and all officials of the provinces
To assemble and come to the dedication.

The same statue that King Nebuchadnezzar
Set up. So the prefects, governors, counselors,
Treasurers, justices, magistrates, and all officials
Of the provinces assemble for the dedication

Of the statue set up by King Nebuchadnezzar
And stand in front of the statue that King
Nebuchadnezzar had set up. A herald comes
And screams: "Peoples, nations, languages!

Magistrates, and all officials of the provinces.
When you hear the sound of the horn, pipe,
Zither, lyre, trigon, harp, drum, and full ensemble
You shall fall down and worship. Whoever does not

Fall down and worship the gold statue will
At once be thrown into a furnace of blazing fire."
As soon as people hear the sound of horn, pipe,
Zither, lyre, trigon, harp, drum, and full ensemble,

All people and nations of every language fall down
And worship the statue of gold King Nebuchadnezzar.

Some Chaldeans begin to slander the Jews.
They tell King Nebuchadnezzar, "O king, live forever!

You ordered that everyone who hears the horn, pipe,
Zither, lyre, trigon, harp, drum, and full ensemble
Must collapse to the ground and worship
Or be thrown into a burning fiery furnace.

There are some Jews whom you made ministers
Of Babylon, Shadrach, Meshach, and Abednego,
They do not heed you. They do not serve your gods
Or worship the statue you have established."

Then Nebuchadnezzar in furious rage orders
Shadrach, Meshach, and Abednego to come
Before the king. Nebuchadnezzar asks,
"Is it true, Shadrach, Meshach, and Abednego

That you do not serve my god or worship
The statue of gold I have set up when you hear
the horn, pipe, zither, lyre, trigon, harp, drum,

And all kinds of instruments? If you do not worship,
You will at once be tossed into a furnace on fire
And what god can save you from my power?"

Shadrach, Meshach, and Abednego tell the king,
"O Nebuchadnezzar, we have not need to answer.
Our God will save us from the fiery furnace
And protect us from your power, O king.

Even if he does not, know O king, we will not serve
Your god or worship the statue you placed there."
Nebuchadnezzar is consumed with rage, his face
Contorted before Shadrach, Meshach, and Abednego.

He commands the furnace be heated seven times
More than its usual heat. He commands the strongest
Army men to bind Shadrach, Meshach, and Abednego
And to throw them in the fire of the furnace.

They bind them in their trousers, shirts, hats
And other garments, bind them and hurl them
Into the fiery flaming furnace. The king's orders
Are urgent. The furnace overheated. A tongue

Of flame kills the men who carry Shadrach,
Meshach, and Abednego. They drop the bound
Into the fire of furnace. The king is astonished.
He rises, telling his comrades, "Did we throw

Three bound men into the fire?" "Surely O king."
"I see four men walking about unbound, unharmed.
The fourth looks like a divinity." Nebuchadnezzar
Comes near the furnace door of the fiery furnace

And calls, "Shadrach, Meshach, and Abednego,
Servants of the Highest God, come out!" So
Shadrach, Meshach, and Abednego come
Out of the fire. The satraps, governors, and royal

Companions gather to see the men whom fire
Ignores. No hair is singed, their shirts the same,
No smell hugs them. Nebuchadnezzar speaks,
"Blessed be the god of Shadrach, Meshach,

And Abednego whose angel saves his servant.
I order any person in any tongue who utters
A blaspheme be torn limb from limb, his house
Demolished. There is one God who saves."

The king promotes Shadrach, Meshach,
And Abednego in the province of Babylon.
In every province, among all peoples, there is
Great prosperity before the wonders of the High God.

Dan. 3.1–30, 4.1–2

Belshazzar's Feast and Darius's Conquest of Babylon

King Belshazzar gives a feast for a thousand lords.
In the presence of the thousand he drinks wine.
They drink wine before the thousand. Half drunk,
Belshazzar orders the gold and silver vessels
His father Nebuchadnezzar took from the Temple
In Yerushalayim so the king and his nobles,
His wives and concubines might drink from them.
The gold vessels that were taken from the Temple
House of God in Yerushalayim and brought there
So the king and his lords, his wives and concubines
Might drink from them. They drink wine and praise
The gods of gold, silver, bronze, iron, wood, stone.

Suddenly, human fingers appear and write
On the plaster of the king's palace wall behind
The lampstand. The king watches the hand
As it scrawls. The king's face darkens. His thoughts
Alarm him. His hip joints go slack, his knees knock.
The king screams for his soothsayers, Chaldeans
And diviners to be brought. "Whoever can tell me
What this writing means will be clothed in purple
and wear a gold chain on his neck. He will rank
Third in the kingdom." Then all the king's sages
Flock in but none can read the writing and tell the king
Its meaning. The king becomes terrified. His face

Turns pale. His nobles are dismayed. Alerted
By the commotion, the queen enters
The banquet hall. She speaks, "O king, live forever!
Do not let your thoughts frighten you. There is
A man in your kingdom who knows the spirit
Of the holy gods. In your father's day he was
Endowed with illumination, understanding
And wisdom of the gods. Nebuchadnezzar,
Your father, chose him as chief of magicians,
Exorcists and diviners. There is to be found
In Daniel (whom the king called Belshazzar)
Enlightened spirit, knowledge and understanding

To interpret dreams, explain riddles, solve problems.
Call Daniel. He will give the interpretation."
Daniel is brought before the king. The king
Addresses Daniel, "You are Daniel, an exile
From Yehudah whom my father the king
Brought from Yehudah. I hear that you have
The spirit of the gods in you, and illumination,
knowledge and extraordinary wisdom are yours.
The sages and enchanters I call in to read
And tell me its meaning knew nothing.
I have heard that you give interpretations
And solve problems. If you can read the writing

And tell me what it means, you will be clothed
In purple, hang a gold chain around your neck,
And be third in the kingdom." Daniel replies
To the king, "Keep your gifts for yourself
And give your reward to others. I will read
The writing for the king and tell its meaning.
O king, the Highest God gives your father
Nebuchadnezzar kingship, grandeur, glory
And majesty. Because of his grandeur,
All peoples, nations, and tongues tremble

And fear him. He kills whom he wishes to
And keeps alive whom he wishes to keep alive.

He raises high whom he wishes and others
Whom he wishes to he brings low. But when
His heart swells with pride and arrogance,
He is deposed from his royal throne. He is
Stripped of glory and driven away from men.
His mind is that of a beast. He lives with wild
Donkeys. He feeds on grass like oxen. His body
Is drenched with the dew of heaven until
He understands that the Most High rules
The kingdom of mortals and chooses to rule
Who he pleases, promotes who he pleases.
You his son, Belshazzar, do not humble yourself.

Although you know all this! You have vessels
Of gold and silver that you took out of the Temple,
The house of God in Yerushalayim, and the king
And nobles, his wives and concubines drink wine
From them and praise gods of silver and gold,
Bronze, iron, wood and stone that do not see, hear
Or understand. But God controls your life breath
And every movement. You do not glorify him.
So his hand appears and inscribes these words.
Here are the words that his hand records:
MENE MENE TEKEL and PARSIN. *Mene*
Means that God has numbered the days of your kingdom
And will bring it to an end. *Tekel,* you are weighed
In the balance and are wanting. *Peres,* your kingdom
Is divided and given to Medes and Persians."
Belshazzar commands and Daniel is clothed in purple.
A chain of gold is hung around his neck. And he
Is proclaimed the third in the kingdom. That same night
Belshazzar is killed. And Darius the Mede receives
The kingdom. He is about sixty-two years old.

Dan. 5.1–30

Four Great Beasts Came Up from the Sea

In the first year of Belshazzar king of Babylon,
Daniel has a dream and visions in mind as he lies in his bed.
Then he writes the dream down. Here is how it begins.
"In my night vision I see the four winds of heaven
Stirring up the great sea. Four mighty beasts, each one
Distinct from the other, emerging from the sea.
The first is like a lion with eagle wings. As I look,
It is lifted off the sea, its wings are plucked off,
It is lifted from the ground, and made to stand
On two feet like a man and given a human heart.

I see another beast. This second one looks like a bear
Raised on one side with three ribs in his mouth
Between his teeth. The order comes, 'Rise, devour
Many bodies.' I see another beast like a leopard.
This animal has four birdwings on its back,
Four heads. He has dominion. There is a fourth beast,
Dreadful, powerful with great iron teeth. He devours,
Stamps on and breaks in pieces everything around him.
He is different from the other beasts. He has
Ten horns and a small one growing between them.

This horn has eyes of a man and an arrogantly-speaking
Mouth. I watch as thrones are set in place. The Ancient
Of Days takes his seat. His garment is white snow,
His hair like lamb's wool, his throne is tongues of flame,
Its wheels of are blazing fire. A river of fire streams out
From his presence. Thousands attend him. Thousands
More stand before him. The court of judges sits and books
Are opened. I look on. The horn uttering arrogant words
Is killed. Its body is destroyed and burned. I look on.
The domino of other beasts is removed, but their lives

Are extended for a season. I watch in night vision.
I see one like a living man emerging from the clouds

Of heaven. He comes to the Ancient One,[1]
Is presented to him and he is given dominion,
Glory and kingship. Now all peoples, nations,
And languages will serve him. His dominion
Is everlasting. It will never pass away.
His kingship is one that will never be destroyed."

Dan. 7.3–14

1. Antiochus IV Epiphanes.

JOEL
Yoel יוֹאֵל

J oel is from Hebrew Yoel, יוֹאֵל. He is one of the twelve minor proph-
ets. Joel is said to be the son of Pethuel. Essentially, nothing is known
of Joel or the author or authors of Joel, and the texts are undated. While
allusions go back to very early text, most commentators suggest a postex-
ilic time. The book of Joel consists of two distinguishable parts. There is
first the description of the plague of locusts and drought that encompasses
Judah and Jerusalem, affecting everyone (1.2–2.11). It comes as some form
of punishment of a recalcitrant people, which can be ended though prayer
and repentance. Joel, like the other prophets, engages in extraordinary
images based on fresh renderings of plain words like "darkness," "moon,"
and "blood" (Joel 2.12–31).

> The sun will turn into darkness
> And the moon into blood before the great
> And terrible day when the lord comes.

We find Joel's line (though uncited) in Acts 2.20 and John's Revelation
6.12, in the famous "opening of the seal." The second part of Joel is an
apocalyptic promise of future blessings (Joel 2.21–28). The force of the
great poetry of the Hebrew Bible is the specificity of sumptuous nature
images in a frame of disaster or joy. Here it is joy.

Joel gives us a path to salvation in Joel 2.32, where God declares,
"Anyone who calls the name of the lord will survive." This line will be

repeated in the New Testament in Paul's Romans 10.13, 1 Corinthians 1.2, and Acts 2.21. Although we have less preserved of Joel than other "minor prophets," a sadly unmerited epithet, he remains, along with Jonah, one our most popular and frequently read Biblical writers.

Pastures of Wilderness Spring

Land, do not fear. Be glad and jubilant.
God will do great things.
The pastures in the wilderness are green with grass.
The trees bear fruit,
The fig tree and vine give abundance.
O children of Zion, be glad.
Be happy in the lord your God.
In early rain you have his kind vindication.

He pours down for you abundant rain,
The early and late rain as before.
The threshing floors will overwhelm in grain.
The vats will overflow with wine and oil.
God says, "I will repay you for the years
Consumed by swarms of locusts,
By cankerworms, grubs and hoppers,
The great army that I let loose amid you

You will eat your fill
And praise the name of the lord your God,
Who has treated you so wondrously.
My people will never again be shamed
And you will know that I am in the midst of Yisrael,
That I the lord am your God
And there is no other, and my people
Shall never again be shamed,

Then I will pour my spirit on everyone.
Your sons and daughters will prophesy.
Your old men will dream dreams,
And your young men have visions.
In those days I will even pour my spirit out
On the male and female slaves.
I shall show portents in the heavens
And on the earth:

Blood and fire and columns of smoke.
The sun will turn into darkness
And the moon into blood before the great
And terrible day when the lord comes.
All who call the name of the lord will be saved.
On Mount Sinai and in Yerushalayim
As the lord promised. Anyone who calls
The name of the lord will survive."

Joel 2.21–32

AMOS
עָמוֹס

Amos is one of the twelve minor prophets in the Hebrew Bible, and often he has been seen as the first of the great prophets. He himself denies that he is a prophet (7.14), so we are left as always in uncertainty. He calls himself a simple herdsman and gatherer of fruit. He is said to be an older contemporary of Isaiah. In the Hebrew Bible he is Amos, עָמוֹס. He denounces the virgin Israel who has fallen, but he also denounces those who become rich at the expense of the poor whom they cheat and keep in their poverty, not even to own a pair of shoes (2.6, 8.6). This theme of compassion for the poor and the duty of the people to care for them makes Amos a most attractive figure. The Book of Amos has a surprising ending, which is felicitous. "They shall plant vineyards and drink the wine thereof; they shall make gardens, and eat the fruit of them" (9.14–15).

Buy the Poor for Silver and the Needy for a Pair of Sandals

This is what the lord God shows me.
There is a basket of summer fruit.
He says, "What do you see, Amos?"
"A basket of summer fruit," I reply.
The lord tells me, "The hour of doom
Is ripe for my people of Yisrael.
Women singing songs in the Temple
On that day will cry lamentations."

The lord says, "So many corpses will be
Thrown everywhere. Be silent.
Hear. You who trample on the needy,
Ruining the poor of the land, saying,
'When will the new moon set
And we can sell grain? And the sabbath
And we can offer wheat for sale?
We'll make an *ephah* small and shekel great

And cheat by tampering with scales
And sell off floor sweepings of wheat.' "
The lord swears by the pride of Yaakov,
"I shall never forget their works.
Shall the earth not tremble for this
And all who live here will mourn,
And all will rise like the Nile,
Be hurled around and sink like the Egyptian Nile?"

"On that day," declares my God,
"I will make the sun go down at noon.
I will blacken the earth on a sunny day.
I will turn your festivals into dirges.
I will cover all loins with sackcloth
And have everyone's head shaved.

It will be like mourning for an only son.
I will make it as mourning for an only son,

As at the end of as a bitter day,
And then I will send famine to the land,
Not a famine of bread or a thirst for water,
But of hearing the words of the lord.
You shall wander from sea to sea
And from north to east. You will wander
Everywhere seeking the word of God,
But you will not find it.

On that day shall the beautiful virgins
And the young men faint from thirst.
Those who swear by the guilt of Samaria
And say, 'As your God lives, O Dan,
And as the way to Beersheva lives,
Even they will fall, and never rise again.'
Yet on a day I shall raise David's fallen huts,
I will repair the gaps in ruined villages.

I will rebuild them strong as in old days
So they will again own the rest of Edom
And all the nations called by my name,"
Says the lord who does all things.
"The time is coming," the lord declares,
"When the plowman will meet the reaper,
And the treader of grapes the sower of seed.
And the hills all flow like the meadows.

I will restore my people of Yisrael.
Ruined cities they will rebuild and live there.
They will till gardens and eat their fruit.
And I will plant them on their soil.
Never again will they be uprooted
From the soil that I have given them."

Amos 8.1–14, 9.11–14

JONAH

Yona   יוֹאֵל

Jonah is from Hebrew Yona, יוֹאֵל, and means "dove." Jonah is set among the minor prophets in the Hebrew Bible. Jonah is the son of Amittai. The period of the piece reverts to the eighth century during the reign of Jeroboam II (876–746 B.C.E.). Everything about this short book defies speculation other than it has survived as a children's book in comic style, and from antiquity to George Gershwin it has been a favorite tale. It appears wholly innocent and unserious, yet it states a miracle and demands our attention. In the end Jonah is one of the most sophisticated books of the Bible, challenging basic social and religious tenets.

It begins with Jonah fleeing to Tarshish, which now is probably in Spanish or Portuguese waters, and he acts like a wise buffoon as he goes to sleep down in the lower side of the hull while desperate sailors scream and plead with him to persuade powerful YHWH to calm the sea. Jonah awakes. Then in a series of loony activities, Jonah magnanimously asks them to throw him into the sea, believing that he has done wrong and this act of penitence may save the sailors and his own soul. The sailors toss him in, the seas cease to rage, and they have thereby discovered the powers of the God of Judah. Waiting is the big fish (a whale by popular tradition), and after three days in "the belly of hell," Jonah sinks deeper in the sea. Jonah utters in a line of major biblical despair, "my soul fainted within me." Then the epiphany. God comes and orders the fish to vomit Jonah up on the dry land. Jonah is great comedy, which now in normally humorless scripture is comic opera. Or ideally, comic opera *ballet*. From Aristophanes to Molière and beyond we know that comedy is the ultimate weapon for social reform.

The Great Fish

Now the word of the lord comes to Yonah
The son of Amittai, saying,
"Go to Nineveh, that great city and proclaim
Their judgment. I know their wickedness."
But Yonah does not sail off to Nineveh,
Does not do the lord's service.
He goes down to Joppa and finds a ship
Going to Tarshish in the west.
He pays the fare and boards with others
For Tarshish, far from the lord's service.

The lord hurls a great wind on the sea,
Such a great tempest the ship is in danger
Of breaking up. The sailors are terrified.
They fling the cargo overboard to lighten it.
But Yonah goes down into the hold
Of the vessel, lies down and falls asleep.
The captain goes to him and says,
"How can you be sleeping so soundly!
Call on your God! Maybe he will be kind
To us and we shall not perish."

The men say to each other, "Let's cast lots
And discover who has brought calamity
Upon us." They cast lots, and the lot falls
On Yonah. They say to him, "You have brought
Us misfortune, what is your occupation?
Where do you come from? What is your country?
And of what people are you?" "I am a Jew,"
He answers. "I worship the lord God of heaven,
Who made both sea and land." The sailors
Are seized with terror and ask him,

"What have you done?" When the men learn
He is fleeing the service of the lord—as so

He tells them—they ask him, "What must we do
For you to calm the sea?" The sea is growing
In stormy rage. He tells them, "Heave me
Overboard and the sea will calm for you.
I know I am the cause the sea has come on you."
Still the men row hard to gain the shore.
They cannot for the sea is gaining intensity.
They cry to the lord, "Lord, please do not let

These men perish because of this man's life.
Do not hold us guilty of killing an innocent!
You, O lord, have brought this about."
And they heave Yonah overboard. The sea calms.
The men fear God even more. They offer
A sacrifice to accompany their vows.
The lord provides a huge fish to swallow Yonah.
He stays in the fish's belly three days
And three nights. Yonah prays to the lord
His God from the belly of his fish. He says:

"In my distress I call to the lord
And he answers me.
From the stomach of Sheol I cry out
And you hear my voice.
You cast me into the deep,

Into the heart of the sea.
The floods encircle me close.
All your breakers and billows
Sweep over me. I thought,
'I am driven away from your sight.

Shall I ever gaze again
On your holy Temple?'
The water closes on me.
The deep surrounds me.
Seaweed twines around my head.

I sink to the root of mountains.
I drop to the land whose bars
Close in on me forever,
Yet you raise my life from the pit.
O lord, my God.

As my life is ebbing away
I remember the lord
And my prayer reaches you
In your holy Temple.
Those who cling to hollow folly

By worshiping false gods,
But I with huge thanksgiving
Will sacrifice to you
And what I vow I shall pay.
Deliverance belongs to the lord!"

The lord commands the fish and it spits
Yonah up and out onto dry land.

Jon. 1–2.10

HABAKKUK

Habakuk חֲבַקּוּק

Habakkuk is from Hebrew Habakuk, חֲבַקּוּק. Habakkuk is the eighth of the twelve minor prophets. It is said to be composed in late seventh century B.C.E. Habakkuk consists of a lament, a vision, and a prayer, and has a central theme: God's purpose. It begins as a dialogue with God. The poems resemble extended Psalms and have a liturgical use. Hence they have been popular in church ceremonies. Martin Luther used "The just shall live by his faith" (2.2–4) as a rallying call for the Reformation. The poems also have their share of wondrous lines that the prophets, when they are not fuming, spill out with magic fluency.

The Just Will Live by Faith

I will stand at my watch post,
I shall station myself on the watch tower,

And wait to see what he will say to me,
How he will answer my complaint.

The lord answers me, saying, "Write down your vision.
Inscribe it clearly on tablets.

The vision is for the appointed time.
It tells the end and does not lie.

If it seems to delay, keep waiting.
It is sure to come and will not delay.

Consider the proud. Their soul is bad,
The good and just live by faith."

Hab. 2.1–4

ZEPHANIAH

Tsefanya צְפַנְיָה

Zephaniah is from Hebrew, Tsefanya, צְפַנְיָה. He is ninth among the twelve minor prophets. Zephaniah states that he is a Cushi, that is, a black Ethiopian. His prophecies are gloomy and vindictive as predicts desolation and clouds of thick darkness for Jerusalem and Israel. He also promises the devastation of enemy nations who have made war with Judah. He is colorful as he describes the salt pits and perpetual punishment for the children of Moab and Ammon who will be condemned to Sodom and Gomorrah as will enemy Assyria. They will be slain by the sword along with sinner Ethiopians. His goal is the salvation of Israel and Zion. He also writes in the end that in the day of the lord there will be singing and rejoicing.

I a Black Ethiopian Prophet Bring You into Song

"From beyond the rivers of Ethiopia,
My suppliants, my scattered ones
Will bring me offerings
And you will no longer be ashamed
Of all your acts in rebelling against me.

On that day I will rid you of those who exult
In pride. You will not again stroll
On my holy mountain.
I will leave living in you a poor
And lowly person who finds refuge

In the name of the lord. The remnant
Of Yisrael will do no wrong
Or babble lies.
Or have a deceitful tongue
Will not occupy your mouths.

Only they will pasture and lie down
And no one will make them fear.
Sing for joy, daughter
Of Zion. Shout O Yisrael.
Delight in and be glad in your heart,

Daughter of Yerushalayim. Be fearless, Zion.
Your God the lord has cleaned you
Of judgments and turned
Away the enemies. The king
Of Yerushalayim is walking with you.

He is a warrior who brings you victory.
He will rejoice in your joy.
He will shout

And sing and dance with you
In jubilation as on a day of festival.

He will soothe and renew you
With his love. I will remove
Disasters from you
That caused long mockery.
At that time I will rescue the lame

And gather wanderers, and win you praise
Among all peoples on earth.
I shall restore
Your fortunes before
Your own eyes!" declares God the lord.

Zeph. 3.10–20

ZECHARIAH

Zehariah זְכַרְיָה

Z echariah is from Hebrew Zehariah, זְכַרְיָה. Zechariah is the eleventh of the twelve minor prophets. His overall concern is God's grace and support as the returning Jews from Babylon to Jerusalem rebuild the great Temple. The work consists of eight night visions. His visions are conveyed by a question-and-answer discussion between Zechariah and the angel (messenger) of the lord, asking that the lord have mercy on the people in the reconstruction in Judah. As in Daniel, Jeremiah, Amos, and Ezra, the tone is apocalyptic, with the expected amazing imagery, horses of all colors, wild lightning laced with arrows, and the blare of trumpets that we hear in the King James Version, in which the traditional "ram's horn" is mistranslated as the "trumpet."[1] The riders on different-colored horses are copied directly into Revelation 6 and the four beasts: we read about a rider on a white horse (6.2), a red horse (6.4), a black horse (6.5), and a pale horse (8), and the name of the rider was Death, and Hell followed. Revelation (Apocalypse) is the fully apocalyptic volume (as its Greek title, Apokalypsis, reveals) in the New Testament, and it owes its marveled and fearful imagery to Zechariah and the other visionary books of the Hebrew Bible.

---

1. The trembling horn of a wild goat is first heard by Jews emanating from a dark cloud over Mount Sinai in Exodus 9.16. Trumpets appear in Israel much later, during periods of Roman occupation of Israel during the time of Jesus.

At Night I See a Man Riding on a Red Horse

At night I have a vision.
I see a man riding on a red horse.
He stands among the myrtle trees
Profoundly rooted in the valley.
Behind him are other horses.
Red, sorrel and white horses.

I ask, "Who are they, my lord?"
The angel speaking with me replies,
"I will show you who they are."
The man standing amid the myrtles
Speaks up and says, "We are sent
By the lord to wander the earth.

We have patrolled the earth.
The entire earth lives in peace."
Then the angel of God says,
"O lord of the armies! How long
Will you withhold pardon for
Yerushalayim and the towns

Of Yehudah whom seventy years ago
You inflicted with your anger?"
Then God replies with kind
And comforting words to the angel
Who spoke with me. "Proclaim
This message. The lord of the armies

Says, 'I am jealous for Yerushalayim,
For Zion. I am furious at nations
At ease. Earlier I was mildly in ire
But they have added to disaster.'"
God says, "With compassion I return
To Yerushalayim. My Temple house

Will be rebuilt there," the lord
Of the armies declares. Measure all
Yerushalayim. My villages
Will overflow with prosperity.
The lord God will comfort Zion
And choose Yerushalayim again.

Zech. 1.8–17

APOCRYPHA

JUDITH

Ιουδίθ   Yehudith   יְהוּדִית

Judith in Greek is Ιουδίθ and in Hebrew, יְהוּדִית. The book and story of Judith are preserved in the Septuagint translation of the Hebrew Bible into Greek in the third or second century B.C.E.—there is uncertainty about date and method of translation—for Greek-speaking Jews of Alexandria who could no longer read Tanakh (the Hebrew Bible) in Hebrew. Those texts which are purely Jewish in nature are called the Apocrypha, meaning "hidden source." Jews are proud of Judith, but lacking an original in Hebrew, even after the Dead Sea Scrolls turned up, it is not part of the Jewish canon.

Judith is a tale of a Jewish heroine widow who sacrifices the honor of her personal body by seducing the Assyrian general Holofernes, getting him drunk, and then in his sleep decapitating him. Thereby she saves her countrymen and also the Kingdom of Judah from alien conquest. Beautiful Judith manages to gain Holofernes' trust by having sex with him. When he is unconscious, she seizes him by the hair, strokes him twice with his own sword, and carries the head away publicly. The feat alarms his armies and they run off. The tale of the weak who destroy the strong recalls David and Goliath, the boy David who faces the huge mocking Goliath.

Judith's People Israel Are About to be Destroyed

Our people are deeply thirsty
And we are compelled to keep our promise.
We made an oath we cannot break.
You are a God-fearing woman. Pray for us.
Pray that the lord sends rain and fills
Our cisterns. For now we are faint with thirst.

Then Yehudith speaks to them.
"Listen to me, I have a plan
That will be retold for generations
To the children of our nation.
Stand tonight at our town gate.
I will go out with my serving maid.

A few days after you have agreed
To deliver the city to our enemies,
God will rescue Yisrael by his own hand.
But do not try to guess what I shall do.
I will say nothing until it is done."
Uzziah and rulers say, "Go in peace.

Let the lord God be with you to avenge
Our enemies." They return to their tents.
Yehudith falls to the earth, puts ashes
On her head and uncovers the sackcloth.
At the instant in Yerushalayim when
Incense is offered in the house of the lord,

Yehudith screams to her lord, saying,
"O lord of my ancestor Shimon to whom
You gave a sword to avenge these strangers
Who ripped off a virgin's garments
To defile her and expose her thighs
Shamefully and pollute her womb

To disgrace her, you claim, 'It was done
To kill their rulers and stain their bed
Of deceit with blood,' and you struck down
Slaves and princes on their thrones. Wives
Were booty, daughters captive. You were
Called for help. O God, my God, hear me, a widow!"

Jth. 8.30–9.4

Beautiful Judith Ravishes Holofernes' Heart

Now after that, she stops
Crying to the God of Yisrael,
And ends her words. Yehudith rises
From where she lay prostrate and calls
Her maid. She goes down
To the sabbath and feast house and pulls off
The sackcloth she is wearing
And removes the clothing of widowhood.

She bathes her body all over
With water, and anoints herself
With precious ointment.
She combs her hair and wears a tiara.
She dresses in glad festive garments
As she wore during the life of her husband
Manasseh. She puts her sandal
On her feet, and adorns herself with anklets

And her bracelets and chains
And her earrings and all her ornaments.
She makes herself beautiful
To seduce the eyes of every man who
Sees her. Then she gives
Her maid a skin of wine and a cruse of oil
And fills a bag with roasted grain,
Lumps of dry fig cakes and fine bread.

She wraps all her dishes
And foods together to carry with her.

Jth. 10.1–5

Judith Leaves the Jewish Camp to Come to Holofernes

When she is ready, Yehudith and her maid
Go out and the men of her city guide her
Until she has gone down the mountain,
Until she has passed the valley and is seen
No more. They go straight along the valley.

An Assyrian patrol meets her and takes her
into custody. They ask,
"Who are your people and where are you from
And where are you going?" She says, "I am a Jew,
But I am fleeing from them. They are about
To hand me over to you to be swallowed up.
I am coming to see Holofernes your commander
Of the army to reveal a true report. I will show him
A way by which he can capture all the hill country
Without losing a man, captured or killed."

Now when the men hear her words and observe
Her face—they find her wondrously beautiful—
They tell her she has saved her life by hurrying
Over to see their lord. "Go at once to his tent.
Some of us will go with you and hand you over
To his hands. When you stand before him,
Do not fear in your heart. Say what you have said
And he will treat you well." They are amazed
By her beauty and so admire children of Yisrael.

Jth. 10.10–16, 10.19

Judith and Holofernes Discourse in His Tent

They choose a hundred men to go with her
And her maid and they take her
To Holofernes's tent. The camp is excited.
Her coming is reported from tent
To tent. They gather around her as she stands
Outside his tent. They wait until he hears
About her. They are plundered by her beauty
And admire the Yisraelites, judging

Them by her. They confide with each other.
"Who can hate this people with women
Like this among them? But it is wiser not
To allow one of their men to live.
They can beguile the universe!" The guards
Of Holofernes and his servants
Emerge. They lead her into his tent. Holofernes
Is resting on his bed below a canopy

Woven with purple and gold, emeralds
And precious stones. They describe
Her to him. He comes out front before
His tent with silver lamps going
Before him. When Yehudith appears before
Him and his servants, they are
Ecstatic over her beauty. She lies on the floor,
Face down in reference to him.

The servants raise her up. Then Holofernes
Tells her, "Courage, woman. Let
No fear be in your heart. I would not hurt
Anyone who chose to serve
Nebuchadnezzar, king of all the earth.
Even now if your people who live

In the hill country had not spurned me
I would not lift a spear against them.

They have done things to themselves. Tell me
Why you have fled them and come
Over to us. You will be safe. Be of good comfort.
No one will hurt you but treat
You well as do servants of lord Nebuchadnezzar."

Jth. 10.19–11.4

Judith Tells Holfernes a Way for His Armies to Reach Jerusalem

"Then I will come and show you how
You will come out with your army
And there will be none to withstand you.
I shall lead you through Yehudah until
You reach Yerushalayim. There I will set
Your throne. You will drive them like sheep
Who have no shepherd. No dog will growl
At you. I received foreknowledge. I heard
About these plans and I am sent to you."

Her words please Holofernes and servants.
They admire her wisdom and say, "No woman
From one end of the earth to the other
Looks so beautiful and speaks such wisdom!"
Then Holofernes tells her, "God did well
To send you ahead of the people and destroy
Those who have despised my lord. You are
Not only lovely to see but wise in speech.
If you do as you say, your God will be my God
And you will live in the palace of King
Nebuchadnezzar and be famous in the world."

Jth. 11.18–23

Holofernes Welcomes Her to His Camp

On the fourth day Holofernes chooses
To have a banquet for his attendants only.
Not an officer is invited.
Then he tells Bagoas the eunuch
Who is in charge of personal affairs,
"Go and persuade the Jewish woman
In your care to join us to eat and drink.

It would be shameful if such a lady
Go without having intercourse with her.
If we cannot seduce her, she will laugh at us."
Bagoas leaves Holofernes and tells her,
"Let this young lady not fear to be near
Holofernes and be honored in his presence
And drink wine with us and be happy

Like an Assyrian woman who serves
In the palace of Nebuchadnezzar."
Yehudith responds, "Who am I
To refuse my lord? Whatever makes
Him happy will be my joy until I die."
So she dresses in her womanly finery.
Her maid goes ahead and spreads

On the ground the lambskins Bagoas
Gave her for her daily eating and sitting.
Yehudith comes in and lies down.
Holofernes's heart is ravished.
His passion is at a peak. He has
Been waiting since the day he
Saw her for a chance to seduce her.

Holofernes says, "Have a drink."
"I will be pleased to drink, my lord.

Today is magnified more in my life
Than any day since I was born."
She takes what her maid prepared
And eats and drinks in his presence.
Holofernes is greatly pleased with her

And he drinks more wine than in
Any single day since he was born.

Jth. 12.10–20

Judith and Holofernes Alone in His Tent

Yehudith is alone in the tent of Holofernes.
He is lying alone on his bed, dead drunk on wine.
Yehudith commands her maid to stand outside

The bedchamber and wait for her to come out
As she does on other days when saying her prayers.
She said the same to Bagoas for the same purpose.

Everyone is gone. No one small or great is left.
Standing by his bed she tells her heart, "O lord
God of might. See this hour of my hands' work

For the exultation of Yerushalayim. It is time
To help your heritage; use my plan to destroy
The enemies who have arisen against us."

She goes to the bedpost near Holofernes's head.
There is a sword hanging there. She takes it down.
She nears the bed, take hold of the hair on his head

And says, "Give me strength today, O lord God
Of Yisrael!" She strikes the neck with all her strength
And cuts off his head. She rolls the body off the bed

And pulls the canopy down from the posts. She leaves
And hands Holofernes' head to her maid. She places it
In her meat bag. The two leave as they do for prayer.

They pass through the camp, circle the valley,
Climb the mountain to Bethulia and reach the gates.
Far off Yehudith shouts to the sentries to open the gates.

"Open, open the gate! God, our God, is with us.
He is still showing his powers in Yisrael and his force
Against enemies as he has done by my hands tonight!"

When the townspeople hear her voice,
They race to the gate
And summons the town elders.

They all run together, young and old. It is impossible
That she is back. They open the gate to welcome them.
They light a fire for light and gather around them.

She shouts in a great voice, "Praise god, O praise him!
Praise him who keeps his mercy for Yisrael,
And destroys our enemies by my hand this night!"

Yehudith pulls the head out of the bag and shows it
And tells them, "Look at the head of Holofernes,
Commander of the Assyrian army. See the canopy

Where he lay in a drunken stupor. The lord struck
Him down by the hand of a woman. The lord lives.
He protected me when I went in and I swear

It was my face that beguiled him into destruction
And he committed no sin of any kind
To this woman to defile and bring me into shame."

Jth. 13.2–16

With Timbrels and Cymbals Judith Sings Her Psalm

Yehudith sings out, "May God listen to timbrels.
Sing to my lord
With cymbals. Tune to him a new psalm.
Exalt him and call
His name. God determines the battle.
He sets up camp
In the midst of his people and he
Delivers me from

The hands of my pursuers. The Assyrian
Come down from mountains
In the north. He comes with myriads
Of a warrior army.
Their multitude block the wadi waters,
Their cavalry covers
The hills and he boasts that he
Will set on fire

My borders, and kill my young men with the sword,
And dash my infants
To the ground, and seize
My children as booty
And take our virgins as a spoil. Almighty God
Foiled them most fully
By the hand of a woman. The towering
Ones did not fall

By the hands of young men. Nor sons of Titans
Smash him, nor giants
Set upon him, but Yehudith daughter
Of Merari weakens him
With the beauty of her countenance undoes him."
She puts away the clothing

Of the widow to exalt to the skies
The oppressed in Yisrael.

Jth. 16.1–7

THE NEW TESTAMENT

MARK

Μᾶρκος

The order of the gospels has traditionally placed Matthew first, followed by Mark, Luke, and John. Although authorship of the gospels is an enigma, we do know that the Markan scriptures precede those of Matthew, which is dependent on Mark. It is a serious error not to begin the gospels with Mark. Richmond Lattimore, the Greek scholar and translator of plays and poetry from ancient Greek, is the first in translating Mark as the first book of the Gospels and the Greek Scriptures.

Mark begins his elemental good news by plunging directly into the stories of John the Baptist and of Jesus tempted for forty days in the desert by Satan (which parallels Moses's forty years in the desert tempted by Baal). It follows his wanderings through the land of Israel, where he takes on disciples and crowds of followers, who accompany him in his ministry. Mark gives us a series of miracles, teachings through parables, and finally the "Passion Week" of Jesus's arrest, trial, death, burial, and disappearance from the tomb.

The Gospel of Mark is most often characterized as having been written by an author whose vernacular Greek is plain and rudimentary. Matthew, Luke, and John are more classical writers. But Mark is in many ways the greatest stylist among the evangelists. Commanding a minimal but compelling diction, he writes with clarity, concision, and dramatic power. The notion that somehow his Greek was inferior to Plato's, a favorite trope of seminarians not trained as classical scholars, is mistaken. Plato is a superb stylist, writing in the sharp and poignant language of his time. All these qualities of common speech and philosophy are part of the miracle of

Mark's style, faithful to the spoken tongue of his day, not to that of Plato, nearly 500 years earlier. Should Robert Frost write English in the speech of Edmund Spenser's sixteenth century *Fairie Queene*? As the presumed author of the earliest gospel,[1] Mark established his plain Frostlike style for later Matthew, Luke, and John.

That Mark used the splendid lively demotic tongue of his time is genial. By using the spoken language of the people, he pioneered the speech of the New Testament. People could understand his "good news," his gospel. Had he chosen to compose the gospel in syntactically complex classical Greek, he would have had no popular audience. Similarly daring, Dante, Chaucer, and Montaigne also chose to write in vernacular Italian, English, and French, rather than in Latin, and thereby created the first great literatures in their homelands. The great Dutch humanist Erasmus praised gospel Greek for its universality, for being the tongue of "the plowboy of the fields."

Mark presents his good news about a Jewish rabbi called "Yeshua" in Aramaic, the language he would have spoken as a first-century Jew. He performs miracles to heal and restore life, and whose death evokes eternal mystery. The first verses quote the prophet Isaiah to prove that Jesus is "the voice crying out in the wilderness" and so he is God's messenger. The common people follow him in Galilee and Judaea, hearing his teaching in aphoristic verse in the manner of the Hebrew Bible wisdom parable. He encourages the desperate. He feeds the hungry and poor.

The gospels speak to the human condition of peasants in a country occupied by the Roman military, in days of mean opportunity. At the heart of the gospels is the wandering rabbi Jesus. He also performs miracles. He cures the leper and the demoniac, the bleeding woman and a paralyzed man on the floor. He restores life to a dead boy and a dead man. He is with all who come to him for medical miracles and spiritual food. There are terrified students[2] who fear for their lives on a boat in a windstorm on the Sea of Galilee until Jesus tells the winds to fall, and there are the masses whom the wandering rabbi feeds with a few loaves and fishes to satisfy

---

1. Matthew, Mark, Luke, and John is the conventional order. But Mark is chronologically first, and Matthew derives in part from Mark.
2. "Student" in Greek is correct, not the subservient "disciples."

them. The primal physical needs of people living close to the edge of life and death show on virtually every page. The book of the gospels is a brief epic of hunger, sickness, despair, and humility. As such it stands in black-and-white contrast to Homer's prosperous gods and soldiers and islanders, whose sensuality, fun, and adventure, rather than an impoverished human condition, excite us. The gospel figures, described in plain Near Eastern Greek, incite our compassion.

Every speaker in the Gospels speaks only Greek. They are all Aramaic-speaking Jews except for the Roman occupiers of Israel, and their tongue is Latin. The fact that the New Testament is preserved only in Greek remains a mystery.

If the Gospels in Greek are not a translation, how can Aramaic-speaking Jesus and Latin-speaking Pontius Pilate converse in Koine Greek? Each generation has its own theories for explaining the enigma. If the texts were composed originally in Greek, with no precursor, then it is likely that they were written late in the century by early Church fathers. It is unlikely we will ever have clear answers, but scholars keep trying.

As a young, itinerant rabbi, Jesus is alert to every frailty. A woman falls to her knees, begging the savior to touch her or her child and enact a cure; the man living in the tombs, possessed by demons, asks Jesus whether he, too, has come to torment him, and then, cured by Jesus, begs, unsuccessfully, to accompany him on his wanderings. The unclean are cleansed, the leper is washed, the hungry receive bread, the prostitute is not scorned, the woman (one of the Miryams, wandering in the garden) discovers a resurrected crucified walking near her, who touches her with hope. All these are the figures of the human landscape that the New Covenant delivers without makeup or guise.

We must also never forget the ultimate drama of each of the canonical gospels: the agony of the last hours of Jesus's life, when the "King of the Jews," an itinerant wisdom rabbi whom the Roman conquerors nail to a T-cross, calls out in despair as he gives up the ghost on a Friday afternoon, shouting in Hebrew, from Psalm 22, line 1, "My God, my God, why hast thou forsaken me?" In response, the earth quakes and the sky blackens and cracks. And the drama of religions has its terrible mystery of death. The story of suffering for the good is a universal theme. To tell it, as we see, the Markan rhetoric is not of learned Cicero, Proust, and Henry James, but in the elegant plain talk of Mark Twain, Emily Dickinson, and Hemingway. On stage are dramatic metaphors of rich and poor, of food and hunger, of the leper seeking cure, the prostitute who loves Jesus's body. And going back to Erasmus's declaration of the plowboy of the fields, Mark's Koine Greek, whatever its source, is the right vehicle for the abundant wisdom poetry of Yeshua son of Yosef and Miryam (Jesus, son of Joseph and Mary).

As noted earlier for the Hebrew Bible, the English names of all figures appear in titles. In the text itself we use their restored names. They were after all not from London or Washington, but from cities and villages along the western coast of Asia Minor.

News

Look, I send a messenger ahead of you
And he will prepare the road,
The voice of one crying out in the desert.
Prepare the way for Adonai[3]
And make his paths straight.

Mark 1.2–3

Dilemmas of the Heart

Why argue in your heart?

What is easier to say to the paralytic?
"Your wrongs are forgiven" or to say,
"Stand, pick up your bed, and walk?"
To know that the earthly son has the power
To forgive wrongs on earth,
I say, "Stand, pick up your bed, and go into your house."

Mark 2.8–11

Old Cloth and New Wine

No one sews an unshrunk patch of cloth
On an old garment
Since the new pulls the patch away from the old
And the tear becomes worse.
No one pours new wine in old skins,
Since the wine splits the skins
And both wine and skins are lost.
No, put new wine in a new skin.

Mark 2.21–22

---

3. Lord. The most common word for God in Hebrew is יהוה, meaning "lord," and is often trans-
lated into English as "YHWH" or the "Tetragrammaton." Tetragrammaton means "four letters,"
referring to the four Hebrew letters in יהוה. It means only "four letters" and is not a translation or
phonetic transliteration of those letters in English letters.

Sower Parable

Look, the sower went out to sow
And it happened that as he sowed
Some seed fell on the road
And birds came and ate it.
Other seed fell on rocky ground
Where there was little soil,
And at once it sprang up
Because it lacked deep soil
And when the sun rose
It was scorched, and because
It had no roots it withered away.
Other seed fell among the thorns
And the thorns sprang up
And choked the sprouts
And it bore no grain,
But some fell into good soil
And it bore grain, growing
And increasing and it yielded
Ninety and one hundredfold.
Who has ears to hear, hear.

Mark 4.3–9

Lamp on a Stand

Is a lamp brought inside to be placed
Under a bushel basket or under the bed
And not set on a lampstand?
Nothing is hidden except to be disclosed
Or secret except to come into light.

Mark 4.21–22

Seed on the Earth

The kingdom of God is like a man throwing seed
On the earth, sleeping and rising night and day
To see the seed sprout and grow
In a way he cannot perceive.
On its own, the earth bears fruit,
First grass, then a stalk,
Then the full grain in the ear.
And when the grain is ripe,
He immediately takes out his sickle.
The harvest has come.

Mark 4.26–29

Parable of the Mustard Seed and the Kingdom of God

To what can we compare the kingdom of God
Or in what parable shall we place it?
Like a mustard seed which is sown on the earth,
Smaller than all the seeds on the earth,
Yet when it is sown it grows and becomes greater
Than all garden plants
And makes branches so big that under its shade
The birds of the sky
May find there a place to nest.

Mark 4.30–32

Child and Bread

Let the children be fed first.
It is not good to take the child's bread
And throw it to the dogs.

Mark 7.27

Child in His Arms

> Whoever welcomes a child
> In my name also welcomes me,
> And whoever welcomes me welcomes
> The one who sent me.

Mark 9.37

Through the Eye of a Needle

> How hard it will be for those with money
> To enter the kingdom of God!
> Children, how hard it is to enter the kingdom of God.
> It is easier for a camel to go through the eye of a needle.

Mark 10.24–25

The First Will Be Last

> There is no one who gives up home or brothers or sisters
> Or mother or father or children or farms
>
> For my sake and for the good news,
> Who will not receive a hundredfold.
>
> In this age you suffer persecutions, losing houses
> And brothers and sisters and mothers
>
> And children and farms
> Yet in the age to come you will gain life everlasting.
>
> Many who now are first will be last
> And the last will be first.

Mark 10.29–31

I Will Die and Be Arisen

We are going up to Yerushalayim
And the earthly son will be handed over to the high priests
And the scholars, and they will condemn him to death
And hand him over to the Romans
And they will ridicule him and spit on him
And flog him
And kill him
And after three days he will rise again.

Mark 10.33–34

Untamed Colt on the Road to Jerusalem

Go into the village before you
And once you are inside you will find a tethered colt
On which no one has sat.
Untie it and bring it.
If someone tells you, "Why are you doing this?" say,
"His master needs it and he will send it back at once."

Mark 11.2–3

Moving Mountains

Have faith in God, I say to you.
If you tell this mountain, "Rise and leap into the sea,"
Have no doubt in your heart.
Believe what you say and it happens.

Mark 11.22–23

The Widow's Copper Coins

That poor widow throws in more
Than all who cast money into the treasury.
They have all thrown in from abundance.

She has thrown in from her poverty.
She gives all that she has to live on.

Mark 12.43–44

The Earthly Son Comes in the Clouds

And then, if someone says to you, "Look,
Here is the messiah, look, he is there,"
Do not believe. False messiahs and false prophets
Will rise up and perform signs and wonders

To mislead the chosen, if they can.
But beware! I have forewarned all to you.
But in those days after that affliction,
The sun will be darkened

And the moon not give its light
And the stars will fall out of the sky
And the powers in heaven will quake.
Then you will see the earthly son coming

On clouds with great power and glory.
Then he will send out angels and gather in
The chosen from the four winds from the end
Of the earth to the deep end of the sky.

Mark 13.21–27

Stay Awake for the Coming

From the fig tree learn the parable.
When its branch is tender again and shoots out leaves,
You know that summer is near.

So when you see these things happening
You know that the earthly son is near the doors.
This generation will not pass away before

All these things have come about.
The sky and the earth will pass away
But my words will not pass away.

But of that day or the hour no one knows,
Neither the angels in heaven nor the son.
Only the father. Be watchful, stay awake.

You do not know when the time will come.
It is like when a person goes on a journey
And puts slaves in charge, to each his task,

And commands the doorkeeper to be watchful.
Be watchful then, you never know when the lord
Of the house comes, in the evening or midnight

Or at cockcrow or dawn, or coming suddenly
He may find you asleep.
What I say to you I say to everyone. Beware.

Mark 13.28–37

Anointed by a Woman in the House of the Leper

Let her be. Why do you bother her?
She has done a good thing for me.
You always have the poor with you,
And whenever you want you can do good for them.
But me you do not always have.
She did what she could.
She prepared ahead of time to anoint my body for the burial.
Wherever in the whole world the good news is preached,
What this woman did will speak her memory.

Mark 14.6–9

Planning the Seder[4] Supper in an Upper Room

Go into the city and you will meet
A man carrying a clay pot of water.
Follow him and wherever he enters tell
The owner of the house, "The rabbi asks,
'Where is my guest room where I may eat
The Pesach supper with my students?' "
And he will show you a large upper room
Furnished and ready. There prepare for us.

Mark 14.13–15

Breaking Matzot Bread and Pouring Wine for the Last Seder Supper

Take bread. This is my body.
Take wine. This is my blood of the covenant
Poured out for the many.
Amain, I say to you.
I will no longer drink the fruit of the wine
Until the day I drink it new in the kingdom of God.

Mark 14.22–25

---

4. The Last Supper is the Seder (from Hebrew) סֵדֶר, or Passover, a ceremonial supper for the Jews in the desert who have just escaped from enslavement in Egypt. They eat unleavened matzot bread because they have no time to let the bread rise. As a Jew, Jesus eats his last Passover Supper with fellow Jews. Later, Christians celebrate communion and his Last Supper by eating a wafer made of unleavened bread.

Before the Cock Crows Twice, Simon Peter Will Deny Him

Today on this same night before the cock crows twice
You will deny me three times.

[Shimon Kefa] But if I must die for you,
I will not deny you.

Mark 14.30–31

Terror and Prayer on the Mountain of Olives

Sit here while I pray.
My soul is in sorrow to the point of death.
Stay here and keep awake.

Mark 14.32, 34

Abba, My Father, Take This Cup from Me

Abba,[5] my father, for you all things are possible.
Take this cup from me.
Not what I will but what you will.

Mark 14.36

Catching Simon Peter Asleep

Shimon Kefa, are you sleeping? Did you not have
The strength to keep awake for an hour?
Stay awake and pray that you are not tested.

Oh, the spirit is ready but the flesh is weak.

Mark 14.37–38

5. Abba is Aramaic for "Father."

Wake, for Betrayal Is Near

Sleep what is left of the night and rest.
Enough! The hour has come.
Look, the earthly son is betrayed
Into the hands of those who do wrong.
Get up and let us go.
Look, my betrayer is drawing near.

Mark 14.41–42

To a Crowd with Swords and Clubs

As against a thief have you come with swords
And clubs to arrest me?
I was with you every day in the Temple, teaching,
And you did not seize me,
Only now you act
So the scriptures may be fulfilled.

Mark 14.48–49

Jesus Responds to the Priest, Citing Daniel and Psalms

And you will see the earthly son seated on the right
of the power
And coming with the clouds of heaven.[6]

Mark 14.62

---

6. Cited from Daniel 7.13 and Psalm 110.1.

Darkness at Noon

Elohi Elohi, lema sabachtani?
My God, my God, why have you abandoned me?[7]

Mark 15.34

Jesus Appears First to Mary Magdalene and Then to the Eleven Disbelieving Students Reclining at the Table

Go into all the world and proclaim the good news to all creation.
Who believes and is immersed will be saved
And who is unbelieving will be condemned.
And signs will accompany the believers.
In my name they will cast out demons
And speak in new tongues.
They will pick up serpents with their hands,
They will drink poison; it will not harm them.
They will lay their hands on the sick who will be well again.

Mark Longer "Orphan"[8] Ending 16.15–18

7. Jesus's cry, "My God, my God, why have you abandoned me?" is in Aramaic, from Hebrew Psalm 22, line 2. In Matthew Jesus utters the same phrase in the original Hebrew. When the Jews were captives in Babylon, they read the Bible in Hebrew, but spoke Babylonian Aramaic, the language from which Hebrew and other Canaanite languages derived.
8. "Orphan" is a polite word for an obviously late Church Father emendation that does not appear in the earliest manuscripts.

MATTHEW

Mattinyahu מַתִּתְיָהוּ

T he authorship and place and date of composition of the Gospel of
Matthew are speculation. In the gospel itself, the writer is identified
as Levi the tax collector. "Matthew" is apparently the apostolic name of
Levi, given to him by churchmen in the second century. Biblical scholar-
ship describes Matthew as steeped in rabbinical reference and learning and
as a Greek-speaking Christian Jew of the second generation. It suggests
that the passages of extreme anti-Semitism, such as "Let his blood be upon
us and upon our children!" (27.25), in which the Jews in the street shout a
curse upon themselves now and on their progeny forever, are later inter-
polations, thereby creating a polemic external to a historical Matthew and
his days in Israel.

We do not know whether Matthew was a Jew or, more likely, a later
Christian writing in the persona of a Jew. Conservative dating of the gospels
has set the gospel as early as possible to provide it a more authentic connec-
tion with actual events. It is difficult to imagine a first-century Christian
Jew raging against fellow Jews, condemning them to eternal damnation
while still hoping to convince them to accept their diabolical depiction in
the gospel. Although dating is a serious guess and here dependent on hints
within the gospel, the story of Jesus suggests a later date by an author or
authors wholly in synch with the new church, which until the composition
of the Gospels possesses solely the Hebrew Tanakh (the Old Testament) as
its Bible and holy scripture. We know only that the gospel of Matthew was
composed decades after 70 C.E., the year of the destruction of the Temple
by Titus referred to in the Gospel.

The other side of the Matthew dichotomy is the extraordinary poet, a poet of earth imagery, ecstasy, and bounding love. His book is aphoristic lyric poetry, as in a sayings book, and extended poetic parables. Matthew is a major world poet. His "Birds of the Sky and Lilies of the Field" is profound and exquisitely beautiful. Surely by happenstance, with the fearful and unexpected "oven" metaphor, he prefigures the truly diabolical Holocaust in "Birds of the Sky and Lilies of the Field":

> And if the grass of the field is there today
> And tomorrow is cast into the oven.

The Gospel of Matthew may be said to be the most aphoristic and poetic of the gospels and closest to a sayings book. He also has a deep pathos and conveys a sense of Jesus as a leader of the poor, of the disenfranchised, in an epic of hunger and hope. Matthew covers many aspects of Jesus's life and mission, including his discourse dealing with death, resurrection, and immortality (24.1–25.46). Many of the critical moments in the New Testament are fully elaborated in Matthew, including the coming of the Magi, the birth of Jesus, the baptizing mission of John the Baptist, John's arrest and execution, and the Passion Week scene of Jesus's arrest, crucifixion, and the risen Jesus. Matthew's most extraordinary literary and philosophical contribution is the Sermon on the Mount (5.1–7.29), including the Beatitudes (5.3–12) and the Lord's Prayer (6.9–13). Constantly citing the Hebrew Bible, Matthew takes his place among the masters of world poetry.

Temptation in the Desert

> One lives not on bread alone
> But on every word coming through the mouth of God.
>
> *Matt. 4.4*

For Those Sitting in the Land and Shadow of Death

> Land of Zvulun and land of Naftali,
> The way to the sea beyond the Yarden,
> The Galil of the foreigners,
> The people who are sitting in darkness
> See a great light,
> And for those sitting in the land and shadow of death
> The light springs into dawn.
>
> *Matt. 4.15–16*

With Fishermen Casting Their Nets into the Sea of the Galilee

> Come, and I will make you fishers of people.
>
> *Matt. 4.19*

Sermon on the Mountain

> Blessed are the poor in spirit
> For theirs is the kingdom of heaven.

> Blessed are they who mourn
> For they will be comforted.

> Blessed are the gentle
> For they will inherit the earth.

> Blessed are the hungry and thirsty for justice
> For they will be heartily fed.

Blessed are the merciful
For they will obtain mercy.

Blessed are the clean in heart
For they will see God.

Blessed are the peacemakers
For they will be called the children of God.

Blessed are they who are persecuted for the sake of justice,
For theirs is the kingdom of heaven.

Blessed are you when they revile, persecute and speak
Every cunning evil against you and lie because of me.

Rejoice and be glad, for your reward in the heavens is huge,
And in this way did they persecute the prophets before you.

Matt. 5.3–12

Salt

You are the salt of the earth.
But if the salt has lost its taste, how will it recover its flavor?
Its powers are for nothing except to be thrown away
And trampled underfoot by others.

Matt. 5.13

Light of the World

You are the light of the world.
A city cannot be hidden when it is set on a mountain.
Nor do they light a lamp and place it below a basket,
But on a stand,
And it glows on everyone in the house.
So let your light glow before people

So they may see your good works
And glorify your father of the heavens.

Matt. 5.14–16

Fulfilling the Words of the Prophets

Do not think that I have come
To destroy the law or the prophets.

I have not come to destroy but to fulfill.
And yes I say to you, until the sky and the earth are gone,

Not one tiny iota or serif will disappear from the law
Until all has been completed.

Whoever breaks even the lightest of the commandments
And teaches others to do the same

Will be esteemed least in the kingdom of heaven,
But whoever performs and teaches them

Will be called great in the kingdom of heaven.
I say to you, if you don't exceed the justice

Of the scholars and the Prushim,[1]
You will never enter the kingdom of heaven.

Matt. 5.17–20

Reconcile with Your Companion

You have heard our people say
To those in ancient times
"You must not murder,"[2]

---

1. Pharisees.
2. Exod. 20.13.

And whoever murders will be liable to judgment.
I say to you, whoever is angry with a companion
Will be judged in court,

And whoever calls a companion a fool
Will go before the Sanhedrin, the highest court,
And whoever calls a companion a scoundrel

Will taste the fire of Gei Hinnom.
If then you bring your gift to the altar
And you remember your companion is angry with you,

Leave your gift before the altar,
And go first to be reconciled with your companion
And then come back and present your offering.

Matt. 5.21–24

Turn Your Cheek

And you have heard it said,
"An eye for an eye and a tooth for a tooth."
But I tell you not to resist the wicked person,
And if someone strikes you on the right cheek,
Turn your other cheek as well.
If someone wants to sue you for your shirt,
Give him your cloak as well.
If someone forces you to go a mile with him,
Go a second mile with him.
Give to who asks you. And do not turn away one
Who wants to borrow.

Matt. 5.38–42

Love Your Enemies

You have heard it said,
"You will love your neighbor and hate your enemy."

I say to you to love your enemies
And pray for those who persecute you
So you may become the children of your father in heaven,
For he makes the sun rise over the evil and the good,
And he brings the rains to the just and the unjust among us.
If you love those who love you, what reward have you?
Do not even the tax collectors do the same?
If you greet only those who are your friends,
How have you done more than others?
Have you done more than the gentiles?
Be perfect as your father the heavenly one is perfect.

Matt. 5.43–48

The Lord's Prayer

Our father who is in heaven,
Hallowed be your name.
Your kingdom come, your will be done
On earth as in heaven.
Give us today our daily bread
And forgive our debts
As we have forgiven our debtors.
And lead us not into temptation,
But rescue us from evil.
[For yours is the kingdom,
And the power and glory forever.]³

Matt. 6.9–13

Forgiving

If you forgive those who have stumbled and gone astray
Then your heavenly father will forgive you,

---

3. This famous two-line ending of the Lord's Prayer is in brackets because this doxology, based on David's prayer in Chronicles 2, does not appear in the earliest Greek texts.

But if you will not forgive others
Your father will not forgive your missteps.

Matt. 6.14–15

Birds of the Sky and Lilies of the Field

Consider the birds of the sky.
They do not sow or reap or collect for their granaries,
Yet your heavenly father feeds them.
Are you not more valuable than they?
Who among you by brooding can add one more hour to your life?
And why care about clothing?
Consider the lilies of the field, how they grow.
They do not labor or spin
But I tell you not even Shlomoh in all his splendor
Was clothed like one of these lilies.
And if the grass of the field is there today
And tomorrow is cast into the oven
And in these ways God has dressed the earth,
Will he not clothe you in a more stunning raiment,
You who suffer from poor faith?

Matt. 6.26–30

Brooding About Tomorrow

Do not worry about tomorrow,
For tomorrow will worry about itself.
Each day has enough troubles of its own.

Matt. 6.34

Splinter in the Eye

Do not judge so you may not be judged,
For by your judgment you will be judged
And by your measure you will be measured.

Why do you gaze at the splinter in your brother's eye
Yet not recognize the log in your own eye?
Why say to your brother,
"Let me take the splinter out of your eye"
When your own eye carries a log of wood?
Hypocrite. Remove the log from your own vision,
And you will see clearly enough
To pluck the sliver from your brother's eye.

Matt. 7.1–5

Pearls and Pigs

Do not give the holy to dogs
Or cast your pearls before pigs.
They will surely trample them underfoot
And turn and tear you to pieces.

Matt. 7.6

Knock and the Door Will Be Opened

Ask and it will be given to you.
Seek and you will find.
Knock and the door will be opened for you.
Everyone who asks receives and the seeker finds,
And the door will be opened to one who knocks.
And who among you if your son asks for bread
Will give him stone?
Or if he asks for fish will give him a snake?
If you, who are cunning, know how to give good gifts
To your children,
How much more will your father of the skies
Give good gifts to those who ask him?

Matt. 7.7–11

Doing for Others

> Whatever you wish others to do for you,
> So do for them.
> Such is the meaning of the law and the prophets.

Matt. 7.12

Narrow Gate

> Go in through the narrow gate,
> Since wide is the gate and spacious the road
> That leads to destruction,
> And there are many who go in through it.
> But how narrow is the gate and cramped is the road
> That leads to life,
> And there are few who find it.

Matt. 7.13–14

Tree and Fruit

> From their fruit you will know them.
> Can you gather grapes from thorns or pick figs from thistles?
> Every good tree bears delicious fruit,
> But the diseased tree bears rotting fruit.
> A good tree cannot yield rotting fruit,
> Nor a diseased tree delicious fruits.
> Every tree incapable of delicious fruit is cut down
> And tossed in the fire.
> So from their fruit you will know them.

Matt. 7.16–20

Wind Battering Houses

> Everyone who hears my words and follows them
> Will be like the prudent man who built his house upon the rock.
> The rain fell and the rivers formed

And the winds blew and battered that house
And it did not fall down
Because it was founded upon the rock.
But everyone who hears my words and doesn't follow them
Will be like the foolish man who built his house upon the sand.
The rain fell and the rivers formed
And the winds blew and battered that house
And it fell down and it was a great fall.

Matt. 7.24–27

No Place to Rest

Foxes have holes in the earth
And birds of the sky have nests,
But the earthly son has no place to rest his head.

Matt. 8.20

Two Sparrows and a Penny

Are two sparrows not sold for a penny?
Yet not one of them will fall to the earth
Without your father,
Even the hairs of your head are each counted.
So have no fear.
You are worth more than many sparrows.

Matt. 10.29–31

Finding Soul

If you love your father or mother more than me,
You are not worthy of me,
If you love your son or daughter more than me,
You are not worthy of me,
And if you do not take up the cross and come along
Behind me, you are not worthy of me.

Whoever finds his soul will lose it,
Whoever loses his soul, because of me, will find it.

Matt. 10.37–39

A Cup of Cool Water for a Child

Whoever accepts you, accepts me.
Whoever accepts me, accepts the one who sent me.
Whoever accepts a prophet in the name of the prophet
Will have the reward of a prophet,
And whoever receives a just person in the name
Of a just person
Will have the reward of the just.
And whoever gives even a cup of cool water
To one of these children in the name of a student,[4]
I tell you none will go unrewarded.

Matt. 10.40–42

Like Children Sitting in the Marketplace

But to what shall I compare our generation?
We are like children sitting in the market places,
Calling out to one another, saying,
"We played the flute for you and you didn't dance.
We sang a dirge and you didn't mourn."
When Yohanan came he was not eating or drinking,
And they say, "He has a demon."
The earthly son came eating and drinking,
And they say, "Look at that glutton and drunk,
A friend of tax collectors and sinners,"
Yet wisdom is justified by her deeds.

Matt. 11.16–19

---

4. "Student," rather than "disciple," is the proper translation from the Greek.

Revealed to Little Children

I praise you, lord of the sky and of the earth,
Because you have hidden these things from the wise
And the learned,
And revealed them to little children.

Matt. 11.25

Father and Son

Yes, father, in this way it was pleasing to you.
All things were given to me by my father,
And no one knows the son but the father,
And no one knows the father but the son
And any to whom the son wishes to reveal it.

Matt. 11.27

Rest for Your Souls

Come to me, all who labor and are sorely burdened,
And I will give you rest.
Take my yoke upon you and learn from me
Because I am gentle and humble in heart,
And you will find rest for your souls
For my yoke is easy and my burden is light.

Matt. 11.28–30

My Love in Him in Whom My Soul Delights

Look, here is the servant I have chosen,
My love in whom my soul delights.[5]
I will place my spirit in him
And he will announce judgment for the foreigners.

5. From Solomon's Song of Songs.

He will not quarrel or shout;

No one will hear his voice in the main streets.

He will not break a bruised reed

Or quench a smoking wick of flax

Until he brings in the victory of judgment.

In his name the foreigners will hope.

Matt. 12.18–21

Bread for Four Thousand on the Shore

I pity the crowd. They have stayed with me

For three days and have nothing to eat.

I don't wish to send them away hungry

For fear they will collapse on their way.

Matt. 15.32

The Keys of the Kingdom

You are blessed, Shimon bar Yonah.[6]

It was not flesh and blood that revealed to you this vision

But my father who is in the heavens.

And I tell you that you are Kefa the rock

And upon this rock I will build my church

And the gates of Gei Hinnom will not overpower it.

I will give you the keys of the kingdom of the skies,

And whatever you close upon the earth

Will be closed in the heavens,

And whatever you open on the earth

Will be open in the heavens.

Matt. 16.17–19

6. Simon son of Yonah. The name "Kefa" in Aramaic/Hebrew means "rock." Kefa in Greek is "Petros," also meaning "rock or stone." In English "Petros" becomes "Peter." Hence Simon Peter was originally Shimon Kefa.

Jesus Speaks to His Students about Their Faith

You fail because of your poor faith.
I say to you, even if your faith is no bigger
Than a mustard seed,
When you say to the mountain to move
It will be moved
And nothing will be impossible for you.

Matt. 17.20

Becoming Like Children

Unless you change and become like children,
You will never enter the kingdom heaven.
But whoever becomes little like this child
Will be greatest in the kingdom heaven,
And whoever in my name accepts a child
Like this one also accepts me,
But whoever leads one of these children to stumble
Who believes in me, for him it would be better
To hang a donkey's millstone around his neck
And be drowned in the depth of the sea.

Matt. 18.3–6

Parable of a Lost Sheep

Take care. Do not despise a little sheep.
I tell you that their angels in the air constantly gaze
At the face of my father who is in the heavens.
What seems right? If you have a hundred sheep
And one of them wanders away,
Will you not leave the ninety-nine on the mountain
And look for the one who wandered?
And if you happen to find it,
You are happier than over the ninety-nine

Who did not go astray.
So it is the wish of your father in the heavens
That none of the little ones be lost.

Matt. 18.10–14

On Earth as in Heaven

I tell you that whatever you close on earth
Will be locked up in heaven

And whatever you free on earth
Will be free in heaven.

If two agree about everything on earth they ask for
It will be done for them by my father in the skies.

Where two or three come together in my name
There I live among them.

Matt. 18.18–20

Entering Jerusalem on a Colt

Go on into the village ahead of you
And soon you will find a donkey tethered
And her foal beside her.
Untie them and bring them to me.
And if anyone should say anything to you,
Say that their master needs them.
He will send them at once.

Matt. 21.2–3

Riding on a Donkey

Say to the daughters of Zion,
Look, your king is coming to you,

Modest and riding on a donkey
And with a colt,
The son of the donkey.

Matt. 21.5

Cursing and Drying Up the Fig Tree

If you have faith and do not doubt,
Not only what happened to the fig tree
Will be in your domain,
But you can say to the mountain,
Rise up and hurl yourself into the sea,
And it will be done.
All things you ask for in prayer with faith
You will receive.

Matt. 21.21–22

Planning the Seder in an Upper Room

Go into the city to a certain man and tell him,
"The teacher says, 'My time is near.
And I will celebrate the Pesach at your house
With my students.'"

Matt. 26.18

Terror and Prayer at Gethsemane[7]

Sit down here while I go over there to pray.
My soul is in anguish to the point of death.
Stay here and keep awake with me.

Matt. 26.36, 38

7. In Hebrew "Gat Shmanim."

Jesus Prays Prostrate, His Face on the Earth

My father, let this cup pass from me,
But not as I wish, but as you wish.

Matt. 26.39

Jesus Goes Off Again and Prays

My father, if this cup cannot pass from me
Without my drinking it,
Let your will be done.

Matt. 26.42

One Walking with Jesus Who Has Cut Off the Ear of the High Priest's Slave

Put your sword back into its place,
For all who draw the sword will die by the sword.
Do you think I don't have the power to call on my father
To send me at once twelve legions of angels?
How else would the scriptures be fulfilled
That say in this way these things must happen?

Matt. 26.52–54

Jesus to the Crowd

Have you come to arrest me with swords and clubs
As if I were a robber?
Day after day I sat in the Temple, teaching,
And you did not take hold of me.
All this is happening so the scriptures
Of the prophets are fulfilled.

Matt. 26.55–56

Jesus Replies to the High Priest Who Has Asked Him If He Is the Messiah

You said it. But I say to you,
From now on you will see the earthly son
Seated at the right hand of the power
And coming upon the clouds of the sky.

Matt. 26.64

Pilate the Governor Questions Jesus

Are you the King of the Jews?
You say so.

Matt. 27.11

Darkness at Noon

Eli, Eli, lema sabachthani?[8]
My God, my God, why have you forsaken me?

Matt. 27.46

8. Psalm 22. Jesus's words are in Hebrew.

LUKE

Loukas   Λουκάς

The Gospel of Luke is the longest of the gospels, and, according to most commentators, the most skillfully constructed one, composed in an elegant Greek at times approaching classical Hellenistic Greek of the first century.

The Gospel of Luke reads as a fluent late text, greatly enlarging the scope of the New Testament. Its immediate source in the Synoptic chain is the unknown Q source, which is presumed to be a sayings gospel, and also a source for Mark and Matthew. Perhaps the most original and beautiful passages in Luke—and there are no counterparts in the other gospels—are the annunciation moment (1.26–38), Mary's visit to Elizabeth (1.39–56), the nativity scene of the birth of Jesus in the manger (2.1–7), and the parable of the Good Samaritan (10.29–37). Along with Luke's narrative genius, extraordinary poetry fills the pages of his book, including the painfully beautiful and moving "The Lost Son" ("The Prodigal Son"). Luke is also a major influence on other poets, including T. S. Eliot, whose "Song for Simeon" begins unforgettably:

> Lord, the Roman hyacinths are blooming in bowls and
> The winter sun creeps by the snow hills;
> The stubborn season has made stand.
> My life is light, waiting for the death wind,
> Like a feather on the back of my hand.
> Dust in sunlight and memory in corners
> Wait for the wind that chills towards the dead land.

Elizabeth Sings Encouragement to Mary

You are blessed among women
And blessed is the fruit of your womb.
How has it happened to me that the mother
Of my lord comes to me?
Look, as soon as the sound of your greeting came
Of my ears, a child in my womb leaps in joy!

Luke 1.42–44

The Magnificat / Song of Mary

My soul magnifies the lord
And my spirit is joyful in God my savior,
For he has looked upon his young slave
In her low station.
Hereafter all generations will call me blessed,
Through his powers the great one did wondrous
Things for me. His name is holy
To those who fear him.
He has shown the strength of his arm,
And scattered those who were proud
In the mind of their heart.
Has toppled monarchs from their thrones
And raised the poor to their feet.
He filled the hungry with good foods
And sent the rich away empty.
He has helped Yisrael his servant and child
Through the memory of his mercy,
Just as he spoke to our fathers,
To Avraham and to his everlasting seed.

Luke 1.46–55

Jesus at Age Twelve Is in the Temple for His Bar Mitzvah, Questioning the Rabbis, When Joseph and Mary Find Him

Why were you looking for me?
Did you not know I must be
In the house of my father the lord?

Luke 2.49

Saying Isaiah's Prophecy in the Nazarene Synagogue[1]

The spirit of the lord is upon me,
Through which he anointed me
To bring good news to the poor.
He sent me to preach release of captives
And vision to the blind,
To let the downtrodden go free,
And to proclaim the year of the lord's favor.

Luke 4.18–19

On Lake Gennesaret with Simon Peter

Go out into the deep waters
And drop your nets and fish.
Do not be afraid. From now on
You will be catching people.

Luke 5.4, 10

Sermon on the Plain

Blessed are the poor
For yours is the kingdom of God.

1. Isa. 6–2, 58.6.

Blessed are you who are hungry now
For you will be fed.

Blessed are you who weep now
For you will laugh.

Blessed are you when people hate you,
When they ostracize you and blame you

And cast your name about as evil because of the earthly son.
Be happy on that day and spring and leap,

For look, your reward is great in the sky.
For in the same way their fathers treated the prophets.

Luke 6.20–23

A Plague on the Rich

But a plague on you the rich,
For you have received your consolation.

A plague on you who are filled now,
For you will hunger.

A plague on you who laugh now,
For you will mourn and weep.

A plague on you when all people speak well of you,
For so did their fathers treat the false prophets.

But I say to you who listen:

Love your enemies, do good to those who hate you,

And praise those who curse you.

Luke 6.24–28

Sayings of Love and Enemies

Praise those who curse you.
Pray for those who abuse you.

When one slaps you on the cheek,
Offer the other cheek as well.

From one who takes your coat,
Do not withhold your shirt.

To all who ask you,
Give what you have.

From one who takes what is yours,
Ask nothing back.

As you wish people to do for you,
Do for them.

If you love those who love you, what grace is yours?
Even sinners love those who love them.

And if you do good to those who do good,
What grace is yours? Sinners do the same.

If you lend to those from whom you hope return,
What grace is yours?
Even sinners lend to sinners for a like return.

But love your enemies and do good,
And when you loan, ask nothing in return.

Your reward will be great.
You will be the children of the highest.

He is kind to the ungrateful as he is to the cunning.
Be compassionate as your father is compassionate.

Luke 6.28–36

Helping the Blind, the Lame, and the Lepers

The blind see again, the lame walk, lepers are cleansed,
The deaf hear, the dead arise,
The poor are told good news.
And blessed is one who does not stumble
And fall into wrong because of me.

Luke 7.22–23

Call Me a Glutton and a Drunk

What are the people of this generation
And to whom shall I compare them?
They are children in the marketplace,
Sitting and calling out to each other, who say,
"We play the flute for you
And you do not dance.
We sing a dirge
But you do not weep."
Yohanan the Baptizer comes and eats no bread
And drinks no wine, and you say, "He has a demon."
The earthly son comes and eats and drinks
And you say, "Look, this man is a glutton and a drunk,
A friend of tax collectors and sinners."
But wisdom is proved right by all her children.

Luke 7.31–35

A Loving Prostitute Who Washes Jesus's Feet with Her Tears and Dries Them with Her Hair

Do you see this woman?
I come into your house.
You do not give me water for my feet,

But she washes my feet with her tears.
You give me no kiss,
But from the time I come in

She has not stopped kissing my feet.
You do not anoint my head with olive oil,
But she anoints my feet with myrrh.

Therefore, I tell you, her many sins
Are forgiven, for she loves much.
But one who is forgiven little, loves little.

Luke 7.44—47

His Mother and Brothers Are Standing Outside and Wish to See Him

My mother and my brothers are those
Who hear the word of God and do it.

Luke 8.21

Curing the Bleeding Woman

Someone touches me. I feel the power
Go out from me.
Daughter, your faith has saved you.
Go in peace.

Luke 8.46, 48

Our Daughter Is Dead

Do not be afraid. Only believe
And she will be saved.

Do not weep. She did not die
But is sleeping.

Child, get up!

Luke 8.50, 52, 54

Instructions for the Twelve on the Road

Take nothing for the road,
No staff, no bag, no bread, no silver,
Not even two tunics.
Whatever house you go into, stay there,
And leave from there.
And whoever does not receive you,
As you go out of that city shake the dust
From your feet
In testimony against them.

Luke 9.3–5

Greatness and the Child

Whoever receives this child in my name
Receives me,
And whoever receives me receives the one
Who sent me.
Whoever is smallest among you all,
That one is great.

Luke 9.48

Seventy Naked Lambs on the Road

The harvest is abundant, but the workers few.
So ask the master of the harvest
To send out workers into his harvest.
Go forth. Look, I send you as lambs
Into the midst of wolves.
Carry no purse or a bag or sandals,
And greet no one along the road.

Whatever house you enter, first say, "Peace to this house."
And if a child of peace is there,
Your peace will stay with that one.
And if not, it will return to you.
Remain in the same house, eating and drinking with them,
For the worker deserves his wages.

Don't wander from house to house.
And when you go into any city and they receive you,
Eat what they set before you
And heal those who are sick and say to them,
"The kingdom of God is near."

Luke 10.2–9

Parable of the Good Samaritan[2]

A man is going down from Yerushalayim[3]
To Yeriho[4] and falls into the hands
Of robbers. They strip and beat him.
By chance a priest walks down the same road
And when he sees him he passes by on the other side.
And a Levite also comes by and sees him
And passes by on the other side.

2. In Aramaic a Samaritan would have been called a "Shamroni."
3. Jerusalem.
4. Jericho.

But a Samaritan Jew on his journey comes near
And when he sees him he pities him.
He goes to him and binds his wounds
And pours olive oil and wine over him,
And sets him on his own beast, and takes him
To an inn where he cares for him.
And on the next day he takes out and gives
Two denarii to the innkeeper and says,
"Take care of him and what costs you still may have,
I will repay when I return."
Which of the three seems to you the neighbor
Of the man who fell before the robbers?

Luke 10.30–36

The Master May Come at Any Hour

Let your loins be girded about and the lamps burning
And be like people waiting for their master
When he comes back from the wedding,
So that when he comes and knocks
They will open for him at once.
Blessed are the slaves whom the lord
On his return finds wide awake.
Amain, I tell you, he will gird himself up
And have them recline to eat and he will come near
And if he comes in the second watch or third watch
And he will serve them. And finds them alert, they will be blessed.
But know this. If the master of the house
Knows what time the thief is coming,
He will not let his house be broken into.
Be ready for the earthly son to come
In the hour when you least expect him.

Luke 12.35–40

Mustard Seed and Kingdom of God

What is the kingdom of God like
And to what shall I compare it?
It is like a mustard seed that a man threw
Into his garden and it grew into a tree,
And the birds of the sky nested in its branches.

Luke 13.18–19

Healing a Man with Dropsy on Shabbat

Who among you who has a son or an ox
Fallen into a well

Will not lift it out immediately
On the day of Shabbat?

Luke 14.5

Choosing Guests at Your Table

He also said to the one who was his host,
When you prepare a lunch or supper,
Do not invite your friends or your brothers
Or your relations or rich neighbors,
For possibly they will invite you in return
And it will be a repayment to you.
When you prepare a banquet invite
The poor, the crippled, the lame, the blind.
Then you will be blessed, for they have not means
To repay you, but you will be repaid
At the resurrection of the good.

Luke 14.12–14

Hate Your Father and Mother, Renounce Everything and Follow Me

If someone comes to me and does not hate
His father and mother and wife and children
And brothers and sisters and even life itself,
He cannot be my student. Whoever does not
Carry the cross and follow me cannot be my student.

Luke 14.26–27

Taste of Salt

Salt is good. But if salt has lost its taste
How can it be seasoned?
It is not fit for the land or a dunghill.
They throw it out.
Whoever has ears to hear, hear.

Luke 14.34–35

Parable of the Lost Drachma

Or what woman who has ten drachmas
If she loses one will not light a lamp
And sweep the house and search carefully
Until she finds it? And finding it, she calls
Together friends and neighbors, saying,
"Celebrate with me, for I have found the coin
I lost." So I tell you, there is joy
Among the angels over one sinner who repents.

Luke 15.8–10

Parable of the Lost Son

There is a man who has two sons.
The younger says to his father, "Father,
Give me the share of the property
That will belong to me." So he divides

His resources between them. And not
Many days later the younger son
Gets all his things together and goes off
To a far country and there he squanders
His substance by riotous living.

When he has spent everything he had,
There comes a severe famine throughout
That country, and he begins to be in need.
And he goes and hires out to a citizen
Of that land, who sends him to his fields
To feed the pigs. He longs to be fed
On the pods the pigs are eating, but no one
Gives him anything. He comes to himself
And says, "How many of the day laborers
Of my father have bread left over and here
I'm starving and dying. I will rise up
And go to my father and I will say to him,
"Father, I have sinned against heaven
And before you. I am no longer worthy
To be called your son. Make me
Like one of your hired hands."
And he rises and goes to his father.

While he is still far in the distance,
His father sees him and is filled
With compassion and tears fall on his neck
And he kisses him. And the son says to him,
"Father, I have sinned against heaven
And before you. I am no longer worthy
To be called your son." But his father tells
His slaves, "Quick, bring out the finest robe
And put it on him, and give him a ring
For his hand and sandals for his feet.
And bring the fatted calf, slaughter it,
And let us eat and celebrate, for my son
Was dead and he has come back to life,

He was lost and he has been found."
And they began to celebrate.

Now the older son is in the fields
And as he draws near the house he hears
Music and dancing. And he calls over
One of his slaves and asks what is going on.
He tells him, "Your brother is here,
And your father has slaughtered the fatted calf
Because he has taken him back in good health."

The son is angry and does not want to go in,
But his father comes out and pleads with him.
But he answers and tells his father,
"Look, so many years I have served you
And never disobeyed an order of yours,
And for me you never gave a young goat
So I could celebrate with my friends.
But when this son of yours came, who ate up
Your property with prostitutes, for him
You slaughtered the fatted calf." Then
His father says, "Child, you are always with me,
And everything that is mine is yours,
But we must be happy and celebrate.
Your brother was a dead man and he lives
And he was lost and has been found."

Luke 15.11–32

Faith Uprooting a Black Mulberry Tree

If you have faith like a grain of mustard seed
You can say to this black mulberry tree,
"Pluck yourself up by the roots and plant yourself
In the sea," and it will still obey you.

Luke 17.6

Coming of the Kingdom of God Mysteriously Inside

> The kingdom of God is not coming
> In an observable way,
> Nor will people say, "Look, it is here!"
> Or, "It is there!"
> For look, the kingdom of God is inside you.

Luke 17.20–21

Majesty and Terror in the Apocalyptic Coming of the Earthly Son

> The days are coming when you will long to see
> One of the days of the earthly son,
> And you will not see it.
> And they will say to you, "Look, there!" or "Look, here!"
> Do not go after them! Do not follow them!
> For as lightning burns at one end of the sky
> And then at the other end of the sky glistens,
> So will be the coming of the earthly son.
> But first he must suffer multiple wrongs
> And be rejected by this generation.
> And as it happened in the days of Noah,
> So it will be in the days of the earthly son.
> The people were eating, drinking, marrying,
> And given away in marriage until the day
> Noah went into the ark and the flood came
> And destroyed all of them. It was the same
> As in the days of Lot. They were eating,
> Drinking, buying, selling, planting, building.
> But on the day Lot went out of Sedom
> It rained fire and sulfur from the sky
> And destroyed everything. So it will be
> On the day the earthly son is revealed.

On that day if a man is on the roof and his goods
Are in the house, let him not come down
To carry them away. And one in the field
Likewise let him not turn back for anything
Left behind. Remember the wife of Lot.
Whoever tries to preserve her life will lose it,
But whoever loses it will bring it to life.
I tell you, on that night there will be two men
In one bed. One will be taken, the other left.
There will be two women grinding meal
At the same place. One will be taken, the other left.
Two men in the field. One will be taken, the other stays.

Luke 17.22–36

The Children Come to Me

Let the children come to me
And do not stop them, for the kingdom of God
Belongs to them.
Whoever does not receive the kingdom of God
Like a child will never enter therein.

Luke 18.16–17

Rewards for Abandoning Family for the Kingdom

There is no one who has left house or wife
Or parents or children for the kingdom of God
Who will not receive back many times more
In this age and in the age to come of life everlasting.

Luke 18.29–30

I Will Die and Be Risen

Look, we are going up to Yerushalayim
And all that has been written by the prophets

About the earthly son will be fulfilled.
He will be handed over to the Romans
And they will mock and insult and spit on him,
And after scourging him they will kill him
And on the third day he will rise again.

Luke 18.31–33

Entering Jerusalem on a Colt

Go into the village just ahead
And as you enter you will find a tethered colt
On which no one has ever sat.
Untie it and bring it here.
If someone asks you, "Why are you untying it?"
You will say, "His master needs it."

Luke 19.30–31

Telling His Students to Speak Out

I tell you,
If you are silent,
The stones will weep.

Luke 19.40

Of Yahweh and the Messiah

How can they say the messiah is the descendant of David
When David himself says in Psalms:
Yahweh said to my lord,
"Sit at my right side
Till I have made your enemies your footstool?"[5]
David calls him lord. How then can he be his son?

Luke 20.41–44

5. Ps. 110.1.

The Widow's Copper Coins

This widow who is poor
Has cast in more than anyone else.
All of them put in gifts from their abundance
While she in her poverty cast in
All the pennies she had to live on.

Luke 21.3–4

Foretelling the Destruction of the Temple by the Romans

As for what you see,
The days will come
When there will be
Not one stone on a stone
Not thrown down.[6]

Luke 21.6

Cosmic Disasters and Coming of the Earthly Son

There will be signs in sun and moon and stars,
And on the earth the dismay of foreign nations
In bewilderment at the sound of the sea
And surf. People will faint from fear
And foreboding of what is coming upon the world,
For the powers heaven will be shaken.
And then they will see the earthly son coming
On a cloud with power and enormous glory.
When these things happen, stand up straight
And raise your heads, for your redemption is near.

Luke 21.25–28

6. Reference is to the Romans' conquest of Jerusalem and burning of the Temple in 70 C.E.

Parable of the Budding Fig Tree

Look at the fig tree and all the trees.
When they sprout leaves, you look at them
And know that summer is already near.
So too when you see these things happening
You know the kingdom of God is near.
I tell you truth. This generation will not
Pass by until all these things take place.
The sky and the earth will pass away
But my words will not pass away.

Luke 21.29–33

Preparing the Passover Meal with His Students

Look, as you go into the city,
A man carrying a jar of water will meet you.
Follow him into the house he enters
And say to the owner of the house,
"The rabbi says to you, 'Where is the guest room
Where I am to eat the Pesach meal
With my students?'" And he will show you
A large upstairs room, already furnished.
Prepare it there.

Luke 22.10–12

The Seder

I greatly desired
To eat this Pesach with you
Before I suffer. I tell you truth,
I will not eat it again until it is fulfilled
In the kingdom of God.

Luke 22.15–16

Take This Cup from Me

Take this cup from me and share it among you.
I say to you, as of now I will not drink of the fruit
Of the vine until the kingdom of God comes.

Luke 22.17–18

Breaking the Matzot Bread

This is my body
Which is given for you.
Do this in remembrance of me.

Luke 22.19

After Supper He Does the Same with the Cup

This cup is the new covenant in my blood,
Which is poured out for you.

Luke 22.20

Foretelling the Hand of the Betrayer

But look, the hand of the betrayer is with me
On the table.
Because the earthly son is going away
As has been determined,
But a plague on that man who betrayed him.

Luke 22.21–22

After a Quarrel among His Students about Who Is the Greatest

The kings of nations lord it over them
And those I power are called benefactors,
But with you it is not so,

Let the greatest among you be the youngest
And the leader the one who serves.
Who is greater?
The one who reclines at the table
Or the one serving?
I am among you as one who serves.

Luke 22.25–27

You Will Eat and Drink at My Table in My Kingdom

You are the ones who have stood by me
In my trials. And just as my father
Has conferred a kingdom on me, I confer on you
That you may eat and drink at my table
In my kingdom, and you will sit on thrones
And judge the twelve tribes of Yisrael.

Luke 22.28–30

Simon Peter, Will You Deny Me?

Shimon, Shimon, look, Satan has demanded
To sift you like wheat,
But I have prayed that your faith not fail you,
And when you return you strengthen our brothers.

Luke 22.31–32

To Simon Peter Who Says He Is Ready to Go to Prison and to Die for Him

I tell you, Shimon Kefa, the cock will not crow today
Until you have three times denied knowing me.

Luke 22.34

Now Go Out with a Purse, Bag, and Sandals, and Buy a Sword

> But now let the one who has a purse
> Let him take it, and also the bag,
> And the one who has no sword,
> Let him sell his coat and buy one.
> For I tell you, what Yeshayahu[7] wrote
> Must be fulfilled in me.
> Even he was counted among the lawless
> And what is said about me will find resolution.

Luke 22.36–37

On His Knees, Praying on the Mountain of Olives

> Father, if you choose, take this cup from me,
> And let not my will but yours be done.

Luke 22.42

To His Students Sleeping after Their Grief

> Why are you sleeping? Get up and pray
> That you may not enter the time of trial.

Luke 22.46

His Student Judas, Leading a Crowd, Comes Up to Kiss Him

> Yehudah, are you betraying the earthly son with a kiss?

Luke 22.48

7. Isa. 5.2.

The Mob Attacking Him

Did you come out with swords and clubs
As if I were a robber?
Each day I was with you in the Temple
You did not lay your hands on me.
But this is your hour, and the power of darkness.

Luke 22.52–53

The Sanhedrin Questions Him

Are you the Mashiah?

I tell you, you will not believe me,
And if I question you, you will not answer.
But from now on the earthly son
Will be sitting at the right hand of the power of God.

Luke 22.67–69

On Golgotha, Place of the Skull, Jesus and the Two Criminals

Father, forgive them.
They do not know what they are doing.

Luke 23.34

To One of the Criminals Who Asks to Be Remembered

Today you will be with me in paradise.

Luke 23.43

Darkness at Noon

Father, into your hands I commend my spirit.

Luke 23.46

On the Road to Emmaus, a Village Seven Miles from Jerusalem, Jesus Sees Two Students Who Do Not Recognize Him

What are these words you are exchanging
With each other as you walk along?
O what fools and slow of heart you are to believe
All that the prophets spoke!
Did not the mashiah have to suffer this
And enter into his glory?

Luke 24.17, 25–26

Back in Jerusalem Jesus Stands in Their Midst

Peace be with you.

Luke 24.36

The Students Are Full of Fear, Looking at Him as at a Ghost

Why are you shaken and why do doubts rise
In your hearts? Look at my hands and my feet
And see I am myself. Touch me and see,
Because a ghost does not have flesh and bones
Which as you see I have.

Luke 24.38–39

After Showing His Hands and Feet Jesus Asks

> Do you have something to eat?

Luke 24.41

After Eating Broiled Fish

> These are my words which I spoke to you
> While I was still with you:
> All that was written about me in the law of Mosheh
> And the prophets and Psalms must be fulfilled.

Luke 24.44

Jesus Cites Torah, Telling His Students Their Mission to Carry the Word

> It is written that the Mashiah is to suffer and to rise
> From the dead on the third day,
> And in his name you will preach repentance
> And forgiveness of sins to all nations,
> Beginning with Yerushalayim.
> You are the witnesses. And look,
> I am sending the promise of my father to you.
> So stay in the city until you are clothed
> With power from on high.

Luke 24.46–49

JOHN
Yohanan   יוֹחָנָן

The Gospel of John is unparalleled in the Bible. The prologue is magi-
cal for believers or nonbelievers; indeed, it is a singular moment in
religious scripture and world literature. As Mark is poignant and dramatic,
Matthew infused with lyricism, Luke accomplished in telling the nativity,
the parables, and singing the poor, John is uniformly spiritual and philo-
sophical. Thematically and structurally, the Gospel of John is remarkably
independent of the three preceding Synoptic gospels. It has dialogues and
discourses not found elsewhere.

In the prologue there is an emphasis on light and darkness, on truth and
lies, which seems to be in harmony with dichotomies found in the Dead
Sea Scrolls of the Essene community. In the richest and most eloquent pas-
sages of spiritual inquiry, there is a strong Gnostic element. In short, John is
a mirror to a time of diverse beliefs and philosophies. Key terms and con-
cepts, from the Neo-Platonist Jew Philo of Alexandria to the scrolls of the
Essenes and the Gnostics, flash in and out of his text with unusual intensity.
Among the Gnostics, John was accepted as one of their own.

John is distinct from the Synoptic gospels in many ways. There is no
Sermon on the Mount. Jesus tells no parables (except of the good shep-
herd), heals no lepers. Demons are not exorcised, there is no Lord's Prayer
or Last Supper, and the notion of religious instruction and moral teachings
found in the Synoptics is transformed into metaphysical discourse. As in
the other gospels, the Book of John does use miracles as "signs" to prove
the powers of the messiah and God. However, by contrast, Jesus is a more
abstracted figure; the presentation of his crucifixion, in contrast to that

of the other gospels, is not of an especially suffering man, tortured and dying for human sin, but of a controlled, even aloof, figure, following his own divine purpose without fear. There are similarities to the language of Apocalypse, which is incorrectly ascribed to John.

The paradoxes of light and darkness, heaven and earth, truth and lies, recall the dichotomies found in the Dead Sea Scrolls of the Essene community. Amid the rich and eloquent passages of spiritual inquiry characterizing John, there is also a Gnostic element with respect to knowledge and inner light. As a mirror to a time of diverse beliefs and philosophies, John emerges as the gospel of being.

John also contains the longest diatribe against the Jews in the Bible (John 8.12–35). No matter where they go or hide, they will be caught. "They are the children of the devil" (John 8:37–39). He echoes Matthew's condemnation of Jews and all descendants (Matthew 27.25). One must always ask, what about ritually circumcised Jesus, "King of the Jews"? If Jesus the Jew is the son of God, his father God is also a Jew. That makes God a child of the devil. The schizoid anti-Jew ambience in the Gospels is totally mad, sad, and tragic. It has never made sense, but it has endured for two millennia.

John helped shape the medieval picture of the Jew. Like the Synoptic evangelists, John is traditionally presumed to be a Jew, and, for apologists, therefore incapable of being anti-Jewish. He is composing around 100 C.E., and by then probably an early church father. He fumes against the Jews as Jewish prophets self-critically do in the Hebrew Bible. Contradictions? Yes. As Koheleth says in Ecclesiastes, "there is nothing new under the sun."

Despite his anti-Judaism, John remains the later philosopher closest to Jewish thought and their Tanakh, taking from the Bible passage after passage to enrich his work. "I am the bread of life" (John 6.35). "I am the way, the truth, and the life" (John 14.6). And for all the stupid anger, John brings the Hebrew Bible vividly back to life like none except John in Revelation, which is pure Jewish apocalypse close to Zechariah and the apocalyptic prophets. But John the evangelist has clarity in each individual meditation. He looks for light. The latter part of John resembles visionary Ecclesiastes and Daniel. The contradictions will never be resolved, but John and the dispersed Johannine movements remain as mysteries. As in the other Gospels and in the Ten Commandments, love will save us, and especially love for the poor, the prostitute, the enemy and the foreigner. One should if possible forget the absurd anti-Semitism and welcome the magical wordsmith and unsurpassed metaphysical philosopher. He is the teacher of being. The Gospel of John is itself literature and lives in all who have absorbed his solitary grandeur. Hear his advice for us on earth (John 12.36):

> While you have light, believe in light
> So you may be the children of light.

In the Beginning Is the Word

In the beginning is the word
And the word is with God,
And the word is God.
He is in the beginning with God.
All things are born through him,
And without him nothing is born.
In him is life
And in life is the light in all people
And light glows in the darkness
And darkness cannot cast it down.

John 1.1–5

Light Is in the World

The true light glowing in all people
Comes into the world.
He is in the world
And through him the world is born,
And the world does not know him.
He goes to his own
And his own does not receive him.
To all who receive him,
Who believe in his name,
He gives a power to become the children of God,
Who are born not from blood
Or from the will of the flesh
Or from the will of a man,
But are born from God.
And the word becomes flesh
And lives among us,
And we gaze on his glory,
The glory of the only son born of the father,
Who is filled with grace and truth.

John 1.9–14

Under the Fig Tree Nathanael Tells Jesus, "Rabbi, You Are the Son of God!" and Jesus Responds

Because I tell you I see you under the fig tree,
Do you believe?
You will see even greater things.
You will see the sky open
And angels of God ascending and descending
Upon the earthly son.

John 1.50–51

At a Wedding in Galilee Mary Tells Jesus They Have No Wine and Jesus Responds with a Plan to Turn Water into Wine

Woman, what is that to me and you?
My hour has not yet come.
Now fill the pots with water,
Pour some of the water out
And take it to the master of the feast.

John 2.4, 7, 8

Seeing Himself as the Temple of the Body

Destroy this Temple
And in three days I shall raise it up.

John 2.19

His Pharisee Friend Nicodemus Asks How He Can Perform Miracles

Unless you are born from above
You cannot see the kingdom of God.
Unless you are born from water and the wind of God
You cannot enter the kingdom of God.

What is born from the flesh is flesh,
What is born from the wind is wind.
Do not wonder that I told you
You must be born again from above.
The wind blows where it wants to and you hear its sound
But you cannot know where it comes from and where it goes.
So it is for everyone born from the wind of God.
You are the teacher of Yisrael and do not know this?

We speak of what we know and we testify to what we have seen,
Yet you do not receive our testimony.
If I tell you of earthly things and you do not believe,
How if I tell you of heavenly things will you believe?
And no one has gone up into the sky
Except the one who came down from the sky,
Who is the earthly son.
And as Mosheh raised up the snake in the desert,
The earthly son must be raised up
So that all who believe in him will have eternal life.

John 3.3, 5–8, 10–15

God's Only Son

God loves the world so much he gives his only son
So that all who believe in him might not be destroyed
But have eternal life.
God does not send his son into the world to judge the world
But so through him the world might be saved.
One who believes in him is not judged
But one who does not believe is judged already
For not believing in the name of God's only son.

John 3.16–18

The Light

And this is the judgment.
Light comes into the world
And people love the darkness rather than the light,
For their works are cunning.
For all who do shoddy things hate the light
And do not come toward the light
So that their works will not be exposed.
But those who do the truth come toward the light
So their works may shine as accomplished through God.

John 3.19–21

To a Samaritan[1] Woman Drawing Water from a Well

Give me a drink.

John 4.7

The Woman Asks Jesus How He, an Orthodox Jew, Can Give a Samaritan Jew a Drink

If you knew the gift of God and who is saying to you,
"Give me a drink,"
You would have asked and he would have given you
Living water.

John 4.10

The Woman Says He Has No Bucket and Asks If He Is Greater than God Their Father

Everyone who drinks this water will be thirsty again.
But whoever drinks the water I give them
Will not be thirsty again.

---

1. The Samaritans in Israel were one of the many Jewish sects.

The water I give them will become in them
A fountain of water springing into eternal life.

John 4.13–14

The Woman Says He Must Be a Prophet

Believe me, woman, the hour is coming
When not on this mountain
Nor in Yerushalayim will you worship the father.
You worship what you do not know.
We worship what we know
Since salvation is from the Jews.
But the hour is coming and it is now
When the true worshipers will worship the father
In spirit and truth,
For the father seeks such people to worship him.
God is spirit
And those worshiping must worship him
In spirit and truth.

John 4.21–24

The Woman Says She Knows a Messiah Is Coming Who Is Called the Anointed

I am he, talking to you.

John 4.26

Answering the Amazed Students Who Tell Him to Eat

I have a food to eat which you do not know.
My food is to do the will of him
Who sent me and to complete his work.

John 4.32, 34

Grain for Eternal Life

Do not say, "Four more months and then comes the harvest."
Look, I tell you, lift up your eyes
And you will see the fields are white for harvest.
Already the reaper is taking his wages
And gathering the grain for the eternal life
So sower and reaper alike may be happy.
The words of the proverb are true:
"One sows and another reaps."
I sent you to reap what you did not labor.
Others work and you enter their work.

John 4.35–38

Healing a Prince Near Death in the Galilee Through Belief

Unless you see signs
You will not believe.

Go, your son lives.

John 4.48, 50

Healing a Man Thirty-Eight Years Sick in Jerusalem by the Sheep Gate

Do you want to get well?

Stand.
Take up your bed
And walk.

John 5.6, 8

To Those Who Are Angry for His Healing on the Sabbath

My father is still doing his work
And I am doing mine.

The son can do nothing by himself unless he sees
The father doing the same,

For what he does the son does likewise.
The father loves the son and shows him everything

That he is doing,
And he will show him greater works than these

So you will marvel.
Just as the father wakes the dead and gives them life,

So the son gives life to whom he will.
The father judges no one.

He has given all judgment to his son
So all will honor the son as they honor the father.

One who does not honor the son
Does not honor the father who sent him.

John 5.17, 19–23

Eternal Life

One who hears my word and believes him
Who sent me
Has eternal life and does not come to judgment,
But passes out of death to life.
A time is coming and it is now
When the dead will hear the voice of the son of God

And those who hear will live.
Just as the father has life in himself,
So he has given the son life to have in himself,
And he has given him authority to judge
Because he is the earthly son.

Do not wonder at this,
For the hour is coming when all who are in their graves
Will hear his voice and will come out:
Those who have done good will go to a resurrection of life,
But those who have done evil

Will go to a resurrection of judgment.
I can do nothing from myself.
As I hear I judge and my judgment is just,
Since I do not seek my will but the will of him
Who sent me.

John 5.24–30

By Lake Tiberius Near Where Jesus Walks on the Sea after Feeding Five Thousand Men with Bread

You look for me not because you see miracles
But because you eat the loaves and are filled.
Do not work for the food that spoils
But for the food that lasts for eternal life,
Which the earthly son will give you,
Since on him God who is father set the seal.

John 6.26–27

The People Ask Jesus Always to Give Them Bread

I am the bread of life.
Who comes to me will not be hungry,

And who believes in me will not be thirsty again.
Yet I say to you,
You see me and do not believe.
All that my father gives me will come to me
And anyone who comes to me I will not turn away,
Since I have come down from the sky
Not to do my own will but the will of him who sends me.
And this is the will of him who sent me,
That I should lose nothing of all he gives me
But raise it up on the last day.
This is the will of my father,
That all who see the son and believe in him
May have eternal life,
And I will raise them up on the last day.

One who believes has eternal life.
I am the bread of life.
Your parents ate the manna in the desert and died.
This is the bread that comes from the heavenly sky,
So anyone may eat it and not die.
I am the living bread
Who comes down from the sky.
Whoever eats this bread will live forever,
And the bread is my flesh,
Which I give for the life of the world.

John 6.35–40, 47–51

Jesus in the Synagogue at Kfar Nahum Says His Flesh Is the True Meat, His Blood the True Drink

Unless you eat the flesh of the earthly son
And drink his blood, you have no life within you.
The one who eats my flesh and drinks my blood
Has eternal life and I will raise that person up

On the last day, for my flesh is the true meat
And my blood is the true drink.

The one who eats my flesh and drinks my blood
Lives in me and I in them.
As the living father sent me and I live
Because of the father,
So the one who eats me will live because of me.
This is the bread that came down from the sky,
Not like what our parents ate and died.
Who eats this bread will live forever.

John 6.53–58

Not Flesh but Breath Keeps Us Alive

Does this shock you?
What if you see the earthly son ascend to where he was before?
Breath[2] keeps us alive.
The flesh is of no help.
The words I spoke to you are the breath of spirit
And are life.
But some among you do not believe.

John 6.61–64

My Teaching Is Not Mine

My teaching is not mine but is his who sent me.
Whoever wants to do the will of God
Will know whether the teaching is from God
Or whether I speak on my own.
The person who speaks only from inside
Seeks a personal glory,
But the person who seeks the glory of God who sent us
Is true and has nothing false inside.

---

2. Breath from the Greek (pneuma), meaning "breath" and by extension "spirit."

Did Mosheh not give you the law?
Yet none of you keeps the law.
Why are you trying to kill me?

John 7.16–19

Who Am I?

You know me and know where I am from,
And I have not come on my own,
But he is true, the one who sent me,
And you do not know him.
I know him because from him I am
And he sends me.

John 7.28–29

Look for Me, but I Am Going Where You Cannot Come

For a little more time I am still with you
And then I go away to the one who sent me.
You will search me out and not find me,
And where I am you will not be able to come.

John 7.33–34

Celebrating the Last Day of Sukkoth in the Temple, He Cries Out

Let anyone who is thirsty come to me and drink!
For one who believes in me, as it says in the scriptures,
"Rivers out of his belly will flow with living water."

John 7.37–38

To a Woman Accused of Adultery, Jesus Stoops Down, Writes with His Finger on the Ground, Rises and Says

The one among you without sin,
Let him first cast a stone at her.

John 8.7

The Woman Tells Jesus She Is Not Condemned

Woman, where are they?
Has no one condemned you?
Neither do I condemn you.

John 8.10–11

Light of the World

I am the light of the world.
Whoever follows me will not walk in darkness
But will have the light of life.

John 8.12

To Those Who Question His Veracity

Even if I testify about myself, my testimony is true.
I know where I came from and where I am going.
And you do not know where I came from
Or where I am going?
You judge according to the flesh.
I judge no one.
And if I do judge, my judgment is true
Because I am not alone,
But I and the father who sent me.
And in your law it is written in Deuteronomy
That the testimony of two people is true.
I am he who testifies about myself,

And testifying about me
Is the one who sent me, my father.

John 8.14–18

Where Is Your Father?

You know neither me, nor my father.
If you knew me,
You would also know my father.

John 8.19

I Am Not of This World

I am going and you will look for me
And you will die in your sins.
Where I am going you cannot come.

You are of things below.
I am of things above.

You are of this world,
I am not of this world.

So I have told you
You will die in your sins.

If you do not believe that I am,
You will die in your sins.

John 8.21, 23–24

Who Are You?

I am what from the beginning I told you.
I have much to say and much to judge,
But the one who sends me is true
And what I hear from him I speak in the world.

When you raise up the earthly son,
Then you will know that I am
And from myself I do nothing,
But I speak as my father taught me.
And the one who sends me is with me.
He does not leave me alone,
For what I do pleases him always.

John 8.25–26, 28–29

To Those in the Temple Who Believe in Him

If you remain with my word,
You are truly my students,

And you will know the truth
And the truth will set you free.

John 8.31–32

Bringing Day to Those Born Blind

Neither he nor his parents do wrong.
He is born blind so the work of God
Might be revealed in him.
We must do the work of him who sends us
While it is day.
Night is coming when no one can work.
While I am in the world,
I am the light of the world.

John 9.3–5

To the Blind Man to Whom He Gave Light

Do you believe in the earthly son?
You have seen him
And he is the one talking with you.

I came into this world for judgment
So those who cannot see may see
And those who see may go blind.

John 9.35, 37, 39

Good Shepherd at the Gate Who Lays Down His Life for the Sheep

I am the gate of the sheepfold
Whoever enters the sheepfold not through the gate
But climbs up and goes in another way
Is a thief and a robber,
But whoever enters through the gate
Is the shepherd of the sheep.

The gatekeeper opens to him
And the sheep hear his voice
And he calls his own sheep by name
And he leads them out.

When he has put all his own outside,
He goes in ahead of them and the sheep follow
Because they know his voice.
They will not follow a stranger, but flee from him.
They do not know the voice of strangers.

John 10.1–5

He Explains the Parable of the Good Shepherd

All who came before me are thieves and robbers.
The sheep do not listen to them.
I am the gate.
Whoever enters through me will be saved
And will go in and go out and find pasture.
The thief comes only to steal and kill and destroy.
I came that they may have life, and have abundance.

I am the good shepherd.
The good shepherd lays down his life for the sheep.
The hired man who is not a shepherd
And is not the owner of the sheep
Sees the wolf coming and leaves the sheep and runs,
And the wolf ravages and scatters them
Since he is a hired man
And cares nothing about the sheep.

I am the good shepherd
And I know my own and my own know me
As the father knows me and I know the father.
And I lay down my life for the sheep.
And I have other sheep which are not from this fold.
And I must also bring them in
And they will hear my voice
And there will be one flock and one shepherd.

Therefore my father loves me
Because I lay down my life to receive it again.
No one takes it from me.
But I lay it down of my own accord.
I have the right to lay it down
And I have the power to receive it again.
This command I have received from my father.

John 10.8–18

Martha[3] Whose Brother Lazarus[4] is Dead Four Days in the Tomb

Our friend Elazar has fallen asleep,
But I am going there to awaken him.

---

3. Marta or Martha from the Greek Martha, from the Aramaic Marta.
4. Elazar or Eleazar from the Hebrew Elazar.

Elazar died and I am happy for you
That I was not there so that you may believe.
But now let us go to him.
Your brother will rise again.

John 11.11, 14, 15, 23

I Am the Resurrection

I am the resurrection and the life.
Those who believe in me, even if they die they will live.
And everyone who lives and believes in me
Will not die into eternity.

John 11.25–26

After Raising Lazarus, Jesus Asks Martha If She Believes

Do you believe this?
Where have you laid him?
Lift the stone.
Have I not told you that if you believe
You will see the glory of God?

Father, I thank you for hearing me,
And I know that you hear me always
But because of the crowd standing here
I speak they believe you send me.

Elazar, come out!

Unbind him and let him go.

John 11.26, 34, 39–44

Mary Who Anoints Jesus's Feet and Wipes with Her Hair

Let her be, so she may keep it for the day
Of my burial.

The poor you always have with you,
But me you do not always have.

John 12.7–8

The Hour Has Come When the Earthly Son Is Glorified

The hour has come when the earthly son is glorified.

Unless a grain of wheat falling into the earth dies,
It remains alone.
But if it dies, it brings forth a great harvest.

Whoever loves life will lose it,
And whoever hates life in this world
Will keep it for life everlasting.

Let anyone who serves me, follow me,
And where I am, there also will be my servant.
Whoever serves me, the father will honor.

John 12.23–26

Now My Soul Is Shaken

Now my soul is shaken
And what shall I say?
Father, save me from this hour?
But I came for this hour.
Father, glorify your name.

John 12.27–28

A Voice Came Out of the Sky

Not because of me has this voice come
But because of you.
Now is the judgment of the world,
Now the ruler of this world will be cast out.
And if I am raised above the earth
I shall draw all people to me.

John 12.30–32

Be Children of Light

For a little time longer the light is with you.
Walk about while you still have the light
So that the darkness may not overtake you.
If you walk in the darkness,
You do not know where you are going.
While you have light, believe in light
So you may be the children of light.

John 12.35–36

Jesus Cries Out to Those Who Love Human Glory More than the Glory of God

Who believes in me does not believe in me
But in the one who sent me.
Who looks at me also looks at him who sent me.
As light into the world I have come
So that who believes in me will not reside in darkness.
And who hears my words and does not keep them
I do not judge
For I have not come to judge the world
But to save the world.

Who rejects me and will not receive my words
Has a judge waiting.

The word I spoke will judge him on the last day.
Because I did not speak from myself
But the one who sent me,
The father has given me his commandment,
What I should say and how I should speak.
And I know his commandment is life everlasting.
So what I say, as the father told me, I say it.

John 12.44–50

At the Supper Table Simon Peter Asks Jesus Why He Has Stripped, Girded His Waist with a Towel, and Is Washing His Students' Feet

What I do for you, you do not know now,
But these things later you will understand.
Unless I wash you, you have no part of me.
One who has bathed need wash nothing except his feet
And he is wholly clean, and you are clean
But not all of you. Not the betrayer.
Not all of you are clean.

John 13.7–8, 10, 11

After Washing Their Feet, Jesus Puts on His Garments and Reclines at the Table

Do you know what I have done for you?
You call me the rabbi and lord,
And what you say is right, for so I am.
So if I your lord and rabbi washed your feet,
You also ought to wash each other's feet.
For I have given you an example
For you to do as I have done to you.

A slave is not greater than his master,
Nor is the sent one greater than he who sent him.

If you know these things,
You are blessed if you do them.

John 13.12–17

At the Table, Troubled in His Soul, He Prophesies His End

I am not speaking of all of you—
I know whom I chose—
But to fulfill the scripture:
The one who ate my bread
Lifted his heel against me.
I tell you now before it happens
So that when it happens
You will believe that I am I.
The one who accepts the one I send
Also accepts me,
And whoever accepts me
Accepts him who sent me.
Amain amain, I say to you,
One of you will betray me.

John 13.18–21

The Beloved Student Leaning on His Chest Asks Jesus, Who Is It?

It is the one for whom I shall dip the matzot bread.
Give it to him.

John 13.26

Jesus Speaks of Goodbye and Love

Children, I am with you a short while.
You will look for me.
And I tell you as I say to the Jews,

"Where I go you cannot also come."
I give you a new commandment
To love each other.
As I love you, you also must love each other.
By this everyone will know
You are my students.
You are my students if you love each other.

John 13.33–35

Answering Simon Peter Who Asks Where He Is Going

Where I go you cannot follow me now,
But you will follow later.

John 13.36

I Am the Way and the Truth and the Life

Do not let your hearts be shaken.
Believe in God and believe in me.
In my father's house there are many rooms.
If there were not, would I have said to you
That I go to prepare a place for you?
And if I go to prepare a place for you,
I will come again and take you to me
So that where I am you may also be.
And where I go you know the way.
I am the way and the truth and the life.
No one comes to the father but through me.
If you had known me, you would have also known my father,
And now you know him and have seen him.

John 14.1–4, 6, 7

Who Believes in Me

Who believes in me will also do the works I do
And you will do ones greater than these,
Because I am going to the father.
And whatever you ask in my name I will do
So that the father may be glorified in the son.
If you ask for anything in my name,
That I will do.

If you love me, keep my commandments,
And I will ask the father for another comforter[5]
To be with you forever,
The spirit of truth that the world cannot accept
Because it cannot see or know it.
You know it because it dwells with you
And in you will be.

I will not leave you orphans.
I am coming to you.
A little time and the world will not see me,
But you will see me.
Because I live, you also live.
On that day you will know I am in my father,
And you are in me and I am in you.
Who has my commands and keeps them loves me.
You who love me will be loved by my father,
And I will love you and reveal myself to you.

John 14.12–21

I Leave You Peace

Anyone who loves me will keep my word,
And my father will love you

---

5. The Paraclete, meaning in Greek "the comforter."

And we will come to you and make our home with you.
Anyone who does not love me
Does not keep the word that you hear,
And what I say is not mine
This I have told you while I remain with you
But the comforter, the holy spirit,
Whom the father will send in my name,
Will teach you all things and recall all things
That I have said to you.

I leave you peace. My peace I give to you.
Not as the world gives, I give to you.
Do not be shaken in your heart or frightened.
You heard what I told you.
"I am going away and I am coming to you."
If you loved me you would be happy
That I am going to the father
Since the father is greater than I.

And now I have told you before it occurs
So when it happens you may believe.
I will no longer talk much with you,
For the ruler of the world is coming,
And he owns no part in me.
But so the world knows I love the father,
What the father has commanded me I do.

Rise up. Let us go from here.

John 14.23–31

I Am the True Vine and My Father Is the Gardener

I am the true vine and my father is the gardener.
Each branch in me bearing no fruit he cuts off,
And each branch bearing fruit he also prunes clean

That it may bear even more fruit.
You are already clean because of the word
I have spoken to you.

Abide in me as I in you.
As the branch cannot bear fruit by itself
Unless it stays on the vine,
You too cannot unless you dwell in me.
I am the vine, you the branches.
You who dwell in me as I in you
Bear much fruit.

Anyone who does not remain in me
Is cast away like a branch and dries up,
And these are gathered and thrown into the fire and burned.
If you dwell in me and my words dwell in you,
Ask whatever you wish and it will be given you.
My father is glorified that you may bear much fruit
And be my students.
As the father has loved me I have loved you.

Dwell in my love.
If you keep my commandments
You will stay in my love,
Just as I have kept the father's commandments
And dwell in his love.
These things I have told you so my joy may be in you
And your joy be full.

John 15.1–11

Love Each Other as I Have Loved You

This is my command,
That you love each other as I have loved you.
No one has greater love than this,
Than to lay down one's life for one's friends.

You are my friends if you do what I command you.
No longer will I call you slaves
Because the slave does not know what the master does.
But you I have called friends
Because all things I heard from my father
I have made known to you.

You did not choose me
But I chose you and appointed you to go and bear fruit
And your fruit will last
And so whatever you ask for in my name he may give you
These things I command you
So you may love one another.

John 15.12–17

A World Hating Us Without Cause

If the world hates you,
Know that before you it hated me.
If you were from the world
The world would love you as its own.
But I have chosen you out of this world
And because you are not of this world
The world hates you.

Remember the word I said to you:
No slave is greater than his lord.
If they persecuted me, they will persecute you also.
If they kept my word, they will also keep yours.
But all this they will do to you
Because of my name,
Because they do not know the one who sent me.

If I had not come and spoken to them,
They would have no sin,
But now they have no cloak to wrap around their sin.

Who hates me also hates my father.
If I had not done among them things
That no one else has done,
They would have no sin.
But now they have seen and hated both me and my father.
And to fulfill the word written in the Psalms,
"They hated me openly and without cause."[6]

John 15.18–25

When the Comforter Comes

When the comforter comes,
Whom I will send you from my father,
The breath of truth who comes from the father,
He will testify about me.
You also will be my witness
Since from the beginning you are with me.

John 15.26–27

I Shall Go Away So the Comforter Will Come

This I have told you so you will not go astray.
They will expel you from the synagogue
And the hour is coming when those who kill you
Will suppose they are serving God.
And they will do this because they know
Neither the father nor me.
But this I have told you so when the hour comes
You will recall that I told you.
I did not tell you at the beginning, since I was with you.
But now I am going to the one who sent me,
And not one of you asks me, "Where are you going?"
But because I have said these things to you,
Sorrow has filled your heart.

---

6. Pss. 35.19 and 69.5.

I tell you the truth: It is better for you that I go away.
If I do not go, the comforter will not come to you.
But if I go away, I will send him to you.
And when he comes he will expose the world
Concerning wrongdoing and justice and judgment:
Wrongdoing, since they do not believe in me;
Justice because I am going to the father
And you will no more see me.
Judgment because the ruler of this world has been judged.

I still have many things to tell you
But you cannot bear to hear them now.
When the spirit of truth comes
He will be your guide to the whole truth.
For he will not speak from himself but what he hears
And will report to you what is to come.
He will glorify me
Since he will take what is mine and report it to you.
All that the father has is mine,
So I said he will take what is mine and report it to you.
In a little while you will no longer see me
And again in a little while you will see me.

John 16.1–16

When I Return Grief Will Turn into Joy

Are you asking each other what I meant by,
"In a little while you will no longer see me
And again in a little while you will see me"?
You will weep and mourn but the world will be joyful.
You will be grieved but your grief will turn to joy.

When a woman gives birth she grieves
Because her hour has come,
But when she has borne her child

She no longer remembers her pain
Because of the joy that a child was born into the world.
So now you are in sorrow, but I will see you again
And your heart will be happy
And your gladness no one will take from you.
And on that day you will ask me nothing.
Whatever you ask the father in my name,
He will give you.
Till now you ask nothing in my name.
Ask and you will receive so your joy may be complete.

These things I have told you in riddles,
But the hour is coming when no longer in riddles
Will I speak to you, but plainly I will declare
Concerning the father.
On that day you will ask in my name.
And I do not say to you I will ask the father on your behalf.
The father loves you because you have loved me
And believed that I have come from God.
I came from the father and have come into the world.
I leave the world again and go to the father.

John 16.19–28

Through Me Have Peace. I Have Conquered the World

Now do you believe?
Look, the hour is coming and it has come
When you will be scattered each on his own
And you will leave me alone.
But I am not alone, because the father is with me.
These things I have said to you
So through me you may have peace.
In the world you have pain. Courage.
I have conquered the world.

John 16.31–33

Jesus Raises His Eyes to the Sky, Converses, and Prays for His Students

Father, the hour has come.
Glorify your son so that your son may glorify you
As you gave him authority over all flesh[7]
So he may give life everlasting to all you have given him.
And this is the life everlasting
So that they may know you, the only true God on earth
By completing the work you gave me to do.
And now glorify me, father, with yourself,
With the glory I had with you before the world was.

I made your name known to the people
Whom you gave me from the world.
They were yours and you gave them to me
And they have kept your word.
Now they know that all you gave me comes from you.
Because the words you gave me I gave them.
And they accepted them,
And they knew the truth that I came from you
And believed that you sent me.
I ask for their sake.
I am not asking for the sake of the world
But for the ones whom you gave me
Because they are yours.
And all that is mine is yours and yours is mine
And I am glorified in them.

John 17.1–10

I Am Not in This World

And I am no longer in the world
But they are in the world,

---

7. Flesh in a larger sense meaning "all the people."

And I am coming to you.
Holy father, keep them in your name,
Which you gave me,
So they may be one as we are one.
When I was with them,
Through your name I kept those whom you gave me.
I guarded them and not one of them was lost
Except the son of perdition
So that the scripture be fulfilled.

John 17.11–12

I Am Coming to You

Now I am coming to you
And these things I say in the world
So my elation be fulfilled in them.
I gave them your word and the world hated them
Since they are not of the world
As I am not of the world.

John 17.13–14

Sanctify Them in the Truth

I do not ask you to take them from the world
But to keep them from the cunning one.[8]
They are not of this world as I am not of this world.
Sanctify them in the truth.
Your word is truth.
As you sent me into the world
So I sent them into the world.
And for them I sanctify myself
So they may also be sanctified in truth.

John 17.15–19

8. The devil.

I Do Not Ask for Them Alone

I do not ask for them alone,
But for those believing in me through their word
That we may all be one
As you, father, are in me and I in you;
That the world may believe that you sent me.
The glory you gave me I gave them
So they may be one as we are one.
I in them and you in me
So they may be made perfect as one,
So the world may know that you sent me
And loved them just as you loved me.

Father, wherever I am I want the ones you gave me
Also to be with me and see my glory,
Which you gave me since you loved me
Before the foundation of the world.
Just father, the world did not know who you were,
But I knew you
And these ones knew that you had sent me.
I made your name known to them
And I shall make it known
So the love you have had for me
May be in them and I in them.

John 17.20–26

Where Everything Is to Happen to Him

Who are you looking for?
I am he.
Who are you looking for?
I told you that I am he.
If you are looking for me, let these men go.
I have not lost one of those you gave me.

John 18.4, 6–9

After Simon Peter Cuts Off the
Slave's Ear

Put your knife back in its sheath.
Shall I not drink the cup the father gave me?

John 18.11

To the High Priest Questioning Him

I have spoken openly to the world.
I always taught in a synagogue and in the Temple
Where all the Jews gather. And in secret
I spoke nothing. Why question me?
Ask those who heard what I said to them.
Look, they know what I said.

John 18.20–21

A Slave Beats Him

If I spoke wrong, testify to the wrong.
But if I spoke right, why do you beat me?

John 18.23

Before Pilate Who Asks, "Are You the King
of the Jews?"

Are you speaking for yourself
Or did others tell you about me?
Am I a Jew?
My kingdom is not of this world.
If my kingdom were of this world
My servants would have fought to keep me.
But now my kingdom is not here.
You say I am a king.
For this I was born
And for this I came into the world

That I might testify to the truth.
Everyone born of truth hears my voice.

John 18.34, 36–37

Pilate Asks, "Where Are You From?"

You would have no authority over me at all
Were it not given to you from above.
Therefore the one who handed me over to you
Has the greater sin.

John 19.11

Near the Cross Stood His Mother Mary and Mary of Magdala

Woman, here is your son.

John 19.26

To One of His Students

Here now is your mother.

John 19.27

Hanging from the Spikes of the Cross

I am thirsty.

John 19.28

Jesus Bows His Head, Giving Up His Spirit, Saying

It is ended.

John 19.30

Near the Empty Tomb Mary of Magdala Thinks She Sees a Gardener. It Is Jesus Who Says

Woman, why are you weeping?
Whom are you looking for?

John 20.15

Mary of Magdala Turns, Crying Out, Rabboni! (My Great Rabbi) and the Risen Jesus Says

Do not hold on to me
Since I have not yet gone up to the father.
But go to my brothers and tell them:
"I am ascending to my father and your father
And my God and your God."

John 20.17

Jesus Appears in the Locked House of His Students

Peace to you.
Peace to you
As the father sent me, so I send you.

John 20.19, 21

He Breathes Over Them and Says

Receive the holy spirit.
For any whose sins you forgive,
Their sins are forgiven.
For any whose sins you do not release
They are not released.

John 20.22–23

After Doubting Thomas Says "Until I See the Mark of the Nails on His Hands and Put My Finger Into the Place of the Nails and My Hand into His Side I Shall Not Believe" and Jesus Says

Peace to you.
Bring your fingers here and see my hands
And bring your hand and put it in my side,
And do not be without faith but of faith.

Do you believe because you have seen me?
Blessed are they who have not seen and believe.

John 20.26–27, 29

GOSPEL OF THOMAS

Gospel of Toma[1]

In 1946 the Dead Sea Scrolls were discovered in caves at Qumran on the
northwest shore of the Dead Sea, yielding copies in Hebrew, Aramaic,
and Greek of biblical documents as well as key scriptures of the Essenes,
who lived on that arid plain. The Dead Sea Scrolls shook the religious
world. A year earlier in 1945, the Nag Hammadi Library was discovered in
a sealed jar buried in a farm in upper Egypt near the town of Nag Ham-
madi, yielding twelve leather-bound papyrus codices containing copies in
Coptic of fifty-two mostly Gnostic tractates. These are the Gnostic gospels,
of which the most famous is the Gospel of Thomas.

Thomas begins with the hidden sayings that the living Jesus spoke and
Judas Thomas the twin recorded. Thomas's original Aramaic name, Toma,
means "twin," as it also does in Syriac and Hebrew. The Gospel of Thomas
is a collection of 114 wisdom sayings in the voice of Jesus. It is appropriate
to begin with number 1, which sets the tone, but the larger order seems to
be arbitrary. It contains no gospel story of Jesus's life but rather a discourse
between himself and his students. The speech has the dialectical flavor of
the ancient world.

Harold Bloom asserts that one of the effects of the Gospel of Thomas is
to "undo the Jesus of the New Testament and return us to an earlier Jesus."[2]

---

1. I have revised these three Gnostic gospels for a literary audience. For an annotated version with
scholarly notes on the three Gnostic gospels, see my *Restored New Testament* (New York: W. W. Norton,
2009).
2. Harold Bloom, "A Reading," in Marvin Meyer, *The Gospel of Thomas* (San Francisco: HarperCol-
lins, 2004), 125.

Given that there are no clear or even vaguely existing sources for the Jesus story in the canonical gospels, the existence of Thomas's wisdom sayings, which appear in like form in the gospels, seems a likely source for wisdom sayings in the gospels. Indeed, the 114 sayings in the Gospel of Matthew could have been key to the combinatory messianic figure of Jesus that the evangelists fleshed out in their own mythic tale of wonder, proselytizing, miraculous healing, crucifixion, and resurrection. Unlike the New Testament gospels, however, the Gospel of Thomas is free of narrative. It contends no virgin birth, and Jesus performs no physical miracles, reveals no fulfillment of prophecy, or announces no apocalyptic kingdom about to disrupt the world order. He is not acclaimed as master or lord or the incarnate and unique son of God. More, Jesus dies for no one's sins and does not rise from the dead on Easter Sunday.

The gospel path to salvation is alien to the Thomas sayings, though Thomas does not exclude later salvation. The secret words of Jesus propose immediate internal salvation now, independent of world and time. Harold Bloom in his "reading" of Thomas in Marvin Meyer's *The Gospel of Thomas: The Hidden Sayings of Jesus*, tells us

> Unlike the canonical gospels, that of Judas Thomas the Twin spares us the crucifixion, makes the resurrection unnecessary, and does not present us with a God named Jesus. No dogmas could be founded upon this sequence (if it is a sequence) of apothegms. If you turn to the Gospel of Thomas, you encounter a Jesus who is unsponsored and free. No one could be burned or even scorned in the name of this Jesus.

Jesus in Thomas lives on in his secret sayings with hidden meanings: "Whoever discovers what these sayings mean / Will not taste death" (1). That is to say, one who uncovers the interpretive keys to these sayings finds true wisdom and knowledge. "There is nothing hidden that will not be revealed." The Gospel of Thomas shares the Gnostic centering on the pursuit and absorption of relative knowledge.

There are two realms in Thomas, the physical and the spiritual. As to personal resurrection, in Thomas's dualistic belief system, the spirit alone, not the body, is saved. And we attain the spiritual through finding the light. Crucially, Elaine Pagels in *Beyond Belief* sees in Thomas the gnostic notion of Jesus as teacher, who is not the light of the world but one who proclaims a divinity of light within us (Thomas 24).

> There is light within a person of light
> And it shines on the whole world.

Thomas, like the letters, is probably an early direct or indirect source for the Gospels, coming perhaps a decade or two decades before the canonical Gospels.

GOSPEL OF TOMA

These are the hidden sayings that the living Jesus spoke and Judas the twin recorded.

Jesus Speaks to His Students

Whoever discovers what these sayings mean
Will not taste death.

Seek and do not stop seeking until you find.
When you find, you will be troubled.

When you are troubled,
You will marvel and rule over all.

If your leaders tell you, "Look, the kingdom is in heaven,"
Then the birds of heaven will precede you.
If they tell you, "It is in the sea,"
Then fish will precede you.

But the kingdom is in you and outside you.
When you know yourselves, you will be known
And will understand that you are children of the living father.
But if you do not know yourselves,
You dwell in poverty and you are poverty.

You who are old in days will not hesitate
To ask a child seven days old about
The place of life, and you will live.
Many who are first will be last and be solitary.

Know what is in front of your face
And what is hidden from you will be disclosed.
There is nothing hidden that will not be revealed.

STUDENTS

Do you want us to fast? How should we pray?
Should we give to charity?
What diet should we observe?

JESUS

Don't lie and don't do what you hate.
All things are disclosed before heaven.
There is nothing hidden that will not be revealed,
Nothing covered that will remain undisclosed.

Blessings on the lion if a man eats it,
Making the lion human.
Foul is the human if a lion eats it,
Making the lion human.

A person is like a wise fisherman
Who cast his net into the sea
And drew it up from the sea full of little fish.
Among the fish he found a fine large fish.
He threw all the little fish back into the sea
And easily chose the large fish.
Whoever has ears to hear should hear.

Look, the sower went out, took a handful of seeds,
And scattered them.
Some fell on the road
And birds came and pecked them up.
Others fell on rock
And they did not take root in the soil
And did not produce heads of grain.
Others fell on thorns
And they choked the seeds and worms ate them.
And others fell on good soil

And it brought forth a good crop,
Yielding sixty per bushel and one hundred twenty
Per bushel.

I have thrown fire on the world,
And look, I am watching till it blazes.

This firmament will pass away
And the one above it will pass away.
The dead are not alive
And the living will not die.
On days when you ate what is dead
You made the dead live.
What will you do when you are in the light?
On the day when you were one you became two.
When you become two, what will you do?

STUDENTS

We know you will leave us.
Who will be our leader?

JESUS

Wherever you are, seek out Yaakov the just.
For him the sky and earth came into being.

Compare me to something
And tell me what I am like.

SIMON PETER

You are like a just messenger.

MATTHEW

You are like a wise philosopher.
Rabbi, my mouth is utterly unable to say
Who you are like.

JESUS

I am not your rabbi.
Since you drank you are intoxicated
From the bubbling spring I tended.

And Jesus takes Simon Peter and withdraws, and speaks three sayings to him.
When he comes back to his friends, they ask him,

STUDENTS

What did Yeshua say to you?

SIMON PETER

If I tell you one of the sayings he spoke to me,
You will pick up rocks and stone me
And fire will come out of the rocks and consume you.

JESUS

If you fast you will bring sin on yourselves,
And if you pray you will be condemned,
And if you give to charity you will harm your spirits.
When you go into any region and walk through the countryside,
And people receive you, eat what they serve you
And heal the sick among them.
What goes into your mouth will not defile you,
But what comes out of your mouth defiles.

When you see one not born of woman,
Fall on your faces and worship.
He is your father.

People may think I have come to impose peace on the world.
They do not know I have come to impose conflicts
On the earth: fire, sword, and war.
There will be five in a house.

There will be three against two and two against three,
Father against son and son against father,
And they will stand alone.

I shall give you what no eye has seen,
What no ear has heard,
What no hand has touched,
What has not arisen in the human heart.

Th. 1–17

Jesus to Students Asking about the End

STUDENTS

Tell us how our end will be.

JESUS

Have you discovered the beginning and now seek the end?
Where the beginning is the end will be.
Blessings on you who stand at the beginning.
You will know the end and not taste death.

Blessings on you who came into being
Before coming into being.
If you become my students and hear my sayings,
These stones will serve you.
There are five trees in paradise[3] for you.
Summer or winter they do not change
And their leaves do not fall.
Whoever knows them will not taste death.

STUDENTS

Tell us what the kingdom of heaven is like.

---

3. The five trees of paradise are also discussed in Manichaean texts and in the Islamic Mother of Books.

JESUS

It is like a mustard seed, tiniest of seeds
But when it falls on prepared soil
It produces a great plant
And becomes a shelter for the birds of heaven.

Th. 18–20

Jesus Tells Mary of Magdala What His Students Are Like

MARY OF MAGDALA

What are your students like?

JESUS

They are like children living in a field not theirs.
When the owners of the field come, they will say,
"Give our field back to us."
The children take off their clothes in front of them
To give it back, to return the field to them.

So I say, if the owner of a house knows that a thief is coming,
He will be on guard before the thief arrives
And will not let the thief break into the house
Of his estate and steal his possessions.

As for you, be on guard against the world.
Arm yourselves with great strength,
Or the robbers will find a way to reach you.
The trouble you expect will come.
Let someone among you understand.
When the crop ripened,
The reaper came quickly with sickle in hand
And harvested it.
Whoever has ears to hear should hear.

JESUS

These nursing babies
Are like those who enter the kingdom.

STUDENTS

Then shall we enter the kingdom as babies?

JESUS

When you make the two into one,
And when you make the inner like the outer
And the outer like the inner
And the upper like the lower,
And when you make male and female into a single being,
So that male will not be male nor female be female,
When you make eyes in place of an eye,
A hand in place of a hand, a foot in place of a foot,
An image in place of an image,
Then you will enter the kingdom.

I shall choose you as one from a thousand
And as two from ten thousand
And you will stand as a single one.

STUDENTS

Show us the place where you are.
We must seek it.

JESUS

Whoever has ears should hear.
There is light within a person of light
And it shines on the whole world.
If it does not shine it is darkness.

Love your brother like your soul.
Protect that person like the pupil of your eye.

You see the speck in your brother's eye
But not the beam in your own eye.
When you take the beam out of your eye,
You will see clearly to take the speck
Out of your brother's eye.

If you do not fast from the world
You will not find the kingdom.
If you do not observe the Shabbat as Shabbat,
You will not see the father.

I took my stand in the midst of the world,
And I appeared to them in flesh.
I found them all drunk yet none of them thirsty.
My soul ached for the human children
Because they are blind in their hearts and do not see.
They came into the world empty
And seek to depart from the world empty.
But now they are drunk.
When they shake off their wine, they will repent.

If the flesh came into being because of spirit,
It is a marvel,
But if spirit came into being because of body
It is a marvel of marvels.
Yet I marvel at how this great wealth
Has come to dwell in utter poverty.

Where there are three deities,
They are divine.
Where there are two or one,
I am with that one.

A prophet is not accepted in his hometown.
A doctor cannot heal those who know the doctor.

A city built on a high hill and fortified can't fall
Nor can it be hidden.

What you will hear in your ear is in the other ear,
Proclaim from your rooftops.

No one lights a lamp and puts it under a basket,
Nor in a hidden place.
You put it on a stand
So that all who come and go will see its light.

When the blind person leads the person,
They both fall into a pit.

You cannot enter the house of the strong
And take it by force without binding the owner's hands.
Then you can loot the house.

From morning to evening and from evening to morning,
Do not worry about what you will wear.

Th. 21–36

Jesus Tells His Students How They Will Be Able to See Him

STUDENTS
When will you appear to us
And when shall we see you?

JESUS
When you strip naked without being ashamed
And take your clothes and put them under your feet
Like small children and trample them,
Then you will see the child of the living one
And you will not be afraid.

Often you like to hear these sayings I tell you
And you have no one else from whom to hear them.
There will be days when you will seek me
And you will not find me.

The Pharisees and scholars have taken the keys
Of knowledge and have hidden them.

They have not entered,
Nor have they allowed those who want to enter
To go inside.

You should be shrewd as snakes
And innocent as doves.

A grapevine has been planted far from the father.
Since it is not strong
It will be pulled up by the root and perish.

Whoever has something in hand will be given more
And whoever has nothing will be deprived
Of the paltry things possessed.

Be wanderers.

STUDENTS
Who are you to say these things to us?

JESUS
From what I tell you, you do not know
Who I am, but you are like the Jews.
They love the tree but hate its fruit
Or love the fruit but hate the tree.

Whoever blasphemes against the father
Will be forgiven,

Whoever blasphemes against the son
Will be forgiven,
But whoever blasphemes against the holy spirit
Will not be forgiven,
Either on earth or in heaven.

Grapes are not harvested from thorn trees
Nor figs gathered from thistles.
They yield no fruit.
A good person brings good
Out of the storehouse
A bad person brings evil things
Out of the corrupt storehouse in his heart
And spouts evil things.
From the abundance of the heart
Such a person brings out evil.

From Adam to the baptizer Yohanan,
Among those born of women,
No one of you is so much greater than Yohanan
That your eyes should not be averted.
But I have said that whoever among you becomes a child
Will know the kingdom
And become greater than Yohanan.

One person cannot mount two horses
Or bend two bows,

And a servant cannot serve two masters,
Or the servant will honor one and offend the other.

No one who drinks old wine
Suddenly wants to drink new wine.
New wine is not poured into old wineskins
Or they may break,
And old wine is not poured into a new wineskin
Or it may spoil.

An old patch is not sewn onto a new garment
Or it may tear.

If two make peace with each other in one house
They will tell the mountain: "Move,"
And the mountain will move.

You are lucky who are alone and chosen,
For you will find the kingdom.
You have come from it and will return there again.

If they say to you, "Where have you come from?"
Say, "We have come from the light,
From the place where the light came into being by itself,
Established itself, and appeared in their image."
If they say to you, "Is it you?"
Say, "We are its children and the chosen of the living father."
If they ask you, "What evidence is there of your father in you?"
Say to them, "It is motion and rest."

Th. 37–50

Jesus Tells When the New World Will Come

STUDENTS
When will the dead rest?
When will the new world come?

JESUS
What you look for has come
But you do not know it.

STUDENTS
Twenty-four prophets have spoken in Yisrael
And they all spoke of you.

JESUS

You have disregarded the living one among you
And have spoken of the dead.

Th. 51–52

Jesus Tells Whether Circumcision Is Useful or Not

STUDENTS

Is circumcision useful or not?

JESUS

If it were useful, fathers would produce their children
Already circumcised from their mothers.
But the true circumcision in spirit
Is fully valuable.

You the poor are lucky
For yours is the kingdom of heaven.

Those who do not hate their father and mother
Cannot be my students,
And those who do not hate their brothers and sisters
And bear the cross[4] as I do
Will not be worthy of me.

Whoever has come to know the world
Was discovered to be a carcass,
And of whoever has discovered a carcass
The world is not worthy.

The father's kingdom is like someone with good seed.
His enemy comes at night and sows weeds among the good seed.

---

4. A common figure of speech for bearing up under burdens or difficulties.

He does not let them pull up the weeds
But says to them,
"No, or you might go to pull up the weeds
And pull up the wheat along with them."
On harvest day the weeds will be conspicuous
And will be pulled up and burned.

Who is lucky?
One who has worked hard and found life.

Look to the living one as long as you live
Or you may die and try to see the living one
And you won't be able to see.

He sees a Pharisee carrying a lamb
As he is going to the land of Yehudah.
He is carrying the lamb around.

STUDENTS

Then he may kill it and eat it.

JESUS

He will not eat it while it is alive
But only after he has killed it
And it has become a carcass.

STUDENTS

Otherwise he cannot do it.

JESUS

So it is with you. Find a place of rest
Or you may become a carcass and be eaten.

Th. 53–60

Jesus Tells Salome Why He Has Climbed on Her Couch, and Eaten from Her Table as if He Comes from Someone

JESUS

Two will rest on a couch.
One will die, one will live.

SALOME

Who are you?
You have climbed on my couch
And eaten from my table as if you are from someone.

JESUS

I am the one who comes from what is whole.
I was given from the things of my father.

SALOME

I am your student.

JESUS

I say, if you are whole you will be filled with light,
But if divided, you will be filled with darkness.

I disclose my mysteries to those who are worthy
Of my mysteries.
Do not let your left hand know
What your right hand is doing.

Show me the stone the builders rejected.
That is the cornerstone.

One who knows all but has nothing within
Has nothing at all.

Blessings on you when you are hated and persecuted,
And no place will be found,
Wherever you are persecuted.

You who have been persecuted in your heart are lucky.
Only you truly know the father.
You who are hungry are lucky
When some other hungry stomach might be filled.

If you reveal what is in you, what you have will save you.
If you have nothing in you
What you don't have in you will kill you.

I shall destroy this house
And no one will be able to rebuild.

Th. 61–71

Jesus Tells a Man Who Asked Him to Tell His Brothers to Share Their Possessions with Him

A MAN

Tell my brothers to share my father's possessions with me.

JESUS (*to the man*)

Who made me a divider?

JESUS (*to his students*)

I'm not a divider, am I?

The harvest is large but the workers few.
Implore the master to send workers to the harvest.

STUDENTS

Master, there are many around the drinking trough
But nothing in the well.

JESUS

There are many standing at the door
But those who are alone will enter the wedding chamber.

The father's kingdom is like a merchant
Who owns a supply of merchandise and finds a pearl.
The merchant is prudent.
He sells his goods and buys the single pearl
For himself. So with you.
Seek treasure that is unfailing and enduring,
Where no moth comes to devour and no worm destroys.

I am the light over all things.
I am all.
From me all things have come
And all things have reached me.
Split a piece of wood.
I am there.
Lift up the stone
And you will find me there.

Why have you come out to the countryside?
To see a reed shaken by the wind?
Or see someone dressed in soft clothes
Like your rulers and your men of power?
They are dressed in soft clothes
And cannot understand truth.

Th. 72–78

To a Woman Who Blesses the Womb that Bore Him and the Breasts that Fed Him

JESUS (*to a woman in the crowd*)
Blessings on the womb that bore you
And the breasts that fed you.

JESUS
Blessings on those who have heard the father's word
And have truly kept it.
A day will come when you will say,
"Blessings on the womb that has not conceived
And the breasts that have not given milk."

Whoever has come to know the world
Has discovered the body
And of whoever has discovered the body
The world is not worthy.

Let a rich man rule,
And a powerful man renounce.

Whoever is near me is near fire,
Whoever is far from me is far from the kingdom.

You see images,
But the light in them is hidden in the image
Of the father's light. He will be disclosed
But his image is hidden by his light.

When you see your likeness you are happy,
But when you see your images that came into being before you
And that neither die nor become visible,
How you will suffer!

Adam came from great power and great wealth
But was not worthy of you.
Had he been worthy, he would not have tasted death.

Foxes have dens and birds nests,
But the human child has no place
To lay his head and rest.

How miserable is the body that depends on a body
And how miserable the soul that depends on both.

The messengers and the prophets will come to you
And give you what is yours.
You give them what you have and wonder,
"When will they come and take what is theirs?"

Why do you wash the outside of the cup?
Don't you know that he who made the inside
Also made the outside?

Come to me.
My yoke is easy and my mastery gentle
And you will find rest.

Th. 79–90

He Tells Those Who Ask How They May Believe in Him

STUDENTS
Tell us who you are so we may believe in you.

JESUS
You examine the face of heaven and earth
But you have not come to know the one before you,
Nor know how to see the now.

Seek and you will find.
In the past I did not tell you what you asked.
Now I am willing to tell
But you do not seek.

Do not give what is holy to dogs.
They might throw them on manure.
Do not throw pearls to swine.
They might turn it into mud.

Seek and you will find.
Knock and the door will open.

If you have money, do not lend it at interest,
But give to someone
From whom you will not get it back.

The father's kingdom is like a woman
Who takes a little yeast, hides it in dough,
And makes large loaves of bread.
Whoever has ears should hear.

The father's kingdom is like a woman
Who is carrying a jar full of meal.
While she walks along a distant road
The handle of the jar breaks
And the meal spills behind her along the road.
She doesn't know it.
She notices no problem.
When she reaches her house she puts the jar down
And finds it empty.

The father's kingdom is like a man
Who wants to put someone powerful to death.
At home he draws his sword

And thrusts it into the wall
To find out whether his hand goes in.
Then he kills the powerful man.

Th. 91–98

Jesus Tells His Students about His Brothers and Mother Standing Outside

STUDENTS
Your brothers and your mother are standing outside.

JESUS
Those here who do the will of my father
Are my brothers and my mother.
They will enter my father's kingdom.

STUDENTS (*showing Jesus a small coin*)
Caesar's people demand taxes from us.

JESUS
Give Caesar the things that are Caesar's,
Give God the things that are God's,
And give me what is mine.

Whoever does not hate
His father and mother
As I do
Cannot be my student.
Whoever does not love his father and mother
As I do
Cannot be my student.
My mother gives me lies,
My true mother gives me life.

Shame on the Prushim.
They are like a dog sleeping in the cattle manger.
It does not eat or let the cattle eat.

You are lucky if you know where the robbers will enter
So you can wake up, rouse your estate,
And arm yourself before they break in.

Th. 99–103

To Those Who Ask Jesus to Pray and Fast

STUDENTS
Come let us pray today and fast.

JESUS
What sin have I committed
Or how have I been undone?

When the bridegroom leaves the wedding chamber,
Then let the people fast and pray.

Whoever knows the father and mother
Will be called the child of a whore.

When you make two into one,
You will become human children. When you say
"Mountain, move," the mountain will move.

The kingdom is like a shepherd
Who has a hundred sheep.
One of them, the largest, goes astray.
He leaves the ninety-nine and looks for the one
Until he finds it.
After so much trouble he says to the sheep,
"I love you more than the ninety-nine."

Whoever drinks from my mouth will become like me.
I myself shall become him
And the hidden will be revealed.

The kingdom is like a man who has a treasure hidden in his field.
He doesn't know it,
And when he dies he leaves it to his son.
The son doesn't know.
He takes over the field and sells it.
The buyer is plowing and finds the treasure,
And begins to lend money at interest to whomever he wishes.

You who have found the world
And become rich,
Renounce the world.

The heavens and earth will roll up before you.
And you who live from the living one will not see death.
Doesn't Jesus say, the world is not worthy
of whoever has found himself?

Shame on flesh that depends on soul.
Shame on soul that depends on flesh.

Th. 104–112

To His Students Who Ask, When Will the Kingdom Come?

STUDENTS
When will the kingdom come?

JESUS
It will not come because you are looking for it.
No one will announce, "Look, it's here,"

Or "Look, it's there."
The father's kingdom is spread out over the earth
And people do not see it.

SIMON PETER

Miryam should leave us.
Females are not worthy of life.[5]

JESUS

Look, I shall guide her to make her male,
So she too may become a living spirit resembling you.
Every female who becomes male
Will enter the kingdom of heaven.

Th. 113–114

5. See also Thomas 96–98 for a different view. Thomas 96–98 goes beyond gender differences. It reflects a traditional view that the female represents what is earthly and mortal as in the earth mother, and the male what is heavenly and divine as in the sky father. Whatever the explanation, it reveals deep prejudice against women in the Abrahamic religions. At least in the Hebrew Bible there are many heroic and salvific women.

GOSPEL OF MARY MAGDALENE
Myriam of Magdala

The Gospel of Mary Magdalene is a wisdom gospel dialogue between Jesus and his follower Mary Magdalene, Mary's vision of the soul's ascent, and a final debate between Mary and the apostles. This rare, brief, mutilated gospel—ten pages are missing—records the most extended conversation between Jesus and a woman that has survived from ancient biblical scriptures. Its leaves disclose the drama of Jesus in his metaphysical cloak, Mary's visionary spiritual trip through the universe, and the envy of the male apostles who listen to her grand recital with distress and anger. The battle pits assertive and courageous Mary against the cynical and derisive students Simon Peter and Andrew. The gospel is a loud clear bell celebrating an early woman in that dangerous mix of early Christian and Gnostic camps.

As scriptures take on Gnostic qualities, the role of women rises. Eve is a hero who asserts not obedience and faith but her right to knowledge. She is not a sinner before God who passes her morose condition along to her descendants but a socially active apostolic figure. In this gospel Mary is not the prostitute or later saint, not the sensual Mary Magdalene whom Jesus loved. She is closer to the Mary Magdalene waiting in Jesus's empty tomb in Mark 16.1–8. But she is less victim and more active as she scraps for her place. As an educated woman, she rebuts Simon Peter's belittling jibes. Peter expresses similar insult in the Gospel of Thomas, saying, "Miryam of Magdalene should leave us. / Females are not worthy of life" (114).

In the gospel, Mary Magdalene takes her place as Jesus's student in what seems to be the inner circle of students. According to the text, when Jesus leaves, other students are weeping, and it is Mary who with enlightened compassion comforts them. Jesus will be with us, Mary Magdalene proclaims, for he has humanized us by making us truly human within. As in the Gospel of Thomas, the message of salvation in the Gospel of Mary is one of a mystical realization of true inward being. She will not demean it by explanations. In her *The Gospel of Mary of Magdala*, Karen King tells us that the gospel "presents a radical interpretation of Jesus' teachings as a path to inner spiritual knowledge."[1]

1. Karen King, *The Gospel of Mary of Magdala: Jesus and the First Woman Apostle* (Santa Rosa, CA: Polebridge Press, 2003), 3.

Jesus to Students Asking about the Nature of Matter

STUDENTS (*speaking to the Messiah*)
Shall matter be destroyed or not?[2]

MESSIAH
Each nature and shaped thing and every creature
Lives in and with each other, and will dissolve
Into distinctive roots, but the nature of matter
Will dissolve into the root of nature.

Whoever has ears to hear should hear.

SIMON PETER
You have revealed all things to us. Tell us more.

MESSIAH
There is no sin, but you create sin
When as in adultery you mingle,
Which is called sin, and which is why the good
Came to be with you, to enter every nature
And restore each nature down to its root.
Sin is why you fall into sickness and die.
You love something and what you love tricks you.
Whoever has a mind should understand.

Matter gave birth to passion without form
Because it comes from what opposes nature
And so confusion rose throughout your body.
That's why I told you then to be courageous.
If you despair, stand up and gaze ahead

---

2. The first six pages are missing from the Coptic manuscript. The extant text begins in the middle of a dialogue between Jesus and his students on the nature of matter. This dialogue includes reflections on Stoic themes.

Before nature's diversity of forms.
Whoever has ears to hear should hear.

Jesus Tells His Students to Go Out and Preach

MESSIAH
Peace be with you, receive my peace.
Take care that no one sends you lost into the wrong,
Saying, "Look over here," or "Look over there."
The human child exists in you.
Follow the child.
And if you look you will find the child.

Go out and preach the message of good news
About the kingdom. Do not seek any rules
Other than what I give you. Establish
No law as lawgivers have done, or by
Those same laws each of you will be bound.

(*The Messiah departs.*)

MARY MAGDALENE (*consoling the students*)
(*The students break into despair and cry deeply*)
How can we go out to the gentiles to preach
The message of good news about the kingdom
Of the son of man? If even they did not spare him,
what can we expect?

MARY MAGDALENE (*stands up and greets each of them and then
responds to each brother*)
Don't cry or break into despair or doubt.
His grace will go with you and protect you,
And let us praise the greatness of his work
For he prepared us, made us truly human.

(When Mary Magdalene says this, she turns hearts to goodness, and they inspect the savior's words.)

SIMON PETER *(challenging Mary Magdalene)*
Sister, we know the savior loved you more
Than any other woman. Tell us what
The savior said to you, his words as you
Remember them. And you alone know them
And we cannot because we never heard them.

Mary Magdalene Tells of Her Vision

MARY MAGDALENE
What is hidden from you I shall reveal to you.
I saw the master in a vision. I said,
"Master, today I saw you in a vision."

MESSIAH *(suddenly appears)*
Blessings on you since you who in no way trembled
When you saw me.
Where mind is, there is the treasure.

MARY MAGDALENE
Master, how does one contemplate a vision?
With soul or with spirit?

MESSIAH
One sees neither with soul nor with the spirit.
The mind, which is between the two, sees vision.

(Mary recounts her vision of the soul's ascent.)

MARY MAGDALENE
I didn't see you descending,
But now I see you rising.

Tell me why you are lying to me.
You belong to me.

SOUL

"I saw you but you did not see or know me,
And for you I am nothing more than
A garment.³ You cannot know who I am."
After the soul says this, she leaves, intensely happy.
The soul approaches the third power, called ignorance.
The power questions the soul, saying,
"Where are you going? You are bound by evil,
You are bound so do not judge."

"Why do you judge me? I haven't judged you.
I was roped up, but I have not bound ropes
On others. Though I wasn't recognized,
I've understood that all will be dissolved,
Both what is earthly and what is heavenly."

When the soul overcomes the third power,
She rises and sees the fourth power. It takes seven forms:
The first form is darkness,
The second, desire, The third, ignorance, The fourth, death wish,
The fifth, fleshly kingdom,
The sixth, foolish fleshly wisdom,
The seventh, wisdom of the angry.
These are the seven powers of wrath.
The powers ask the soul,
"Where are you coming from, you who murder mortals,
And where are you going, you who destroy realms?"

"What binds me is slain and what surrounds me
Destroyed. My desire is gone. Ignorance is dead.

---

3. This garment, which clothes the soul, is made up of all of the features that characterize bodily existence in this world. The soul puts on this garment upon entering the world and removes it when leaving the world. Compare with the seven heavenly spheres (often for the sun, moon, and five known planets—Mercury, Venus, Mars, Jupiter, and Saturn) described by ancient astronomers and astrologers.

In a world I am freed through another world.
In an image I was freed through a heavenly image.
The fetter of oblivion is temporary.
From now on I shall rest through this age in silence."

*(After Miryam says this she grows silent. Shimon Kefa and Andreas doubt
Miryam's word.)*

SIMON PETER

For the savior has told her all these things.

ANDREAS

Andreas answers, saying to the brothers,
"Say what you will about what she said.
I still don't think the savior said all this.
These teachings are very strange ideas."

SIMON PETER *(expressing like concern)*
He asks the others about the savior:
"Did he actually speak with a woman in private,
Without our knowledge? Should we all now turn
And listen to her? Did he prefer her to us?"

MARY MAGDALENE *(crying, addresses Simon Peter)*
My brother, Shimon, tell me what you think.
Do you think that I made all this up myself
Or am lying about the savior?

LEVI *(answering for her, says to Simon Peter)*
Kefa, you are always angry. Now I see you
Arguing against this woman like an enemy.
If the savior made her worthy, who are you
To turn her away? Certainly the savior
Knows her well. That is why he's loved her more
Than we are loved. We should all be ashamed

And become the perfect person and assume it.
As he commanded us, preach the good news,
And never invent a rule or law other
Than what the savior has spelled out for us.

(*When Levi says this, they leave and go out to teach and preach.*)

Gospel of Judas

The Gospel of Judas (Yehudah Iskariot in Hebrew) was discovered in Egypt in the 1970s, in Coptic translation from a Greek gospel probably composed between 130 and 180. By 180 the heresiologist Irenaeus of Lyon had already condemned Gnostic scripture as demonic. The Gospel of Judas, like the gospels of Thomas and Mary, is a series of conversations between Jesus and others. In the Gnostic Gospel of Judas, the apostle Judas is the human hero, and he is Jesus's one enduring confidant among the twelve angry and bumptiously suspicious disciples. Jesus laughs at their jealousy and ignorance. But to Judas he tells his own future and that of Judas. Judas will undertake the infamous task of turning the mortal body of Jesus over to the authorities for crucifixion, after which the real Jesus, the spiritual Jesus, will return to the light of the divine.

The Gospel of Judas does not take us away from messianic Christianity, which has found the messiah foretold in Isaiah, but it has removed from Judas, and hence from Judaism, the inherited stain, iterated as a wicked cliffhanger tale in the canonical gospels, that will justify two millennia of persecution and executions of the descendants of the last prophet Jesus and his true companion Judas, which in Hebrew means "the Jew." The linchpin of enduring anti-Semitism in the New Testament is Judas, the traitor. The word Judas is a curse, and Jews are demonized as "Christ-killers." In the Gospel of Judas, Judas is a hero and Jesus does not die. The Gospel of Judas possesses a Shakespearean fantasy. The friend reluctantly obeys the king's commandment. From their stormy mountain of dialogue and surrender, Judas descends to the streets of Jerusalem and performs his scapegoat mission. As Jesus reveals to Judas, his mortal body, not the true spiritual body, will be handed over. At the time of crucifixion, the spirit of Jesus will already have ascended to the cloud above.

The Secret Revelation

Here is the secret revelation Yeshua
Had with Yehudah Iskariot in one week
Three days before the Pesach celebration.

JESUS (*of mysteries beyond this world*)
When Yeshua came to live upon the earth
He did dynamic miracles and wonders
For the salvation of the peopled world.
While some traveled along the way of justice,
Others ambled about in their transgressions,
And so he called for twelve students to help.
He spoke to them about the mysteries
Beyond the world and what would happen when
The end came upon them. And frequently
He wouldn't come himself before his students.
Mingled among them they would find a child.

JESUS (*astonishing his students*)
One day in Yehudah[1] I come to my students.
I find you all sitting together.
You are all practicing group piety.
When I come near, you are giving a prayer
Of thanks over the bread. I laugh.

STUDENTS
Rabbi, why do you laugh at us
For giving thanks? Are we in error?

JESUS
I don't laugh at you.
You are acting not of your own will
But so that through these things your God will know
Your offerings of praise.

---

1. Judea.

STUDENTS

Rabbi, you are the son of our own God.

JESUS

How do you know me?
I say to you, no generation of the people
Who walk among you will know who I am.

STUDENTS (*angry*)

When the students listened to all of this,
They break into anger and fury.
They begin to execrate him in their hearts.

JESUS (*noticing their deep ignorance and interior weakness*)

Why has your agitation made you furious?
The God who operates inside you spurs
The anger in your souls. Let anyone of you
Endowed with strength among the beings on earth
Produce the perfect human, and stand near Yehudah
So I can gaze upon him face to face.

ALL THE STUDENTS

We have that strength.
Here their beings of spirit don't dare to stand
Before him, except for Yehudah Iskariot.
He is able to stand before the figure
But cannot look him in the eye and turns
His face down and away.

STUDENTS

I know who you are and where you come from.
You are from the deathless realm of the aeon
Of Barbelo (Yahweh), the holy source of all,
And my mouth is unworthy to utter
The ineffable name of him who sent you.

JESUS (*seeing Judas brooding about what is exalted, he speaks to Judas privately of his fate*)

"Come here and I shall tell you mysteries
Of the kingdom, not that you will go there,
But you will journey through extended grief,
For someone will replace you to complete
The circle of the twelve before their God."
Yehudah said to him, "When will you give
Me these secrets? And when will the great day
Of light spread dawn upon the generation?"
But by the time he spoke, Yeshua was gone.

STUDENTS

Rabbi, after you left us you disappeared.
Where did you travel to, what did you do?

JESUS

I went to a holy and great dominion of another generation.

STUDENTS

What is the great generation
That lies above us, holier than we are,
And one that doesn't glitter in our world?

JESUS (*laughing at them*)

Why are you mumbling in your hearts
About the strong and holy generation?
Amain, I tell you, no one born in this aeon
Will be able to glimpse that generation,
And no army of angels from the stars
Will have dominion over that generation,
And no person of mortal birth can join it,
Because that generation is not from what has come to be
The ones that make up the people among you
Are from here, from the human generation
Power powers through which you rule.

(*When his students heard this, each of them sank, spirit in turmoil, and could not utter a word. And on another day Jesus came up to be among them.*)

STUDENTS

Rabbi, we've seen you in a night vision,
In great dreams last night.

JESUS

Why have you fled into hiding?

STUDENTS (*envisioning the Temple*)

We've seen a giant house. It has
A great altar inside. They are the twelve men
We think that they are priests. There is a name,
And crowds of people are waiting at the altar
Until the priests present the offerings.
We were there too.

JESUS

And what are these priests like?

STUDENTS

Some fast for two weeks,
Some sacrifice their children, others their wives,
All under ruses of humility or praise.
Some sleep with men, and others murder.
And some perform a multitude of sins
And lawless acts. And yet these men before
The altar constantly invoke your name,
And in their own practice of sacrifice
They fill the altar with their offerings.

(*After their speech they are silent and troubled.*)

JESUS (*speaking about the temple and sacrifices at the altar*)

Why are you troubled?
I say to you, all the priests standing

Before the altar proclaim my name.
Again I say to you, my name has been set down
In writing in the generations of the stars
Through our generations.
They operate, planting trees that bear no fruit,
Shamefully, and do so in my name.

Those whom you have seen presenting offerings
Before the altar are the ones you are.
That is the God you serve, and you are those
Twelve men you also saw. Cattle you saw
Brought in for sacrifice mirror the many
People you lead astray before that same
Altar. The ruler of the world will stand,
Using my name like that, and generations
Of those with faith and piety stand loyal
By him. Yet after him another man
Will stand before you from the fornicators,
Another from the children slayers, and
Still another from those who sleep with men,
From those who keep the fast, and from all
The others, from the people of pollution,
Lawlessness, and error. Some say,

We are like angels. They are stars bringing an end to all.
And to this generation's human beings
It is announced, "Look, now God has received
Your sacrifice from a priest's hands," meaning
A minister of error. But it is the lord
Of the universe who commands and speaks.
On the last day they will be shamed and punished.

Cease from sacrificing what you have on the altar,
Since they command over your stars,
Over your angels, and already have reached
Their conclusion there.

Let them be in front of you and let them go generations
A baker cannot feed all of creation under heaven.

STUDENTS

Master, help us, save us.

JESUS

A star assigned to you and everyone
that has not come. A spring of water
for the tree of this aeon after a time
but this has come to water
God's paradise and the enduring generation,
Since it won't defile the walk through life
Of that generation, forever and forever.

JUDAS

Rabbi, what kind of fruit does this generation yield?

JESUS

The souls of each human generation will die.
However, when these people end the time
Within the kingdom and the spirit leaves them,
Their bodies die but their souls will stay alive,
And they will be risen above.

JUDAS

And what will all the other human generations do?

JESUS

It is impossible to sow seed upon rock and harvest fruit.
That is the action of the defiled peoples
And of wisdom that has corrupted the hand creating mortal people
So their souls may ascend to eternal realms above.
No authority or angel or power can see
The realms like this great holy generation.

(*Jesus leaves.*)

JUDAS (*his vision*)
Rabbi, as you have heard the others, hear me.
I have had a vision.

JESUS (*breaking into laughter*)
You who are the thirteenth Daimon,
Why do you try so hard?
But speak to me and I shall be here to hear you.

JUDAS
In my vision I saw myself
And the twelve students stoning me
And persecuting me most grievously.
I also came to the place where you were.
I saw a house of such cosmic dimension that my eyes
Could not perceive the scope.
Great people surrounded it,
And that house had a single room
And in the middle of the house there was a crowd.
Rabbi, take me in along with all these people.

JESUS
Yehudah, your star led you astray.
No person of mortal birth is worthy
To go into the house that you have seen.
It IS for the holy, and solely for them.
Neither sun nor moon will have dominion there, nor day,
And yet the holy will live there forever
In the eternal realm with holy angels.
Look, I have revealed to you the mysteries
Of the kingdom and I have taught you
About the error of the stars,
And send to the twelve aeons.

JUDAS

What will happen to me?

Rabbi, could my seed, my heritage,
Fall under the control of the archons,
Who rule this world?

JESUS

Come here that I may . . .
But you know deepest sorrow when you see
The kingdom and all of its generation.

JUDAS

What good to me is what I have received,
Since you have kept me separated from that generation?

JESUS

You will become the thirteenth
And you will be cursed by other generations.
In the end you will rule over them.
In the last days they will oppose you
So you will not rise up to the holy generation,
The cosmology of the spirit.

Come here so I can teach you
What no person has ever seen.
There exists a great and boundless realm
Whose horizons not even a generation
Of angels has looked upon. And therein
Is the great invisible spirit,
Which no eye of an angel has ever seen,
No thought of heart has ever comprehended,
And it was never called by any name.

Then a luminous cloud of light appeared.
The spirit said, "Let an angel exist

And he will become my attendant."
A great angel, the enlightened divine self-generated,
Emerged from the cloud.
Because of him four other angels came
Into existence from another cloud,
And they became attendants for the angel,
The self-generated angel, who said,
"Yehudah, Let Adamas be born,"
And Adamas merged into being. And he created
The first luminary for him to reign over.

He told them, "Let angels be born
To serve him," and myriads suddenly came into being.
He said, "Let an enlightened Aeon be born,"
And he came into being.
Then he created the second luminary
To reign over him together with myriads
Beyond number to serve and offer worship.
This is how he created other enlightened Aeons.
He made them to reign over them
And he created for them myriads of angels
Beyond number to serve and offer worship.

Adamas and luminaries. Adamas
Was in the first luminous cloud
That no angel has ever seen among all
Those who are called "God."
He was after the image and after the likeness of the angel.
He made the incorruptible generation of Seth appear
To the twelve luminaries, twenty-four of them.
He made seventy-two luminaries appear
In the incorruptible generation
In accordance with the spirit's will.
Then the seventy-two luminaries
Made three hundred sixty luminaries
Appear in the incorruptible generation,

In accordance with the spirit's will
That their number might be five for each.

The twelve aeons of the twelve luminaries
Constitute their father, with six heavens
For each aeon, so there are seventy-two
Heavens for the seventy-two luminaries,
And for each of them five firmaments.
This comes to three hundred sixty firmaments.
They were given dominion
And a great army of angels beyond number,
For glory and adoration, and also
Virgin spirits for glory and adoration
Of all aeons, heavens, and their firmaments.

Cosmos, chaos, and underworld
The worldly multitude of those immortals
Is called the cosmos—corruption, inviting
Decay—called by the father and the seventy-two
Luminaries who are with the self-generated
And his seventy-two aeons. In the cosmos
Appeared the first human with mind,
With his incorruptible powers.
And the Aeon who appeared with his generation,
The aeon in whom is the cloud of knowledge
And the angel, is called El (God), an aeon,

And later it was said, "Let twelve Angels be born
To govern chaos and the underworld."
And look, from the cloud came
An angel. His face flashed with fire, his countenance
Was defiled with blood, and his name was Nebro,
Meaning rebel. Others call him Yaldabaoth.[2]

---

2. The names *Yaldabaoth* and *Sakla* are well known in other Sethian Gnostic texts. On *Nebro*, compare
Nebruel in the Holy Book of the Great Invisible Spirit and Manichaean texts, as well as *Nimrod* in the
Hebrew Scriptures in the Greek of the Septuagint, *Nebrod*.

Another angel, Sakla, also came from the cloud.
So Nebro made six angels, with Sakla,
To be his assistants, and each of these
Produced twelve angels in the heavens,
Each one possessing a section of the sky.

Rulers and angels of the underworld
The twelve rulers spoke with the twelve angels,
"Let each of you and let them be a generation
Of five angels: The first is Seth, who is called the Christ.
The second is Harmathoth, who is . . .
The third is Galila.
The fourth is Yobel. The fifth is Adonaios.
These are the five ruling the underworld,
And first of all they rein over chaos.

At last came creation of people on the earth.
Sakla said to his angels,
"Let us make a human being after the likeness
And after the image [of God]."
They fashioned Adam and his wife Eve,
Who in the cloud is known as Zoe which means life
And by this name all generations
Seek the man, and each of them calls the woman
By their own names. Sakla commanded solely
the generations. The ruler said to Adam,
"You shall live for a time with your children."

JUDAS

What is Adam's destiny?
What worth is our human life?

JESUS

Why do you ponder these things?
Adam and his generation have lived their span
Of life. He received his kingdom
With the longevity in keeping with his ruler.

JUDAS

Does the human spirit die?

JESUS

This is why God told Mihael
To give the people spirits only on loan
So that they might offer service,
But the great one ordered Gavriel to grant spirits
To that great generation
Whose sole commanding ruler
Was their spirit and their soul.
And therefore, the other souls.

JESUS (*speaking of the destruction of the wicked*)
Light, chaos around the spirit in flesh
among the generations of the angel!

But God had knowledge given to Adam
And those with him so that the kings
Of chaos and the underworld might not
Impose dominion over them.

JUDAS

So what will those generations do?

JESUS

For all generations the stars bring happenings
Into their consummation.
When Sakla completes the span of life assigned him,
Their first star will sparkle with generations,
And they will finish what it is said they shall do.
They will fornicate in my name,
Will slaughter their children,
And they will in my name. And your star
Will rule over the thirteenth aeon.

(*Jesus laughed.*)

JUDAS

Rabbi, why are you laughing at us?

JESUS

I don't laugh at you but at the error of the stars,
Because these six stars are wandering about
With these five planetary combatants,
And they will all be destroyed with their offspring.

JUDAS

Those who have been bathed in your name,
What will they do?

JESUS

Amain, I say to you about this bathing in my name.
Amain, I say to you, Yehudah,
Those who offer sacrifices to Sakla await every evil,
But you will surpass all of them.
You will sacrifice the man who contains me.[3]
Already your horn is raised,
Your anger is on fire,
Your star is passing by and your heart has grown strong.

Amain I say to you,
Your last days are darkening. Grieve the ruler.
He will be destroyed.
And then the image
Of the great generation of Adam will be exalted.

Before there was heaven, Earth, and angels
And that generation coming from the eternal realms existed.
Look. You have been told everything that is.

---

3. The man who contains or bears Jesus is thought to be the fleshly, mortal body that carries around the inner, spiritual person of Jesus for a period of time.

Raise your eyes and look at the cloud
And at the light within it and the stars
Surrounding it. The star that leads the way is *your* star.
Yehudah raised his eyes
And saw the luminous cloud
And he entered into the cloud.

Those standing on the ground heard
A voice coming from the cloud, saying,
"Great generation image."[4]

(*Yehudah hands Jesus over.*)

Their high priests murmured because he
Had gone into the guest room to pray.
Yet some of the scribes were there, watching sharply
And carefully in order to arrest him
While at prayer. They were afraid of the Jews,
Who esteemed him as a prophet.
They came near Yehudah, and said to him,
"What are you doing here? You are Yeshua's student."
He answered them just as they wished.
Yehudah received some money
And then he handed Yeshua over to them.

4. In this passage it appears that Jesus experiences a transfiguration or ascension.

SAUL

Shaul   שָׁאוּל   Παῦλος

Paul, the Pharisee Jew from the tribe of Benjamin, is correctly seen as
the founder of the emerging Jewish sect called Christianity, named
for the Messiah whom Isaiah and others predicted would come and bring
peace, safety, and meadows of grain and honey to the happy people of
Judaea. Paul was certain that Jesus was the Isaiah-foreseen Messiah. But
his coreligionists did not find an afterlife in Torah. But Pharisee Paul, with
Platonist ideas of eternity, saw an afterlife not only of spirit but of body in a
new Jerusalem in the heavens. Paul gave us knowledge through faith, hope
for salvation and a heavenly dominion. He expanded Christianity itself to
include the pagans, who were largely Greek, and no longer required to
observe the Sabbath, dietary law, and above all circumcision.

Paul was born in the cosmopolitan city of Tarsos (Acts 22.3) into a Hel-
lenistic Jewish family and from the tribe of Benjamin. His birth name was
Saul (Shaul) and was later Paul from Greek Pavlos. His first language was
Greek, as it was for most of the Jews of Alexandrian North Africa, Rome,
Greece, and Anatolia. A Jew, circumcised on the eighth day, he describes
himself as belonging to the tribe of Benjamin (Romans 11.1) and a Phari-
see (Philippians 3.5; Acts 26.5). It is said that he was schooled in Hebrew
at a local synagogue school. He was also trained in Greek grammar, Sto-
icism, and basic works of other Greek philosophical schools. Wherever
he obtained his main instruction, in Hellenistic Tarsos, in Jerusalem, or
elsewhere, Paul was skilled in rhetoric, Jewish law, and Greek philosophy,
which pervaded the thinking of most religious sects in the Greco-Roman
territories. He apparently went to Jerusalem early for guidance under the

liberal Rabbi Gamaliel (Acts 26.4), said to be the grandson of the Pharisee reformer Hillel. In Jerusalem Paul states, "I am verily a man *which am* a Jew, born in Tarsus, *a city* in Cilicia, yet brought up in this city at the feet of Gamaliel" (Acts 22.3, KJV).

Paul was born early in the common era and died around the year 60. Paul wrote his letters before the gospels were composed, and knew nothing about Jesus's thought, deeds, events, nothing except that Jesus was the Isaiah-foreseen savior. Surely an eager scribe emended the disparate passages that tell women to stay home, obey their husband, and shut up. Indeed, Paul frequently writes in the letters about his close friendships with his trusted women. If there were a problem in a new temple he would send his most reliable woman as his apostle to solve the problem or found a new one. The traditional Vatican view that women cannot be members of the

Apostle St. Paul by El Greco (Domenikos Theotokopoulos).

clergy because Paul chose only males as his apostolic founders is not based on Paul's letters, the only true authority.

Paul gave us the basic tenets of what would become Christian dogma: knowledge and redemption and justification through faith, salvation, and resurrection. He believed that Jesus was the son of God, that he died to save us, and that he would return soon to save us all on earth. He is the most philosophic of New Testament figures, and his poetic sermon letters read like Greco-Roman rhetorical epistles. He is also the lonely historic figure of the Bible, bequeathing us not a new cult but worldwide Christianity.

Faith Love and Joy

Therefore, since we are justified by faith,
We've peace with God through our lord Yeshua
The Mashiah. Through him we have by faith
Our access to this grace in which we stand.
We exult in the hope and glory of our God.
We exult also in our afflictions, knowing
Afflictions carry us to enduring patience,
And patience to a quality of character,
And quality to hope. Hope does not fail
Because God's love has poured into our hearts.
Through the holy spirit we have been given.

Rom. 5.1–5

In Weakness and Trembling

When I came to you, my brothers, I came
Not with eloquence or superior wisdom
When I announced to you God's mystery.
I determined to know nothing among you
But Yeshua the Mashiah, the crucified.
I came to you in weakness and deep fear
And trembling. Yet my speech and ministry
Lay not in the persuasion of my words
Of wisdom but in revealing the spirit
And power so that your faith may not rest
On men's wisdom but on the power of God.

1 Cor. 2.1–5

Freedom in Slavery

From all men I am free and made myself
A slave to all, and so gain more from them.
To Jews I've been a Jew that I may win
The Jews. To those who are under the law

(Though I am not under the law myself)
I'm like one under the law that I may gain them.
For those outside the law I am like one
Outside the law, yet not outside the law
Of God but with the law of the Mashiah
That I may gain the ones outside the law.
To the weak I was the weak to win the weak.
To all men I became all things to save
A few of them. I do it for the good news
And so that I might also share its blessing.

1 Cor. 9.19–23

ON PAUL'S "OF LOVE"

In the Vulgate translation from the Greek, Jerome mistranslates *agape* into
caritas, meaning "charity." "Love" becomes a Pauline charity argument for
church tithing. It simply means love, and in all possible senses: bodily and
spiritually. Paul is a world poet. He has Gerard Manley Hopkins's passion
and exact articulation, and when he is fully baroque he is John Milton,
creating his own poetics of Paradise.

Of Love

If I speak in the tongue of men and angels
But have no love, I am but sounding brass
Or a clanging cymbal. If I have prophecy
And understand all mysteries and all knowledge
And if I have all faith to remove mountains
But love I do not have, then I am nothing.
If I give all my goods to feed the poor
And give my body to be burned, and love
I do not have, in all I have gained nothing.

Love suffers long and love is kind. Love has
No jealousy and cannot boast and has
No pride. Love isn't crude and doesn't seek

Things for itself, is not provoked to anger,
Nor counts up wrongs. Not gloating in misdeeds,
Its happiness is truth. Love bears all things,
Believes all things; it hopes and it endures.

Love never falls. Yet prophecies will cease
And tongues turn dumb and knowledge also vanish.
We know only in part, we prophesy
Only in part, yet when perfection comes,
Then what is but a part will disappear.

When I was a child I spoke like a child,
I thought like a child and reasoned like a child.
When I became a man I put an end
To childish things. For now we look into
An enigmatic mirror. One day we will gaze
Face to face. Now I know in part, but then
I will know in full even as I am fully
Known. Now faith, hope, and love remain,
These three. Of these the greatest one is love.

1 Cor. 13.1–13

Paul's Vision of Jesus

I have to boast. No good can come of it
Yet I'll know visions and apocalypses
About the lord. I know about a man
Who fourteen years ago knew the Mashiah.
Was it in body? I don't know. Was it
Outside the body? I don't know. God knows,
But he was caught up into the third heaven.
And heard ineffable words that no man
Can be allowed to speak. For such a man
I'll boast, but for myself I will not boast
Except in weaknesses. But if I care
To boast, I shall not play the role of fool

Since I speak truth. I stop. I will refrain,
Not wanting anyone to credit me
With something more than he can see and hear,
Above all with my flood of revelations.

2 Cor. 12.1–7

Day of the Lord Will Come Like a Thief in the Night

Concerning times and seasons, there's no need
To write to you, my brothers. You yourselves
Know accurately that the day of the lord
Will come like a thief in the night. They say,
"Peace and security." Then doom arrives
Like birth pangs in the belly of a woman,
And they cannot escape. But you, my brothers,
Are not in darkness for that day to catch
You like a thief. You all are sons of light
And sons of day. We are not of the night
Or dark. Therefore, let us not sleep like others
But be awake and sober. They the sleeping
Sleep through the night. The drunks get drunk again
At night. But we belong today, are sober,
And wear a breastplate of our faith and love,
Wearing a helmet of our hope of salvation,
But God did not choose us for anger but
To gain salvation through our lord Yeshua
Mashiah, who died for us. So if awake
Or sleeping, we shall live with him. Comfort
Each other and give strength as you do now.

1 Thess. 5.1–11

JAMES

Iakavos   Ἰάκωβοσ   Jacob   Yaakov   יַעֲקֹב

T he work is thought to be anonymous, of late first- or early second-
century composition by a Christian Jew. In contrast to Paul's letters,
where the crucifixion and resurrection are central, there is curiously no
reference to cross, resurrection, or salvation in this missive. All parabolic
exempla of moral comportment are to Torah. Here the word is spoken
to God. In surviving documents of this intertestamental period of reli-
gions in ferment, there is no clear demarcation between inspired Jewish
and Christian pseudepigrapha and the scriptures later determined to be
canonical.

James is an insight into faith and works, and the necessity of the latter
to justify the former, and into the purpose of works, which is alleviation
of the suffering of the poor. It finds its argument from a wealth of biblical
parables, from faithful Abraham, whose deeds justified him, to Rahab the
good prostitute, who endangered her life for Jericho. There is throughout
a dexterous harmony of wisdom proverbs intricate in the verse.

James's letter is a sermon essay speaking in high poetic discourse to the
poor. During this period, Christian (Messianic) Judaism was increasingly
attempting to distance itself from its Jewish foundation. Except for the
slight Christianizing salutations at the beginning of Chapters 1 and 2, as
with most new Jewish sects during a period of tremendous ferment, this
marvel of wisdom, philosophy, theology, and poetry should be taken as a
superior example of Jewish pseudepigrapha composed during the intertes-
tamental period. The emerging Christian movement had no testament of

its own other than the Hebrew Bible, which it interpreted as a prophetic book in which the messiah was realized in Jesus Christ. The stunning letters of James and John are major philosophical and literary documents. James's emotive wisdom poetry finds expression in primal nature as his preferred metaphor.

Sun Rises with Burning Heat and the Flower of Grass Shrivels

Yaakov slave of God and of the lord
Yeshua the Mashiah to the twelve tribes
In their diaspora, I send you greetings.
My brothers, think of it as happiness
Whenever you face falling into trials,
And know that testing of your faith creates
Endurance. Let endurance be perfected.
Complete it through your work, and you will lack
In nothing. But if anyone is short
In wisdom, let him ask for it from God,

Who gives to all and generously without
Reproach, and it will be accorded him.
But ask in faith and never doubt. The one
Who doubts is like a sea wave tossed about
By blowing winds. And let the doubter know
That one who vacillates is no way sound,
And wavering gets nothing from the lord.
Let the lowdown boast of being raised up

And let the rich man fall in lowliness
And pass away like a flower of the field.
The sun rises with burning heat and shrivels
The grass. Its flower falls and the beauty
Of its appearance perishes. The rich
Amid their busywork will also fade.
My brothers, do your favoritizing acts
Go with your faith in Yeshua Mashiah.

In shabby clothes in the synagogue
Who is our glorious lord? If a man comes
Into your synagogue with rings of gold
Around his fingers and in splendid robes,

And then a poor man comes in filthy rags,
You look at him in all his splendid robes
And say, "Sit here in a good place," and to
The shabby man you say, "Stand there, or sit
Under my footstool." Do you make distinctions
Among yourselves and judge your crafty thoughts?

James 1.1–11, 2.1–4

Faith and Works

What good is it, my brothers, if you say
That you have faith but have no works?
Can faith save you? If a brother or sister
Is naked, short of daily food, and one
Of you says, "Go in peace. Keep warm and eat,"
But you give nothing for the body's needs,
What good is it? So even faith, if by
Itself and not backed up by works, is dead.
Someone will say, "You have the faith, and I
Have works." Show me your faith apart from works
And I will show you from my works my faith.

A man is justified by works and not
By faith alone. Likewise Rahav the whore
When she took in the messengers and sent
Them on an undetected road she too,
Was she not justified? Just as the body
Without spirit is dead, so also faith,
If not accompanied by works, is dead.

James 2.14–18, 24–26

God Not for the Proud but the Lowly

Where do those wars and quarrels among you
Come from? Are they not from the pleasures warring

Inside your bodies? You desire and don't
Possess. You envy, murder, and yet you still
Do not possess it. You fight and make war.
You do not have because you fail to ask.

You ask and don't receive because you ask
Wrongly so you can spend it on your pleasures.
Adulterers, do you not know that friendship
With things of the world makes you enemy
Of God? And do you think it meaningless
When it says in Genesis: "The spirit he sent
To live in us is jealous cravings." But grace
He gives is stronger as in Proverbs:
God opposes the proud and graces the lowdown.

James 4.1–6

The Rich Have Cheated and Killed the Laboring Poor

Come now, you rich men. Weep, wail, howl
Over the miseries coming to you. Your wealth
Is rotted, fled, your clothes eaten by moths,
Your gold and silver rusted and their rust
Will testify against you, feed on your flesh
Like fire. You've stored your treasures for the last
And final days. Listen! The workmen's pay
For mowing fields which you held back by fraud
Cries out. The cries of harvesters have reached
The ears of Yahweh Tzvaot. You lived
On earth in luxury and self-indulgence,
And nourished your hearts on the day of slaughter.
You have condemned and murdered the just man.
He who is left cannot resist your force.

James 5.1–6

Suffer in Patience

Be patient, brothers, till the coming of
The lord. And look, the farmer's waiting for
The precious fruit out of the earth. Be patient
Until it drinks the first and later rains.
Be patient. Gather strength, make your hearts firm.
Drawing near is the coming of the lord.
And brothers, do not groan against each other
For fear you may be judged. And look, the judge
Is standing at the doors! As an example
Of suffering and patience, brothers, see
The prophets who spoke in the name of God.
Look, we call blessed those who have endured.
You have heard of the endurance of Job,
And you have seen the purpose of the lord,
How the lord is generous and takes pity.

James 5.7–11

JOHN

Ioannes   Ἰωάννης   Jonathan

Traditionally, the three letters of John are said to have been written by the same John, son of Zebedee, who wrote the Gospel of John and the Book of Revelation. Modern critics reject common authorship of the three so-called Johannine letters. As for authorship of each letter, the name or names are also unknown. Certain is that the author or authors of the letters were older authority figures in the Johannine sect of early Christian Jews. Dating is less problematic in that since there is frequent reference to and citing from the John gospel, the letters were written no earlier than in the last decade of the first century and possibly, as some think, well into the second (110 C.E.).

The first of the letters ascribed to John is a sermon, without epistolary salutation or conclusion. It is addressed to a troubled and disintegrating Johannine congregation with secessionist teachers who preach docetic ideas that cast doubt on the human nature of Jesus on the cross (is this a man or a divine facsimile?), on his suffering, and on whether or not such uncertain suffering has cleansed his followers from sin. The author condemns the antichrists, deceivers, and false prophets who doubt that Jesus came in the flesh, by recalling the gospel's "the word became flesh" (John 1.14).

The letters of John are a highlight of the New Testament. The style is plain, direct, forceful, and elegant. They are philosophical, and the theme that binds them is love and intelligence. We are fortunate to have these brilliant letters by another figure we call John.

God Is Light

This is the message we have heard from him
That we announce to you, that God is light,
In him no darkness lives in any way.
If we say we share fellowship with him
While we are walking in the dark, we lie
And do not practice truth. But if we walk
In light as he is in the light, we share
A fellowship with one another. Then
The blood of Yeshua his son cleans us
From every sin. Yet if we say we have
No sin, we fool ourselves and truth is not
In us. If we confess our sins, he who
Is good and faithful will forgive our sins
And cleanse us of all wickedness. If we
Say we are free of sin we transform him
Into a liar. His word is not in us.

1 John 1.5–10

Whoever Loves a Sister or Brother Stands in Light

My love, I write you no new commandment
But one you know from the beginning
And is the word you have heard.
I write a new commandment that is true
In him and you because the darkness passes
And light is true and is already shining.
Whoever says, "I am in light" and hates
His brother, he is in the darkness now.
Whoever loves his brother stands in light.
In him there is no cause for him to stumble,
But he who hates his brother is in darkness

And in the darkness walks and doesn't know
Where he is going. Darkness blinds his eyes.

1 John 2.7–11

Who Doesn't Love Remains in Death

Do not wonder, my brothers, that the world
Hates you. We know that we have passed
Out of death into life because we love
Each other. He who doesn't love remains
In death. But all who hate each other are
Clear murderers. And every murderer,
You know, has no eternal life in him.

1 John 3.15–17

He Lay Down His Life For Us

We have known love by this, that he lay down
His life for us. We should lay down our lives
For our brothers. Now anyone who has
His world possessions and comes on a brother
In need and closes all his heart to him,
How can the love of God be in that man?
My little children, let's not love in word
Or tongue but in our deeds and in our truth.

1 John 3.16–18

God's Love in Us

My loves, let us love one another since
Love is from God, and everyone who loves
Is sprung from God, and he knows God. But he
Not loving can't know God, since God is love.
In this way God's love was revealed in us,

And he sent his only engendered son
Into the world that we might live through him.
Love is in this, not in that we've loved God
But he loved us and gave his son to be
As a propitiation for our sins.
My loves, since God loved us, then we should love
Each other. No one ever has seen God,
But if we love each other, God resides
In us, and in us his love is made perfect.

1 John 4.7–12

To the Jews

Πρὸς Ἑβραίους Yehudim יְהוּדִים Hebrews עבריים[1]

As a highly educated Alexandrian, steeped like Paul in Platonist notions of eternity, this first Messianic exegete of the Hebrew Bible prepares the way for the study of one full Bible, which will contain both covenants with equality rather than selective praise and scorn. The author of Jews is also a fervid apologist for the emerging Jesus movement. He takes a lovely mythical moment in the tale of Abram (before God made him Abraham), and incredulously turns the obscure and undeveloped figure of Melchizedek into a full-blown prefiguration of Jesus Christ. In this way the anonymous erudite grammarian once again follows the needlessly justificatory practice of looking hard and wishfully at Hebrew Bible scripture, through Septuagint translation, to prove the presence of the messiah. In the instance of Jews, the focus is on a few verses in Genesis and a verse in Psalms. In Jews, the division between literary creation and its commentary breaks down, for the work is both. Somehow Jews, which was falsely said to be by Paul, found itself among the accepted epistles. Had Jews not carried its earlier Pauline attribution, it would not have made it into the canon. Jews, composed in cosmopolitan Alexandria by a nameless Christian Jew, is a unique, undeclared, and secret achievement of the New Testament.

---

1. "Jews" refers to Christian or Messianic Jews of a congregation, not to "unconverted" Jews. The presumed audience is unknown. Some argue that both Christian Jews and Jews are the intended readers; others argue gentiles. The traditional title of this document is "Letter to the Hebrews." The word 'Hebrew' in modern English refers only to language, not to person or people. Paul in modern English was a Jew, not a Hebrew. Today the word "Hebrew" for a Jew is derogatory, what dictionaries label "offensive." The correct title in English for the book is not "Letter to the Hebrews" but "Letter to the Jews."

Worship in the Earthly Tent

A sukkoh was pitched and graced with a menorah,
A table and a setting out of bread,
And named a holy place or sanctuary.
Behind a second curtain was the tent,
And named the holy of the holy places.

Behind the second curtain stood a gold
Incense altar and ark of the covenant
Entirely overlaid with gold. It held
A golden jar with manna and the rod
Of Aaron that had blossomed. And also

The tablets of the covenant. Above
It were the keruvim of glory, shading
The seat of mercy. About all these things
It is impossible to name each piece.

Jews 9.2–5

Blood of the Messiah Sealing the Covenant

Now Mashiah has come as the high priest
By way of a greater and perfect tent
Not made by hands, not hands of this creation,
And not by blood of goats and bulls but through
His unique blood. He entered once into
The holy place to gain for us eternal
Redemption. But if blood of goats and bulls
And sprinkled ashes of a heifer hallow
Those who have been defiled so that their flesh
Is purified, how much greater is the blood
Of the Mashiah. Through eternal spirit
He gave himself blameless to God to purify
Our conscience far away from mere dead works
That serve us when we worship living God.

Jews 9.11–14

ACTIVITIES OF THE MESSENGERS
(ACTS OF THE APOSTLES)

Like the four gospels, Acts is an anonymous book. It is the fifth book, sometimes called the "fifth gospel," of the New Testament in the common arrangement, and covers the first three decades of church events from after the death of Jesus to Paul's appearance in Rome. In dynamic Rome of conflicting sects and peoples, the narrative suddenly stops, as if this well-composed book were a first large fragment of a larger story. This fifth gospel has profoundly determined succeeding attempts at reconstructing the story of Christianity, beginning with Irenaeus's *Adversus haereses I*, or *Against Heresies I* (ca. 180), and Eusebius's *Ecclesiastical History* (third to fourth century). Unlike the gospels, God in his earthly presence is more significant than Jesus. The anonymous author is celebrated by his cognomen "Paul," and with the triumph of the church of Saint Paul.

Acts was composed well after 80 and the place of composition is unknown. More significant than where it was written is its vast geography, which also tells the spread of early Christendom. Acts is correctly called "colorful" and "vivid" in its narrations, from the astonishingly gruesome punishment of death to Ananias and Sapphira (5.1–11), who lied about their wealth when giving the tithe, to tales of martyrdom, arrests, miraculous escape, and missionary ships on the dangerously stormy Mediterranean. It is a page turner. In his incarnation in Acts, Paul is no longer a confessing memoirist but the main character in the first Christian novel. Missionary Paul is an epic and episodic hero like Odysseus. Acts is the lively story of Saul, a Pharisee Jew, who at Damascus becomes Messianic Paul, who sets out on his holy mission of return to Rome and God in the great Odyssey of Christendom.

Simon Peter in the City of Jaffa

I was in the city of Yafo, praying,
And in the ecstasy of a vision I saw
Coming down an object, like a big linen sheet,
Being let down by the corners from the sky,
And it came close to me. As I looked at it closely
I saw four-footed beasts of the earth
And reptiles and birds of the sky.

And I heard a voice saying to me,
"Stand up, Shimon Kefa. Kill and eat." But I said,
"Surely not, lord, since I have never let anything
Common and unclean enter my stomach."
The voice answered a second time from the sky:
"What God made clean, don't make unclean."

This happened three times and then everything
Was drawn up again into the sky. And look,
Suddenly three men stood before me in my house,
Sent to me from Caesarea. And the spirit told me,
"Go with them, without worrying about distinctions
Between us." These six brothers also came
And we entered the man's house, and he reported
How he saw an angel standing in his house,
And it said, "Send to Yafo and summon Shimon
Whose surname is Shimon Kefa. He will give you words
To save all of you and save your household."

And as I began to speak, the holy spirit
Fell on them as it had on us in the beginning.
And I remembered the word of our rabbi,
How he had said, "Yohanan dipped with water,
But you will be dipped in the holy spirit."
If God gave them the same gift he gave us

When we believed in rabbi Yeshua the Mashiah,
Who was I to block the ways of God?

Acts 11.5–17

Saul Speaks His Life

I am a Jew born in Tarsos of Kikilia,
Brought up in the city at the feet of Gamliel,
Instructed in the strictness of our ancestral law,
And I was zealous for God as you are today.
I persecuted the followers of this new way
Even to the death, binding and putting in jail
Both men and women, as the high priest
And entire council of elders can testify to.
From them I also received letters sent
To the brothers in Damesek. And I went there
To bind and lead them away and bring them back
Bound to have them punished in Yerushalayim.

Acts 22.3–5

A Brilliance from Above

And while I was traveling and coming near
Damesek at about the noon, it happened
That suddenly out of the skies a great light
Shone around me, and I fell to the ground
And I heard a voice saying to me, "Shaul, Shaul,
Why are you persecuting me?" And I answered,
Saying, "Who are you, sir?" And he said to me,
"I am Yeshua the Natzrati, whom you persecute."
And the ones with me saw the light but didn't hear
The voice speaking to me. Then I said,
"What can I do, lord?" And the lord said to me,
"Stand up and go to Damesek and there
You will be told about all things that you

Were chosen to do." And because the glory
Of that light prevented me from seeing,
I came to Damesek with my companions
Leading me by the hand. Then Hananyah,
Who was a devout man about the law
And well esteemed by all the Jews there,
Came to me and stood near. "Brother Shaul,"
He said, "Recover your sight!" At that moment
I recovered my sight and saw him. He said,
"God of our ancestors has appointed you
To know his will and to see the just one
And to hear the voice from his mouth,
Because you will be a witness before
All people about what you have seen and heard.
And now, why delay? Stand up, be dipped
And wash away your sins, calling his name."

Acts 22.6–16

Battling the Crew

Now on the fourteenth day of being tossed
And drifting in the Adriatic Sea,
The night was coming and around midnight
The sailors thought we might be nearing land,
And they took soundings. Twenty fathoms deep.
Sailing a little further, they took soundings.
Fifteen fathoms. Fearing we might be driven
Onto rocky shores we let down four anchors
From the stern and prayed for day to come.
Now the sailors were trying to flee from
The ship, and had lowered the lifeboat down
Into the sea, pretending they were dropping
The anchors from the bow. But Shaul said
To the centurion and to the soldiers,
"Unless these men remain here in the ship

You cannot be saved." Then the soldiers cut
The lifeboat's ropes and let it fall away.

Acts 27.27–32

Shipwreck

When day was coming on us, Shaul urged
Everyone to eat our rations. "Today
Is our fourteenth day of waiting, worried,
Tasting nothing. Now I ask you to eat
What's left. It will help you survive, and none
Of you will lose a hair from your heads."
On saying this he took bread and thanked God
Before everyone. He broke it and ate.

Then all were animated and took food.
We were two hundred seventy-six souls
In all. After eating their fill, they lightened
The ship by throwing grain into the sea.
When day came they didn't recognize land,
But they saw a bay and a beach, and there
They hoped to ground the ship. So they let go
The anchors, leaving them in the sea,
And at the same time loosened the ropes
On the rudders and hoisted the mainsail
Into the wind, and steered for the beach.

But they struck a shoal concealed in the waters
And ran the ship aground. The bow was stuck
And unmovable while the stern was breaking up
By crashing waves. The soldiers had a plan
To kill the prisoners so none might flee
By swimming off. But the centurion, wanting
To save Shaul, ordered those who could swim
To jump overboard first and make for land.

The rest to follow, some on floating boards,
Others on pieces torn from the ship. And so
It happened that all got safely to the land.

Acts 27.33–44

REVELATION / APOCALYPSE
Apokalypsis Ἀποκάλυψις

Apocalypse is the alternate title of Revelation, and in verse 1.1 appears the word "Apocalypse" from the Greek Ἀποκάλυψις (apokalypsis), meaning "Revelation," "disclosure," and literally an "uncovering." The title conveys the visionary and apocalyptic nature of the book.

Visionary writing is a habit of the Hebrew Bible, found in Isaiah, Ezekiel, and Jeremiah, and in the Book of Daniel, which contains four formal apocalypses. The apocalyptic form is found in virtually all religions of the world, be it as murals in a Tibetan monastery or in the Egyptian Book of the Dead. These allegorical works, usually prompted by some historical conflict, have enormous spatial dimensions. In Apocalypse, characters float between earth, heaven, and hell, and, and with Christ's help, the good, on defeating the wicked, enter the fulfillment of a New Age. God declares himself the Alpha and the Omega, and he appears with the mystery of the seven stars in his hand. The four Horsemen of the Apocalypse ride by. A woman gives birth in midair. The angel Michael fights the dragons. Christ and his army throw the beasts of evil into a lake of fire, whereupon a heavenly Jerusalem descends to replace the earthly city, and the millennium arrives.

There is a crypt in a monastery on Patmos, the Greek island to which John was exiled for two years, and in a small cave at the edge of this crypt John is said to have composed Apocalypse. Ephesos on the Asia coast is other candidate. Apocalypse is peopled by angels, monsters, four-headed beasts, who may represent Satan or a Roman emperor, a woman clothed with the sun, representing the faithful people of God, or the great whore of Babylon, representing nefarious Rome. In sharp contrast to the gospels, God, rather than Jesus, has at peak moments a dominant role and roaring voice. It is like reading sublime passages in Daniel. Rather than making Rome the overt demonic enemy and risking more slaughter, the author chose the whore of Babylon and her cohorts as the abhorrent figures. Not only is this visionary book of the future and of heaven and hell anti-Roman, but also the Roman soldiers are symbolized as demon monsters of hell, Rome is Babylon, and the beast, whose code name is 666 (13.18), is not the Babylonian Captivity of Israel in the sixth century B.C.E. but primarily a wicked Caesar Augustus, who became the first emperor of Rome. As an epic poem, Revelation takes its place, along with *Gilgamesh* and *Paradise Lost*, as an extraordinary literary work.

Alpha and Omega

Grace be with you and peace from one who is,
And one who was, and one who is to come,
And from the seven spirits before his throne,
And from Yeshua the Mashiah, faithful
Witness who is the firstborn of the dead
And is the ruler of the kings of the earth.
To him who loves us and freed us from our sins
By his own blood, and who made us a kingdom,
And made priests labor for the God and father,
To him glory and dominion forevermore.

Look, he is coming with the clouds, and every eye
Will see him, and even they who stabbed him,
And all the tribes of the earth will mourn him.

"I am the Alpha and the Omega," says the lord,
"Who is and who was and who is coming,
And who is the ruler of all, the pantokrator."

Rev. 1.4–8

John's Vision

I Yohanan your brother, who through Yeshua
Share with you suffering and kingdom and endurance,
Was on the island called Patmos for the word
Of God and testimony of Yeshua.
I was fixed in the spirit on the lord's day
And I heard behind me a great voice like a ram's horn
Saying: "What you have seen, write in a book
And send it off to the seven churches.
To Efesos, Smyrna, Pergamos, and Thyatira,
To Sardis and Philadelphia and Laodikeia."

Rev. 1.9–11

Jesus Amid Seven Gold Lamps

And I turned to see the voice speaking to me,
And when I turned I saw seven gold lamps,
And in the midst of the lamps was one like
The earthly son clothed in a robe down to his feet,
And girt around his breasts with a gold belt.
His head and his hair were white like white wool
Like snow and his eyes like a flame of fire,
His feet like fine bronze as if fired in a furnace
And in his right hand he held seven stars
And from his mouth came a sharp two-edged sword
And his face was like the sun shining in its power.
When I saw him I fell at his feet like a dead man
And he placed his right hand on me and said,
"Don't be afraid. I am the first and last
And the living one, and I have been dead,
And look, I am alive forevermore
And I have the keys to death and of hell.
So write what you have seen and what you see
And after this what is about to happen.
The mystery of the seven stars you saw
In my right hand, and seven golden lamps.
Seven stars are angels for the seven churches
And seven golden lamps are the seven churches."

Rev. 1.12–20

An Emerald Rainbow Around a Throne in Heaven

After this I looked, and there a door opened
In the sky, and the voice of the first I heard
Was a ram's horn speaking with me saying,
"Come up here and I will show you what
Must happen after this." At once I was enveloped
In the spirit and saw a throne standing in the sky
And one seated on the throne. The one seated
Looked like stone of jasper and carnelian,

And around the throne was a rainbow like an emerald.
And around the throne were twenty-four thrones
And seated on the thrones were twenty-four elders
Clothed in white garments, and on their heads
Were gold crowns. The throne poured out
Lightning flashes and voices and booming thunder,
And before the throne were seven lamps of fire
Burning, which are the seven spirits of God,
And before the throne a sea of glass like crystal.

And in the middle and around the throne
Were four live animals teeming with eyes
In front and in back. The first was like a lion
And the second animal was like a calf
And the third animal had a human face,
The fourth creature was like a flying eagle.
And each of the live animals had six wings
And were full of eyes around them and inside,
And day and night they never ceased saying,
Holy, holy, holy, lord God the pantokrator,
The one who was and is and is to come.
And when the animals gave glory and honor
And thanks to the one seated on the throne
And to the one who lives forevermore,
The twenty-four elders cast their crowns
Before the throne, and said,
"Our lord and God, you are worthy
To receive this glory, honor, and power,
For you made all things, And by your will
They were and were created."

Rev. 4.1–11

The Scroll and the Lamb

And I saw in the right hand of him sitting
On the throne a scroll written on the inside
And on the back, and sealed with seven seals.

And I saw a strong angel who cried out
In a great voice, "Who is worthy to open
The book scroll and break its seven seals?"

And no one in the sky or on the earth
Or under the earth could open the book
Or look at it, \and I wept much since no one
Was found worthy to open the book
Or look at it. And one of the elders said to me,
"Don't weep, see, the lion from the tribe
Of Yehudah, the scion of David, has conquered
And will open the book and its seven seals."

I saw, between the throne and the four animals
And elders, a lamb standing as if slaughtered,
With seven horns and seven eyes which are
The seven spirits of God sent all over the earth.
And he came and took it from the right hand
Of the one seated on the throne. And when he took
The book the four animals and twenty-four elders
Fell before the lamb, each holding a harp and gold bowls
Filled with incense, which are the prayers of saints.

And they sang a new song, saying,
You are worthy to take up the book scroll
And to open the seals upon it
Since you were slaughtered and by your blood
You bought people for God
From every tribe and language and nation,
And for our God
You made them be a kingdom and priests
And they will reign over the earth.

I looked and heard the voices of many angels
Around the throne and animals and the elders,
And they numbered myriads of myriads

And thousands and thousands, saying in a great voice,
"Worthy is the lamb who was slaughtered
To receive the power and the riches
And wisdom and strength and honor
And glory and blessing."

And every creature which is in the sky,
On the earth and under the earth and on the sea,
And everything in these, I heard them saying,
To the one seated on the throne and to the lamb,
"Blessings and honor and glory and dominion forevermore."
And the four animals said, "Amain,"
And the elders fell down and worshiped.

Rev. 5.1–14

Seven Seals

And I saw the lamb open one of the seals
And I heard one of the four animals saying
In a voice that seemed like thunder, "Come!"
And I saw, and look, a white horse
And its rider had a bow and was given a crown
And he went out conquering and to conquer.
And when the lamb opened the second seal,
I heard the second animal saying, "Come!"
Another horse of fire red came out.
Its rider was ordered to take peace away
From earth so men might kill each other,
And he was given an enormous sword.

And when the lamb opened the third seal,
I heard the third animal saying, "Come!"
And I saw, and look, a black horse,
And its rider held a pair of scales in his hand.
And I heard what seemed to be a voice
In the midst of the four animals, saying,

"A measure of wheat for a single denar
And three measures of barley for a single denar,
And do not damage the olive oil with wine."

And when the lamb opened the fourth seal,
I heard the voice of the fourth animal saying,
"Come!" and I saw, and look, a pale green horse,
And the name of his rider was Death, and Hell
Was following him. Power was given them
Over a quarter of the globe to kill
By sword and by hunger and by death
And by the wild beasts of the earth.

And when the lamb opened the fifth seal,
I saw under the altar the souls of those
Who were slaughtered for the word of God
And the testimony which they held.
And they cried out in a great voice saying,
"How long, O absolute ruler, holy and true, Zacharia
Will you wait to judge and avenge our blood
From those who live upon the earth?"
They were each given a white robe and told
To rest a little time until the number was reached
Of their fellow slaves, brothers and sisters
Who are to be killed as they were killed.

When the lamb opened the sixth seal I looked
And there took place a great earthquake
And the sun became black like sackcloth of hair
And the full moon became like blood,
And the stars of the sky fell to the earth
As the fig tree drops its unripe fruit
Shaken by a great wind. And the sky
Vanished like a scroll rolling up
And every mountain and island of the earth
Was torn up from its place and moved.

And the kings of the earth and the great men
And commanders of thousands and every slave
And the free hid in caves and mountain rocks,
And said to the mountains and rocks, "Fall on us
And hide us from the face of him who is sitting
On the throne and from the anger of the lamb
Because the great day of his anger has come,
And before him who has the force to stand?"

Rev. 6.1–17

Angel and Censer of Fire

And when the lamb opened the seventh seal,
There was a half hour of silence in the sky.
I saw the seven angels standing before God
And they were given seven ram's horns.
And another angel came and stood by the altar,
With a gold censer, and was given much incense
To offer with the prayers of all the saints
On the gold altar which was before the throne.

And coming with the prayers of the saints,
Then the smoke of varied incense arose
Out of the hand of the angel before God.
And the angel took the censer and filled it
With fire from the altar and threw it down to earth,
And there came thunders and voices and lightning
Flashes and earthquake. The seven angels
Holding the ram's horns prepared to blow them.

The first angel blew the ram's horn. There came hail
And fire mingled with blood and it was thrown
To the earth, and a third of the earth burned up,
And a third of the trees burned up, and all green grass caught fire.
And the second angel blew the ram's horn
And something like a great mountain on fire

Was cast into the sea. A third of the sea was blood
And a third of the creatures in the sea died,
Who had been alive. A third of the ships sank.

And the third angel blew the ram's horn.
From the sky a great star fell, a blazing torch,
And the star fell on a third of the rivers
And across the springs of the waters,
And the name of the star is called Wormwood,
And a third of the waters became wormwood
And many people died from the waters
Because they were made bitter.

And the fourth angel blew the ram's horn
And a third of the sun was struck by it,
And a third of the moon, a third of the stars,
And a third of their light was darkened,
And the day lost a third of its brilliance
And likewise the night.

And I looked and I heard an eagle flying
In mid-sky, crying out in a great voice,
"Despair despair despair to the inhabitants
Of the earth at the blasts of more ram's horns
That the three angels are about to blow."

Rev. 8.1–13

A Star Fell from the Sky

And the fifth angel blew his ram's horn
And I saw a star fall out of the sky
And down to the earth, and the angel was given
The key to the shaft of the bottomless pit.
He opened the shaft of the bottomless pit
And smoke rose from the shaft like fumes

From a great furnace. And the sun was darkened
And the air was darkened from the smoke
Of the shaft. And out of the smoke came locusts
Upon the earth, and they were given powers
Like the powers of scorpions of the earth.

They were told not to damage the earth's grass,
Or any green thing, or any tree, but only people
Who don't wear the seal of God on their foreheads.
They were told not to kill them but to torture them
For five months, and their torture should equal
The scorpion's torture when it strikes a person.
And in such days the people will seek death,
But not find it, and they will desire to die
But they won't fall into escape to death.
The locusts looked like horses prepared for war.
On their heads it was like the crowns of gold
And their faces were like the faces of people,
And they had hair like the hair of women,
And the teeth in their jaws resembled lions.
Their breastplates seemed to be made of iron,
And the noise of their wings was like the noise
Of many horse chariots galloping into battle.

And they have tails like scorpions and stings,
And in their tails the power to harm people.
They have a king over them who is the angel
Of the abyss, whose name in Hebrew is Abbadon
And in Greek he has the name of Apollyon.
The first despair is over. After the first,
Look, there are still two more despairs to come.

And the sixth angel blew his ram's horn,
And I heard a voice coming from the four horns
Of the gold altar standing before God,
Telling the sixth angel who held the ram's horn,

"Release the four angels who are bound
At the great river Euphrates." The four angels
Were freed, prepared for the hour and day
And month and year to kill a third of the people.
And the number of cavalry of their armies
Is two hundred million. I heard their number.

And so I saw the horses in the vision
And the riders on them were wearing breastplates
Of fire red and hyacinth blue and yellow sulfur
And the heads of horses were like heads of lions
And fire, smoke and sulfur came from their mouths.
From these three plagues a third of humankind
Was killed by the fire and smoke and sulfur
Spewing from their mouths. The power of the horses
Resides in their mouths and in their tails
Because the tails are like serpents with heads
And with their terrible heads they harm.

The rest of the people who had not been killed
In the plagues did not repent of the work
Of their hands so they might go on worshiping
The demons and the idols of gold and silver
And bronze and stone and wood, which cannot
See or hear or walk. And they did not repent
Of their murders or their poison sorceries
Or their dirty copulations or their thefts.

Rev. 9.1–21

An Angel Clothed in Cloud

I saw another strong angel coming down from
The sky, clothed in cloud, and the rainbow
Was on his head, and his face was the sun,
And his feet like pillars of fire, In his hand

He held a little book open. He planted his right foot
On the sea and his left foot on the land
And cried out in a great voice like a roaring lion.

When he cried out, the seven thunders spoke
In their own voices. When the seven thunders spoke,
I was about to write, but heard a voice in the sky,
Saying, "Seal what the seven thunders have spoken
And do not write them down." Then the angel,
Whom I saw standing on the sea and on the earth,
Lifted his right hand to the sky and he swore
By him who is alive forevermore,
Who created the sky and what lives in it,
And the sea and what lives in it, and he said
That the time will be no more. But in the days
Of the sounding of the seventh angel, when he
Is about to blow his ram's horn, right then
The mystery of God will be fulfilled
As he informed his slaves who were the prophets.

And the voice I heard from the sky again
Spoke to me, saying, "Go take the open scroll
In the hand of the angel standing on the sea
And on the earth." And I went to the angel,
Telling him to give me the little book.
And he said to me, "Take it and eat it
And it will make your stomach bitter,
But in your mouth it will be like sweet honey."
And I took the book from the angel's hand
And ate it and in my mouth it was as sweet
As honey but it made my stomach bitter.
Then they said to me, "You must prophesy
Again about many peoples and their tongues,
And about many nations and their kings."

Rev. 10.1–11

The Seventh Ram's Horn

And the seventh angel blew his ram's horn
And there were great voices in the sky, saying,
The kingdom of the world is now the kingdom
Of our lord and his Mashiah,
And he will reign forevermore.
And the twenty-four elders, sitting on their thrones
Before God, fell on their faces and worshiped God,
Saying, We thank you, lord God the pantokrator,
The one who is and was,
Because you have taken your great power and become king.
The gentile nations raged and your anger came
And also the time for judging the dead
And giving wages to your slaves, the prophets
And your saints, and to all who fear your name,
The small and the great,
And to destroy the destroyers of the earth.
Then the temple of God in the sky was opened
And the ark of his covenant was seen in his temple
And there came lightning flashes and voices
And thunders and an earthquake and great hail.

Rev. 11.15–19

Beast from the Sea

Then I saw a beast coming up from the sea,
With ten horns and seven heads and on his horns
Ten diadems, and on his heads were the names
Of blasphemy. The beast I saw was like a leopard,
His feet like a bear and his mouth like the mouth
Of a lion. And the dragon gave him his power
And his throne and fierce power of dominion.

One of his heads seemed to be stricken to death
But the wound causing his death was healed

And the whole world marveled after the beast.
They worshiped the dragon since he had given
Dominion to the beast, and they worshiped the beast,
Saying, "Who is like the beast and can battle him?"

He was given a mouth to speak great things
And blasphemies. And he was given dominion
To act for forty-two months. Then he opened
His mouth to utter blasphemies against God,
Blaspheming his name and his tenting place,
And those who have set their tent in the sky.

He was given powers to battle the saints
And to overcome them, and was given powers
Over every tribe and people and tongue and nation.
All who dwell on the earth will worship him,
Each one whose name has not been written since
The foundation of the world in the book of life
Of the slaughtered lamb. Who has an ear, hear Yirmiyahu:
He who leads into captivity goes into captivity.
He who kills with the sword will be killed by the sword.
Such is the endurance and faith of the saints.

Rev. 13.1–10

Beast from the Earth

Then I saw another beast rising from the earth
And he had two horns like a lamb and he spoke
Like a dragon. He exercises all the dominion
Of the first beast before him, and makes the earth
And its inhabitants worship the first beast,
Whose wound of death was healed. He does great portents,
Even making a fire plunge from the sky
Down to the earth in the sight of the people.
He fools the inhabitants on the earth
By means of the portents he contrives to make

On behalf of the beast, creating an image
To show the beast as wounded by the sword
Yet coming out alive. And he had the power
To give breath to the image of the beast
And the image of the beast could even speak
And cause all who would not worship the beast
To be killed. He causes all, the small and great,
The rich and poor, the free ones and the slaves,
To be marked on the hand and the forehead
So that no one can buy or sell without the mark,
The name of the beast or number of his name.
Here is wisdom. Who has a mind, calculate
The number of the beast, which is the number
For a human. And the number is 666.[1]

Rev. 13.11–18

Lamb on Mount Zion

Then I saw, and look, the lamb standing on
Mount Zion and with him one hundred forty-four
Thousand who had his name and the name of
His father written on their foreheads. And
I heard a voice out of the sky like the voice
Of many waters, like the voice of great thunder,
And the voice I heard was like the voice of harpists
Playing on their harps. They sing a new song
Before the throne and before the four animals
And the elders, and no one could learn the song
Except the hundred and forty-four thousand
Who have been bought from the earth. These are
The men who were not defiled by women,
Since they are virgins. They follow the lamb

---

1. The number of the beast corresponds in Hebrew to a code, which may be the name of Nero Caesar or Caesar Augustus, probably the latter because the ram horns was Augustus's code. The number may have been 626.

Wherever he goes. These were bought from men
As a first fruit of God and the lamb. And in
Their mouths no lie was found. They are blameless.

Then I saw another angel flying in midair
With an eternal gospel to proclaim
To those inhabiting the earth and each nation,
And tribe and tongue and people, saying
In a great voice,
Fear God and give him glory.
The hour of his judgment is come,
And worship him who made the sky and earth,
The sea and the springs of water.
Another angel, a second, followed, saying,
Great Babylon is fallen, is fallen.
She made all nations drink her wine of passion
And her filthy copulations.

Another angel, a third, followed them, saying
In a great voice, "All those who worship the beast
And his image and receive a mark on the forehead
Or on the hand, even those humans will drink
The wine of the wrath of God, which is poured
Undiluted into the cup of the anger
Of their God, and they will be tormented
In fire and in sulfur before the holy angels
And before the lamb. The smoke of their torment
Will rise forevermore, and there's no rest
Day and night for any who worship the beast
And his image or wears the mark of his name."
Such is the endurance of the saints, who keep
The commandments of God and faith in Yeshua.

And I heard a voice out of the sky, saying,
"Write. Blessed are the dead who from now on

Die in the lord." "Yes," the spirit says to them
"So they may rest from their labors.
Their works will follow after them."

Rev. 14.1–13

The Great Whore on a Scarlet Beast

Then came one of the seven angels who held
The seven bowls and he spoke with me, saying,
"Come, I'll show you the judgment on the great whore
Sitting on the many waters, with whom the kings
Of the earth have copulated, and with the wine
Of her copulations the dwellers of the earth
Have got drunk." He took me off to a desert
In the spirit. I saw a woman sitting
On a scarlet beast who was filled with the names
Of blasphemy, with seven heads and ten horns.

The woman was wearing purple and scarlet
And was adorned with gold and precious stones
And pearls. She held a gold cup in her hand,
Full of the abominations of filth
Of her harlotry. On her forehead a name
Was written:
Mystery Babylon the Great
The Mother of the Whores
And the Abominations of the Earth.[2]

And I saw the woman drunk on the blood of saints
And from the blood of the witnesses of Yeshua
I was amazed, looking at her with wonder.

The angel said to me, "Why do you marvel?
I will tell you the mystery of the woman

---

2. The great whore is often a metaphor for "a godless city" as in Isaiah 1.21 and 23.16–17, or Rome of the emperors, or Babylon of the kings.

And the beast with seven heads and ten horns
Who carries her. The beast you saw was
And is not and is about to come up out of
The bottomless abyss and go to his perdition.
And the inhabitants of earth will be stunned,
Whose names have not been written in the book
Of life from the foundation of the world,
When they see the beast that is and is not
And is to come. Here is the mind with wisdom:
The seven heads are seven mountains where
The woman sits on them. They are seven kings.

Five have fallen, one is, the other has not
Yet come, and when he comes, short is the time
He must stay. The beast who was and is not,
He too is the eighth and comes from the seven
And goes to his perdition. The ten horns
You saw are ten kings who did not yet take
A kingdom, but they will have their kingdom
As kings for one hour along with the beast.
These are of one mind and render the power
And dominion to the claws of the beast.
They will make war with the lamb and the lamb
Will conquer them, because he is the lord
Of lords and king of kings. Those on his side
Are the called and the chosen and the faithful."

Then the angel said to me, "The waters you saw
Where the whore sits, there are peoples and crowds
And nations and tongues. The ten horns you saw
And the beast, they will all hate the whore
And will make her desolate and naked,
And eat her flesh and will burn her up with fire.
For God put in their hearts to do his will
And act with one mind to give their kingship
Until the words of God will be fulfilled.

And the woman you saw is the great city
With dominion over the kings of the earth."

Rev. 17.1–18

All Nations Have Drunk the Wine of Copulation with Fallen Babylon

After this I saw another angel coming down
Out of the sky and with great authority
And the earth was lighted with his glory.
And he cried out in a powerful voice, saying,
"Fallen fallen is Babylon the great.
She has become a home for demons
And a prison of every foul spirit
And a prison of every foul bird
And a prison of every foul and
Detested beast, since all the nations
Have drunk the wine of passion
Of her copulation, and the kings
Of the earth have copulated with her,
And the merchants of the earth
Have grown rich on her lechery."

Rev. 18.1–3

Of Merchants, Captains, and Seafarers Who Mourn and Now Cry Out

Then I heard another voice out of the sky, saying,
Come out of her, my people,
So you will not join in her sins,
So you won't take on her plagues,
Because her sins are piled up and reach the sky.
God has remembered her iniquities.

Render to her as she has rendered,
Mix her a double portion

In the cup she has mixed.
As she gloried in the luxury of the flesh,
Give her equal torment and sorrow.
In her heart she says,
"I sit, a queen.
I am not a widow
And will never know grief."
But soon the plagues will come to her,
Death and sorrow and famine,
And in fire she will burn,
For powerful is the lord God who has judged her.

The kings of the earth, who copulated
With her and lived in lechery, will weep
And beat themselves over her when they see
The smoke of her burning. Standing far off
Because they fear the torment, they say,
Despair despair is the great city
Babylon, the strong city,
For in an hour your judgment came.

The merchants of the earth cry out and mourn
Over her, since no one buys their cargo now,
Cargo of gold and silver and precious stones
And pearls and fine linen and purple cloth
And silk and scarlet and every cedar wood
And every ivory vessel and every vessel
Of precious wood and bronze and iron and marble
And cinnamon and spice and incense and myrrh
And frankincense and wine and olive oil
And fine flour and wheat and cattle and sheep,
And horses and chariots and bodies and souls.
And the autumn fruit your soul longed for
Has gone from you,
And all the luxurious and the brilliant
Are lost to you and never will be found.

The merchants of these things, who became rich
From her, will stand far off because they fear
Her torment, her weeping, and her mourning,
Which say,
Despair despair is the great city
Who was clothed in fine linen
And purple cloth and scarlet
And decorated with gold
And precious stone and pearl.
In an hour that wealth was desert.
And all captains and seafarers on the ship
And sailors and all those who work the sea
Stood far off and cried out as they saw
The smoke of her conflagration, saying,
What city was like this great city?
And they threw dust upon their heads
And they cried out with tears and groans,
Despair despair is the city,
Where all who owned ships on the sea
Grew rich from her prosperity.
In an hour came only desolation.

Heaven and saints, celebrate her downfall,
And apostles and prophets, for God has judged
Against her for you. Then one strong angel
Picked up a boulder like a great millstone
And hurled it down into the sea, saying,
With such violence Babylon will be cast down
And will be found no more.
And the voices of harp players and singers,
The pipers and ram-horn blowers
Will be heard no more in you,
And the artisan of any trade
Will be found no more in you,
And the sound of the mill
Will be heard no more in you,

And the light of a lamp
Will shine no more in you,
The voice of the groom and bride
Will be heard no more in you.

Your merchants were the great men of the earth
And all nations were fooled by your sorcery.
In her was the blood of prophets and saints
And all those who were slaughtered on the earth.

Rev. 18.4–24

Rider on a White Horse

I saw the sky open, and look, a white horse
And the rider on him called Faithful and True,
And in the right he judges and makes war.
His eyes are flames of fire, and on his head
Many diadems, with names written known
Alone by him. And he wore a mantle
Dipped in blood and his name is called the word
Of God. The armies in the sky followed him
On white horses, clothed in fine linen white
And clean. And from his mouth goes a sharp sword
To smite the nations. He will shepherd them
With a rod of iron. He will trample the wine press
Of the fury of the anger of God, the pantokrator.
He wears on his mantle and on his thigh
A name written:
King of kings and lord of lords.

Rev. 19.11–16

Into the Lake of Fire

I saw an angel standing in the sun
And he cried out in a great voice, saying,
"To all the birds flying in the middle air,

Come, gather for the great supper of God
To eat the flesh of kings and flesh of captains
And flesh of strongmen and flesh of horses
And of their riders and flesh of both the free
And slaves and small and great." I saw the beast
And kings of the earth and their armies poised
To make war against the rider on his horse
And against his armies. Then the beast
Was captured and with him the false prophet
Who had worked miracles on the beast's behalf
And so deceived those who received the mark
Of the beast and those who worshiped the image
Of the monster. The two of them were cast alive
Into the lake of fire burning with sulfur.
The rest were killed by the sword of the rider
On the horse, the sword that came from his mouth;
And all the flying birds gorged on their flesh.

Rev. 19.17–21

Angel with a Great Chain in His Hand

I saw an angel coming down from the sky.
He was holding a great chain on his hand
And the key of the bottomless pit. He seized
The dragon, and ancient snake, who is the devil
And Satan; he bound him for a thousand years
And cast him into the bottomless pit
And closed it tight and sealed it over him
So he couldn't fool the nations any more
Until the thousand years should be fulfilled.
After that he must be released a short time.

Then I saw thrones, and those who sat on them
Were given the power to judge. I saw
The souls of those beheaded for their testimony
To Yeshua and for the word of God

And those who had not worshiped the beast
Nor the image of him and did not take
His mark on their forehead and on their hand,
And they came to life and reigned with Yeshua
For a thousand years. The rest of the dead
Did not come to life until the thousand years
Were over. This is the first resurrection.

Rev. 20.1–5

Devil in Sulfur and Fire Forever

Blessed and holy are they who take part in
The first resurrection: on these the second death
Has no power. They will become priests of God
And of Yeshua and with him they will reign
A thousand years. And when the thousand years
Should be fulfilled, Satan will be released
From his prison and will come out to fool
The nations in the four corners of the earth,
Gog and Magog, to lead them into battle,
Whose number is like the sand of the sea.
Then they climbed up and over the width
Of the earth and encircled the encampment
Of the saints and their beloved city,
But fire came down from the sky and consumed
The attackers. The devil, who had fooled them,
Was cast into the lake of fire and sulfur
Where both the beast and the false prophet are
And will be tormented forevermore.

Rev. 20.6–10

Of the Dead Written in the Book

I saw a throne great and white, and sitting
On it was he from whose face fled the earth
And the sky, and no place was found for them.

I saw the dead, the great and small. They stood
Before the throne and there the books were opened.
Another book was opened, which is the book
Of life. The dead were judged according to
Their works as they were written in the books.
The sea gave up the dead in it, and hell
Gave up the dead in it, and they were judged,
Each one according to their works. And Death
And Hell were cast into the lake of fire.
This is the second death, the lake of fire.
And anyone not written in the book
Of life was cast into the lake of fire.

Rev. 20.11–15

A New Jerusalem Descends from Heaven

And I saw a new sky and a new earth,
For the first sky and the first earth were gone
And the sea was no more. I saw the holy
City, the new Yerushalayim, coming down
Out of the sky from God who prepared her
Like a bride adorned for her groom. And then
I heard a great voice from the throne, saying,
"Look, now the tent of God is with them. They'll be
His people, and he God will be with them,
And he will wipe away each tear from their eyes
And death will be no more. And grief and crying
And pain will be no more. The past has perished."

Rev. 21.1–4

I Am the Alpha and the Omega

And he who sat upon the throne said, "Look,
I made all new." And he said, "Write, because
These words are true and faithful." And he said
To me, "It's done. I am the Alpha and the Omega,

The beginning and the end. And to the thirsty
I will give a gift from the spring of the water
Of life. The victor will inherit these things
And I will be his God and he will be
A son. But to the cowards and unbelieving
And abominable and murderers and copulators
And sorcerers and all who are false, their fate
Will be the lake burning with fire and sulfur,
Which is the second death."

Rev. 21.5–8

A City Clear Gold Like Clear Glass

One of the angels came with the seven bowls
Full of the seven last plagues, and he spoke
With me, saying, "Come, I will show you the bride,
The wife of the lamb." And he took me away
In spirit onto a mountain great and high,
And showed me the city of holy Yerushalayim
Coming down out of the sky from God,
Wearing the glory of God, and her radiance
Like a precious stone, like a jasper stone
And crystal clear. She has a great and high wall
With twelve gates and at the gates twelve angels,
Their names inscribed on them: the twelve tribes
Who are the sons and daughters of Yisrael.

On the east three gates and on the north three gates,
On the south three gates and on the west three gates.
The walls of the city have twelve foundations,
And on them twelve names, the twelve apostles of the lamb.
The angel speaking to me had a gold
Measuring rod to gage the city and her gates
And walls. The city lies foursquare, its length
And width the same. He gaged the city with
The reed, twelve thousand furlongs in length,

Her length and width and height the same. He gaged
Her wall a hundred forty-four cubits,
By human measurement like the angel's.

The wall is built of jasper and the city
Clear gold like clear glass. The foundations of
The city are adorned with precious stones,
The first foundation jasper, the second sapphire,
Third of agate, fourth of emerald, fifth of onyx,
The sixth carnelian, seventh of chrysolite,
The eighth beryl, ninth of topaz, tenth of chrysoprase,
Eleventh jacinth and the twelfth amethyst.
The twelve gates are twelve pearls, each gate
A single pearl, and the great square in the city
Is clear gold like diaphanous glass.

I saw no temple in her, for the temple
Is lord God the pantokrator and the lamb.
The city has no need of sun or moon
To shine on her, for the glory of God
Illuminated her and her lamp is the lamb.
The gentile nations will walk around
Through her light, and the kings of the earth
Bring glory into her. Her gates will never
Be shut by day, and night will not be there.
Her people will bring the glory and honor
Of nations into her. But no common thing
Will enter her, or anyone who stoops
To abominations and lies, but only those
Written in the book of life of the lamb.

Rev. 21.9–27

River of the Water of Life

The angel showed me a river of the water
Of life shining like crystal and issuing
From the throne of God and of the lamb.
Between the great plaza and the river
And on either side stands the tree of life
With her twelve fruits, yielding a special fruit
For every month, and the leaves of the tree
Are for healing the nations. All curses
Will cease to exist. The throne of God
And of the lamb will be in the city.
His slaves will serve him; they will see his face. His name
Will be on their foreheads. And night will not
Be there and they'll need no light of a lamp
Or light of sun, for the lord God will glow
On them, and they will reign forevermore.

Rev. 22.1–5

I'm Coming Quickly!

Then he said to me, "These words are faithful
And true, and the lord God of the spirits of
The prophets sent his angel to show his slaves
Those things which soon must take place.
Look, I'm coming quickly! Blessed is the one
Who keeps the words of this book's prophecy."
I Yohanan am the one who heard and saw
These things. And when I heard and saw I fell
And worshiped before the feet of the angel
Showing me these things. And he said to me,
"You must not do that! I am your fellow slave
And of your brothers and prophets and those
Who keep the words of this book. Worship God."
And he tells me, "Do not seal the words
Of prophecy of this book. The time is near.

Let the unjust still be unjust, the filthy
Still be filthy, the righteous still do right,
And the holy one be holy still. Look,
I'm coming quickly, and my reward is with me
To give to each according to your work.
I am the Alpha and the Omega, the first
And the last, the beginning and the end."

Rev. 22.6–13

To the Tree of Life

Blessed are they who are washing their robes
So they will have the right to the tree of life
And can enter the city through the gates.
Outside will be the dogs and sorcerers
And copulators and murderers and idolators
And everyone who loves to practice lies.

Rev. 22.14–15

I Am the Offspring of David the Bright Morning Star

I Yeshua sent my angel to you
To testify these things for the churches.
I am the root and the offspring of David,
The bright morning star. The spirit and bride
Say, "Come." Let you who hear say, "Come."
Let you who thirst come, and let you who wish
Take the water of life, which is a gift.

Rev. 22.16–17

Come, Lord Jesus!

I give my testimony to all who hear
These words of the prophecy of this book.
If anyone adds to these, then God will add

To them the plagues recorded in this book.
If anyone takes away from the words
Of this book's prophecy, God will cut off
Their share of the tree of life and the holy
City, those things recorded in this book.[3]
And he who is the one who testifies
To all this says, "Yes, I am coming quickly!"
Amain. Come, lord Yeshua! And may
The grace of lord Yeshua be with you all.

Rev. 22.18–21

3. These last commands and warnings are from Deuteronomy 4.2 and 12.32.

FULL CONTENTS

THE NEW TESTAMENT

GLOSSARY

Abba. Father.
Adonai. Lord.
Aharon. Aaron.
Amminadav. Amminadab.
Amorah. Gomorrah.
Amotz. Amos.
Andreas. Andrew.
Anan. Hannas.
Arrepah. Orpah.
Arimathaia. Arimathea.
Avaddon. Abbadon.
Avraham. Abraham.
Avram. Abram.
Avarim. Abarim.
Avednego. Abednego.
Avshalom. Absalom.
Avva. Abba, Father.
Azur. Azor.

Baal Zebub. Beelzebub.
Baal Zebul. Beelzebul.
Bar. Son.
Bar Abba. Barabbas.
Bar Nabba or Barnabba. Barnabas.
Barsabbas.
Bar Shavvat or Bar Shabbat.
Barsabbas.

Bar Talmai. Bartholomew.
Bar Yohanan. Barjona.
Bat. Beth.
Bavel. Babel.
Ber Sheva. Bersheba.

Devorah. Deborah.

Efesos. Ephasos.
Elazar. Eleazar or Lazarus.
Eliezar of Damasek. Eliezar of
Damascus.
Eliyahu or Eliyah. Elijah or Elias.
Elisheva. Elizabeth.
En Geddi. Ein Gedi.
Ever. Heber.

Galil. Galilee.
Gat Shmanim. Gethsemane.
**Gei Hinnom, Gei Ben Hinnom,
Gehenna.** Hell.
Gilvoa. Gilboah.
Gulgulta. Golgotha.

Havah. Eve.
Ha Vashan. Bashan.
Heshvon. Heshbon.

Iakavos. Jacob, James.
Ihezekel. Ezekiel.
Ionnes. Yonatan. John, Jonathan.
Izevel. Jezebel.

Jael. Yael.

Kanaan. Canaan.
Kefa or Shimon Kefa. Cephas (Latinization) or Peter or Simon Peter or Simeon Peter.
Keriot. Iscariot.
Kfar Nahum or Kefar Nahum. Capernaum.

Levi. Levi, Matthew.
Loukas. Luke.
Loukios. Lucius.

Magdala (town on Sea of Galilee). Mary the Magdalene (from Magdala).
Markos. Mark.
Marta. Martha.
Mashiah. Messiah.
Mattityah. Mattathias.
Mattityahu, Mattai. Matthew.
Merivah–Kadesh. Meribaj Kadesh.
Miryam. Mary.
Mishach, Michzael. Meshach.
Moav. Moab.
Moavite. Moabite.
Mosheh or Moshe. Moses.

Naftali. Naphtali.
Nakdeimon. Nikodemos, Nicodemus.
Natan. Nathan.
Natanel. Nathanael.
Natzeret. Nazareth.
Natzrati. Nazarene.
Nevo. Nebo.

Oved. Obed.

Parush. Pharisee.
Pesach, Pesah. Passover.
Pilatus. Pilate.
Plistim. Philistine.
Prushim or Perushim. Pharisees.

Sanhedrin. Council.
Sarai. (becomes) Sarah.
Seder. Easter meal.
Sedom. Sodom.
Shavvat, Shavvas, Shabbat, Shabat. Sabbath.
Shaddai, El Shaddai, El Shadai. God, God Almighty, God of the Mountains.
Shflela. Shephela.
Sheva. Sheba.
Shir ha Shirim. Song of Songs.
Shafat. Shaphat.
Shaul. Saul, Paul.
Shehem. Sychar or Syhem.
Sheol. Hell.
Shet. Seth.
Sheva. Sheba.
Shiloah. Siloam.
Shimon. Simon or Simeon.
Shimon Kefa. Simon Peter.
Shimshon. Samson.
Shlomit. Salome.
Shlomoh, Shlomo. Solomon
Shomron. Samaria.
Shomroni. Samaritan.
Shomronim. Samaritans.
Smuel. Samuel.
Sukkah. Sukkoth. Sukkot or Tabernacle or Festival of the Booths.

Theofilos. Theophilus.
Toma. Thomas.

Torah. The Torah is the Pentateuch (Five Books of Moses) and also signifies the Old Testament.

Vaal. Baal.
Vaal-hamon or Vaal Hamon. Baal-hamon.
Vath Ravvim. Bath Rebbim.
Veer Sheva. Beersjeva.
Venyamin, Benyamin. Benjamin.
Veth Lehem. Bethlehem.
Voaz. Boaz.

Yaakov. Jacob, James.
Yahweh, Yahveh, YHWH for *Adonai*, God.
Yannai. Jannai.
Yeriho. Jericho.
Yeshayahu. Isaiah.
Yeshua. Joshua, Jesus.
Yafo, Jaffa, Jaffa. Joppo.
Yapheth. Japheth.
Yarden. Jordan.
Yavesh. Yabesh.
Yehu. Jehu or YHWH.
Yehoniah. Jechoniah.
Yehoshua. Joshua.
Yehudah, Yehuda. Judas, Juda, Judah, Jude.
Yehudah. Judea.
Yehudit. Judith.

Yehudah man of Keriot. Judas Iscariot.
Yeriho. Jericho.
Yermeya, Yermeyahu. Jeremiah.
Yerushalayim. Jerusalem.
Yeshayahu, Yeshayah. Isaiah.
Yeshua. Joshua, Yehoshua, Jehoshua, Jesus.
Yeshua the Mashiah. Jesus the Christ.
Yeshua ben Yosef (Hebrew). Jesus son of Joseph.
Yeshayahu, Yeshayah. Isaiah.
Yirmiyahu, Yirmiyah. Jeremiah.
Yisai. Jesse.
Yishmael. Ishmael.
Yisrael. Israel.
Yitzhak. Isaac.
Yoel. Joel.
Yonhah. Jonah.
Yov. Job.
Yohanan. John.
Yona. Jona.
Yonah. Jonah.
Yonatan. Jonathan.
Yosef. Joseph.

Zakai. Zacchaeus.
Zavdai. Zebedee.
Zeharyahu, Zharyahu. Zacharias or Zechariah.
Zvulun. Zebulun.

BIBLIOGRAPHY

Ackroyd, Peter R., and Christopher F. Evans, eds. *The Cambridge History of the Bible: Vol. 1, From the Beginnings to Jerome.* Cambridge: Cambridge University Press, 1970.

Alter, Robert. *Ancient Israel: The Former Prophets: Joshua, Judges, Samuel, and Kings: A Translation with Commentary.* New York: W. W. Norton, 2013.

———. *The Art of Biblical Poetry.* New York: Basic Books, 1987.

———. *The Book of Psalms: A Translation with Commentary.* New York: W. W. Norton, 2007.

———. *The David Story: A Translation with Commentary of 1 and 2 Samuel.* New York: W. W. Norton, 1999.

———. *Genesis: Translation and Commentary.* New York: W. W. Norton, 1996.

———. *Strong As Death Is Love: The Song Of Songs, Ruth, Esther, Jonah, and Daniel: A Translation with Commentary.* New York: W. W. Norton, 2015.

———. *The Wisdom Books: Job, Proverbs, and Ecclesiastes: A Translation with Commentary.* New York: W. W. Norton, 2010.

Alter, Robert, and Frank Kermode, eds. *The Literary Guide to the Bible.* Cambridge, MA: Harvard University Press, 1987.

Barnstone, Willis. *The Apocalypse.* New York: New Directions, 2000.

———. *The Other Bible: Gnostic Gospels, Dead Sea Scrolls, Wisdom Texts, Christian Apocrypha, Jewish Pseudepigrapha, Kabbalah.* San Francisco: Harper and Row, 1984.

———. *The Poetics of Translation: History, Theory, Practice.* New Haven: Yale University Press, 1993.

———. *The Restored New Testament: A New Translation with Commentary.* New York: W. W. Norton, 2009.

Barnstone, Willis, and Marvin Meyer, eds. *The Gnostic Bible.* Boston: Shambhala Books, 2003.

Bates, Ernest Southerland. *The Bible, Designed to be Read as Living Literature: The Old and the New Testaments in the King James Version.* New York: Simon and Schuster, 1993.

Bloom, Harold. "A Reading." In Marvin Meyer, *The Gospel of Thomas: The Hidden Sayings of Jesus.* San Francisco: Harper San Francisco, 1992.

Carroll, Robert, and Stephen Prickett. *The Bible: Authorized King James Version.* Oxford: Oxford University Press, 2008.

Castelli, Elizabeth A. et al., eds. *The Postmodern Bible: The Bible and Culture Collective* New Haven: Yale University Press, 1995.

Coogan, Michael D., ed. *The Oxford Encyclopedia of the Books of the Bible.* 2 vols. New York: Oxford University Press, 2011.

Crossan, John Dominic. *The Essential Jesus: Original Sayings and the Earliest Images.* San Francisco: HarperCollins, 1994.

Danker, Frederick W. *Multipurpose Tools for Bible Study.* Rev. ed. Philadelphia, PA: Fortress, 1993.

Fishbane, Michael. *Biblical Interpretation in Ancient Israel.* Oxford: Clarendon Press, 1985.

Freeman, David Noel, ed. *The Anchor Bible Dictionary.* 6 vols. New York: Doubleday, 1992.

Frye, Northrop. *The Great Code: The Bible and Literature.* Harcourt Brace Jovanovich, 1982.

Gabel, John B., Charles B. Wheeler, Anthony D. York, and David Citino. *The Bible as Literature: An Introduction.* Oxford: Oxford University Press, 2005.

Gillingham, Sue E. *The Poems and Psalms of the Hebrew Bible.* Oxford: Oxford University Press, 1994.

Gunn, David M., and Danna Nolan Fewell. *Narrative in the Hebrew Bible.* Oxford: Oxford University Press, 1993.

Hammond, Gerald. *The Making of the English Bible.* New York: Philosophical Library, 1983.

Hargreaves, Cecil. *A Translator's Freedom: Modern English Bibles and their Language.* Sheffield, UK: JSOT Press, 1993.

Jewish Publication Society. *Tanakh, the Holy Scriptures: The New JPS Translation According to the Traditional Hebrew Text.* Philadelphia: Jewish Publication Society, 1986.

Josipovici, Gabriel. *The Book of God: A Response to the Bible.* New Haven, CT: Yale University Press, 1988.

McDonald, Lee Martin. *Forgotten Scriptures: The Selection and Rejection of Early Religious Writings.* Louisville, KY: Westminster John Knox Press, 2009.

Meyer, Marvin, ed. *The Nag Hammadi Scriptures: The Revised and Updated Translation of Sacred Gnostic Texts Complete in One Volume.* New York: HarperOne, 2007.

Moore, Stephen D. *Literary Criticism and the Gospels: The Theoretical Challenge.* New Haven, CT: Yale University Press, 1989.

Pagels, Elaine. *The Gnostic Gospels.* New York: Random House, 1979.

———. *The Gnostic Paul: Gnostic Exegesis of the Pauline Letters.* Philadelphia: Fortress Press, 1975.

————. *The Origin of Satan: How Christians Demonized Jews, Pagans, and Heretics*. New York: Vintage Books, 1995.

————. *Revelations: Visions, Prophecy, and Politics in the Book of Revelation*. New York: Viking, 2012.

Prickett, Stephen. *Origins of Narrative: The Romantic Appropriation of the Bible*. Cambridge: Cambridge University Press, 2005.

————. *Words and the Word: Language, Poetics and Biblical Interpretation*. Cambridge: Cambridge University Press, 1986.

Rosenberg, David. *A Literary Bible: An Original Translation*. Berkeley: Counterpoint Press, 2010.

Spong, John Shelby. *Liberating the Gospels: Reading the Bible with Jewish Eyes: Freeing Jesus from 2,000 Years of Misunderstanding*. San Francisco: HarperSanFrancisco, 1996.

Steiner, George. *After Babel: Aspects of Language and Translation*. Oxford: Oxford University Press, 1992.

Trobisch, David. *The First Edition of the New Testament*. New York: Oxford University Press, 2000.

Tyndale, William, trans. *Tyndale's New Testament*. Edited by David Daniell. New Haven, CT: Yale University Press, 1989.

Vermés, Géza. *The Changing Faces of Jesus*. New York: Viking Compass, 2001.

————, trans., ed. *The Complete Dead Sea Scrolls in English*. New York: Allen Lane/Penguin Press, 1997.

————. *Jesus the Jew: A Historian's Reading of the Gospels*. Philadelphia: Fortress Press, 1981.

SOURCE TEXTS

Aland, Kurt, and Barbara Aland, eds. *The Greek New Testament*. 4th ed. Stuttgart, Germany: Deutsche Bibelgesellschaft, 1993.

Eliger, Karl, and Wilhelm Rudulph, eds. *Biblia Hebraica Stuttgartensia*. Stuttgart, Germany: Deutsche Bibelgesellschaft, 1998.

INDEX